BLACK PLAQUES

PLAQUES

MEMORIALS TO MISADVENTURE

LONDON

JOHN AMBROSE HIDE

The
History
Press

First published 2019

The History Press
The Mill, Brimscombe Port
Stroud, Gloucestershire, GL5 2QG
www.thehistorypress.co.uk

British Library Cataloguing in Publication Data.
A catalogue record for this book is available from the British Library.

ISBN 978 0 7509 8995 4

Typesetting and origination by The History Press
Printed and bound in Great Britain by TJ International Ltd

CONTENTS

AUTHOR'S NOTE

This collection of stories from the past makes use of the vocabulary and social graces of former days – that is to say, the physically sick called for a physician and the mentally sick a lunatic asylum or madhouse, while voyeurs patronised freak shows, felons were sent to gaol, the thirsty headed to an alehouse (and subsequently a boghouse), and the lecherous sought not a sex worker but a bawd, harlot, whore or strumpet.

On a similar cautionary note, it is hoped that the expressed premise of bringing to light a mixed buffet of succulent historical exploits will appeal to a particular class of inquisitive gourmand, however courtesy obliges mention that thanks to the lavish detail provided in the depictions, there may exude from this book a tang more gamey than to some readers' tastes.

Dates are given in modern style and both the spelling and punctuation of quoted material are modernised if it helps clarity.

The photograph of a detail from Jean Cocteau's mural in the Church of Notre Dame de France is used with the kind permission of the church as well as the Comité Jean Cocteau.

INTRODUCTION

The Black Plaques portrayed in this book are not to be found proudly mounted on a wall, and as will swiftly become clear, for good reason. What with their commemoration of a brutal execution outside Westminster Abbey, the selling of sex toys in St James's Park, and an intruder at Buckingham Palace with Royal undergarments stuffed down his crotch, this is not the sort of subject matter that authorities choose to grace a building's facade or depict on a visitor information board. In fact, many people might hope that such indecorous and inconvenient episodes remain quietly overlooked.

But Black Plaques jog such artful lapses of memory. At a stroke, London's familiar streets and buildings are cast in a quite different light when imprinted – of necessity by proxy, with these Memorials to Misadventure, thus drawing long overdue attention to awkward moments history has done its utmost to discreetly ignore, misrepresent, or prompt a timely bout of amnesia – happily, circumstances that offer fertile conditions for stories of exquisite ripeness.

My motivation to lavish Black Plaques on London arose after a visit to that icon of the city, St Paul's Cathedral, for it was only sometime *after* a visit, I happened to discover that in 1514 a man imprisoned at the building's medieval precursor was murdered by virtue of a red hot needle thrust up his nose. And not only that; the perpetrators of this impolite enterprise were churchmen who endeavoured to bestow the bloody scene with the semblance of suicide – for which the corpse then stood trial in the Lady Chapel. Such a startling sequence of events is not considered worthy of even a footnote in the official history of the Cathedral – a weighty tome with the proportions of a paving slab – so needless to say, neither does it feature anywhere in today's 'visitor experience'. My discovery left me with the feeling that I had been denied the opportunity to stand where events took place and quietly contemplate the mother of all nosebleeds.

While this inglorious affair came as news to me, it is by no means unknown to scholars of the Tudor period, however their focus is not unexpectedly directed towards learned interpretations of the episode's context and consequences, as opposed to the nitty-gritty of its unpleasant operation at what is now a global tourist attraction. Similarly, the Cathedral's governing body concerns itself with priorities far loftier than acquainting visitors with earthy tales of brain-skewering on the premises, yet this was a tale needing to be told about St Paul's and a commemorative plaque – inevitably one both unofficial and incorporeal – was the means to correct this oversight.

When it came to delving into the dustbins at other locations, it soon became apparent that this was not an isolated instance in which the powers that be had covered a compromising stain with carefully placed rug. And so as a matter of public duty I began to bestow Black Plaques – each one a vignette of an unbecoming event at a particular locale, where the blot in question is at best obscured, at worst obliterated from common consciousness, and its uncomfortable truths are distilled into a compendious inscription. Thus, Black Plaques London offers an antidote to run-of-the-mill guidebook spiel on sites such as Covent Garden, Regent Street or Banqueting House, and besmirches the reputation of umpteen less prominent addresses. At many of the sites there are no physical remains that relate to the dishonourable deeds depicted – as is the case with the prison at the

The Great Fire of 1666 expunges reminders of an awkward episode at St Paul's.

old St Paul's – which of course has helped those unsavoury blotches to fade into obscurity.

While perched on the threshold, this is an opportune moment to mention that among the words of remembrance offered herein, nostrils are by no means the only bodily orifice to be poked with something. Eligibility criteria for Black Plaques place no subject off-limits and some of the dedicatory epigraphs are richly laden with lewd and lurid details that are perhaps not everyone's cup of tea; even this introduction is soon to make an insightful deviation into what London Underground's indefatigable cleaners refer to as *Code Two*.

For those still reading, so as not to cause misunderstanding I should also give forewarning that Black Plaques are not simply a generous slice of forbidden fruit. Granted, they shine a spotlight on women's breasts offered up to the caresses of a dead man's hand, and boys' buttocks yielding to the vigorous attentions of the Bishop of London, but moments of indelicacy such as these are counterbalanced by altogether more sober and sobering sagas. I explain this uneasy mixed bill of levity and gravity shortly, but beforehand it is instructive, and I hope not too wearying, to engineer an encounter between conventional (and in London, most commonly blue) plaques and their troublesome new in-laws.

Should a visitor from outer space assess the track record of our species solely by reading commemorative plaques, it is not controversial to conclude that they would form a thoroughly undeserved impression of Earth's self-ordained 'wise' hominids. But labouring under this inordinately generous view, our interplanetary guest might query why these unpredictable blue blobs tend to mark merely the house (or 'site of the house') in which our exemplary specimens 'lived'. Such a discerning extraterrestrial and I cannot be alone in wondering what links the four walls that enclosed our paragon of virtue's domestic, sleeping and ablutionary arrangements with their praiseworthy endeavours. Furthermore, humankind exhibits the inconvenient habit of moving house, so the notably peripatetic Charles Dickens has bagged eight plaques in London solely for places in which he lived (or even 'stayed'). Dickens' reputation justifies such a number but perhaps the seventeenth-century 'Master Astrologer' William Lilly ought to have foreseen that were he more domestically mobile, he might be better remembered. (Lilly is commemorated with a sole plaque mounted on the disused Strand/Aldwych Underground station – a place I fancy he would not have been familiar with.) Plaques such as these do not explicitly identify where something of significance took place; they are not pinpointing what you might call hallowed ground.

At the risk of rocking the commemorative boat yet further, I suggest the habit of marking the place of someone's birth or death is even less meaningful. I am sure that my interstellar associate would graciously concur, judging the former to be an achievement for which they could scarcely claim credit and the latter to represent the least commendable act of their entire lives. By way of illustration, our hospital facades are conspicuously devoid of a mosaic of memorials yet a blue plaque on the handsome six-storey house at No. 32 Elm Park Gardens in Chelsea infers that a Mr and Mrs Cripps resided at the property in 1889 when their son Stafford made his appearance in the world. Many years later he became: 'Sir Stafford Cripps – Statesman – born here', and while it might be diverting to speculate that perhaps a heavily pregnant Mrs Theresa Cripps was only visiting No. 32 when she became indisposed, a quick investigation reveals nothing so beguiling, and conventional expectations ring tediously true. This was indeed Sir Stafford Cripps's parents' home – that is until young Stafford reached the tender age of 4, when the family upped sticks and moved elsewhere. With that in mind, quite what should be gleaned from this plaque eludes me, while our alien anthropologist would surmise that Earth's two-legged primates celebrate privilege by birth.

However, it can at least be declared that No. 32 Elm Park Gardens consists of the very bricks and mortar that echoed with Cripps junior's first faltering speech, because in some cases the backdrop for the dedicatee's passage through their mother's birth canal has long been demolished. In Marylebone, painter and poet Dante Gabriel Rossetti has the misfortune of a plaque on a 1920s building to record the outcome of Mrs Frances Rossetti's labour during the 1820s. Here, the commemorative boat has keeled over. (Incidentally, for those unaware that Rossetti had his long-dead wife exhumed, a Black Plaque carefully digs up this morbid tale.)

While much of this haphazard situation arises from plaques erected by preceding generations and present-day reticence in toppling them, the examples highlight the difficulty of fittingly memorialising individuals at a single location with a token smattering of words. Thus, in preference to commemorating people, Black Plaques mark sites where, to put it bluntly, *shit happened*. Reminding ourselves not only of names but events makes for a much more potent experience; stand outside Westminster Abbey and picture the scene when a man was burned alive on the spot and ghosts from the past can suddenly seem alarmingly close. Perhaps the absence of a physical plaque or information board makes the effect more compelling because the experience is a private and personal one, driven by the power of imagination. However, it would be prudent to first confirm the precise whereabouts beside the Abbey to avoid visualising the gruesome spectacle of April 1555 while stood on the site of a nineteenth-century boghouse in which a Member of Parliament was discovered, breeches ornamenting his ankles, in the receptive company of a young guardsman burdened by similarly disordered dress.

As subject matter for illustration, artists favoured the execution at Westminster (see page 321) over its boghouse.

Admittedly, some of those individuals commemorated with real-world plaques also performed the feats for which they are famed where they lived, however this is seldom the message portrayed. Of all plaques across London, approximately 85 per cent mark solely where someone was born, lived, died or a combination of that terse trio. Yet, were William Lilly's plaque to proclaim not 'Master Astrologer Lived In A House On This Site' but 'Piss Prophet Practised From This Site' then I imagine it would attract significantly more attention. For it was from the comfort of his home that Lilly 'read' clients' urine samples, including one originating from the terminally ill leader of Parliament John Pym. (Lilly skipped the unpalatable business of actually examining Pym's piss and simply used the time it showed up as the basis for his planetary computations. He astutely recognised that the moon's position signified that Pym would die – and lo and behold, so he did.) Lilly also possessed great prowess for detecting witches from their wee, though his prognostications regarding any imminent plague or fire (as conspicuously occurred in 1665–66) were less clear-cut and he instead prudently forecasted how 'for many hundreds of years yet to come', England would experience plague, fire, feasting, famine, war, peace and mole infestations.

The Strand's abandoned Tube station (which Lilly perhaps had indeed anticipated through swarms of subterranean mammals) basks in a fresh golden light when one is sufficiently au fait to picture Lilly peering at pots of piss. And if that brief sketch has whetted an appetite for piss prophets then a quick leak reveals that such opportunism affords them a warm welcome into this hall of shame, where the number one exponent of testing (and disturbingly, tasting) urine has a Black Plaque on Berwick Street in Soho.

It ought now be apparent from the digression into forecasting the future by dint of the erstwhile contents of someone's bladder, that instead of offering a few fleeting

One of William Lilly's 1651 forecasts that 'doth perfectly represent the future condition of the English nation'.

words, Black Plaques probe deep into the meat and potatoes. After all, it would be decidedly frustrating to behold a plaque that declared merely: 'Theresa Berkeley – Renowned Whipper – Dispensed Discipline Here', so I hope their more generous, picturesque narratives stimulate exquisitely vivid scenes in the mind's eye.

But those prophets who trousered the profits of piss might be granted one revelation that is entirely credible and pertinent; with their acute grasp of human psychology these self-appointed soothsayers would recognise that the demand for their services – supplying surrogate sense and meaning in a chaotic and cruel world – is perennial. Today, this rich vein is tapped with great skill and subtlety by a diverse range of more hygienic merchants, for whom punters piss only their cash. Bookshelves (and web servers) groan under the weight of wisdom readily dispensed to satiate this craving to understand ourselves and our surroundings, and the subject category of Black Plaques London is not immune to the phenomenon. For this reason, there is one aspect in which Black Plaques take their lead from conventional plaques: trustworthiness.

Storytelling of the ilk 'Secret', 'Hidden' or 'I Didn't Know That About' London constitutes a crowded and at times homogeneous field, and the reason that another contender has presumed to muscle its way in can be summarised: caveat emptor. Be it seeking truth from a piss prophet or publication: buyer beware. And the unholy trinity of reasons for caution are: legend, folklore and mythology. London, perhaps more than anywhere else, has an extensive, tangled and deeply ingrained web of anecdotal lore – a not inconsiderable obstacle for anyone who ventures to penetrate the mysteries of the obscure or taboo. Where facts are flimsy, legend gets busy and when repeated sufficiently it can become stubbornly set in stone as historical 'truth' – quite literally so in the case of one monument described later. Countless Londoners enjoy a hazy awareness that a kink in the Piccadilly Line swerves around a plague pit, Sir Christopher Wren aligned St Paul's Cathedral with Temple Church for arcane masonic purposes, and Adolf Hitler earmarked Du Cane Court in Balham as his London HQ (although the Führer apparently also favoured Senate House in Bloomsbury as well as

Whiteleys Shopping Centre in Bayswater). Cyberspace, that renowned conveyor of questionable truths, has a voracious appetite for such eminently repeatable gobbets and the longterm future of these whimsies looks assured – their constant regurgitation allowing further 'improvement'. Elements of undeniable fact add to their plausibility: there are indeed plague pits in London (as there are seemingly unexplained bends in Underground tunnels), Wren chose not to build St Paul's on medieval foundations, and not every substantial modern building in London was detrimentally remodelled by the Luftwaffe. But such proverbial grains of truth do not an anecdote make, and wishful embroidering has introduced glaring discrepancies with the mundane truth. (To deal summarily with the aforementioned plague pits, purely because they occupy such a privileged position in the canon of London mythologising: the meeting of a Tube train tunnel and plague pit is yet to occur. And while on the subject of potential spoilers: Black Plaques fully recognise the existence of ghosts – in the shadowy recesses of the human imagination; ditto, little green men or, for that matter, women.)

Far be it from this author to rehearse the socio-psycho-logical factors behind the creation and survival of myths, but among London's clangers a great number arise through misunderstanding (and a straightforward example is pro-vided by London's primary execution site – Tyburn, where felons were *not* tied and burned) and perhaps even bypass the grain of truth (Victorian ghost stories and Dan Brown novels demonstrate inconspicuous leaps to non-fiction) but persist through prejudice (*viz.* a daft Yank snapping up the wrong London Bridge from wily Brits). Were it not for bigotry such red herrings would long be netted and filleted.

Yet they also linger through laziness. For some, the folkloric delicacies are so delightful it is best not to investigate them too thoroughly for fear of finding them at variance with the facts – a situation deftly handled by invoking the time-honoured get-out clause: 'according to legend'. Woe betide those who subject their storytelling to scrutiny because once the magic is punctured, it becomes needlessly bothersome to 'un-discover' that inconvenience and no amount of linguistic sleight of hand can redeem it. Without doubt, cultivating mythology in this book would have been a straightforward matter, while cutting through it introduced the disadvantageous complication of laborious effort, but what that toil uncovered is no less colourful and has added frisson for being factual. Indeed, laying bare the manner in which myths arose is vastly more engrossing than the myths themselves, as may be discovered in some of the bunkum-busting bombshells dropped amongst these pages.

Be that as it may, I feel duty-bound to confess great torment overcoming the conspiratorial urge to slip in a magnificent new confection of my own manufacture in this collection to set loose among London legend – and some of the stories that follow might encourage the impression that I succumbed to that temptation. But suffice to say, much like the responsibility involved in erecting a plaque on a building, the conferral of Black Plaques comes with the wearisome burden of getting the facts right.

And with that being unequivocally and courageously declared, as the commemorative words that follow lay bare, to err is congenitally human, so any blunders herein are manifestly the author's and his alone.

The interests of trustworthy public edification are not the only quality that Black Plaques share with their respectable real-world counterparts. There is something to be said for stumbling upon a plaque that suddenly piques one's interest, and this sense of serendipitous discovery is the rationale for presenting Black Plaques in similarly unpredictable order. Nothing is to be gained from arbitrarily grouping narratives thematically, geographically or chronologically, whereas by diving head first into a pair of knickers at Buckingham

Palace, then turning the page to unearth bodies beneath Kennington Park, etc, I hope readers are swept along in an exhilarating roller coaster ride. Moreover, by meandering through London in this way, readers may discover connections for themselves – be they overt, such as the imaginative gambits employed by men across the ages to either gratify their sexual ambitions or appease a deity (or a subtle combination of the two); opaque, for instance how the Strand station site also housed a theatre in which two cross-dressing young gentlemen had an infamous outing (in both senses); or obscure, for example, some intimate uses for German white wine. For the convenience of those who seek material of specific special interest, or wish to revisit a story but recall only that it entailed, say, an unhappy brush with erotic asphyxiation, fulfilment may be found in the comprehensive index.

To wrap up this bout between decorous public plaques and the indecorous sub-species presented here, the two share one further quality: neither make any claim to be

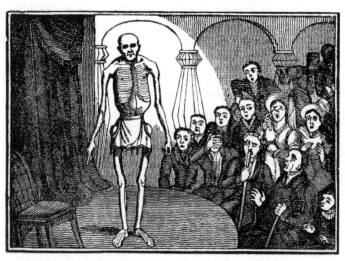

The exhibition of an enfeebled Frenchman is indexed under: Seurat, Claude Ambroise, Pall Mall, freak show and skeleton, 'living'.

exhaustive. These pages could be filled solely with either places of execution, the former sites of gay molly-houses or even the premises of piss prophets, and in a roundabout way such books already exist. The Black Plaques Executive Committee – the official body charged with determining the sites to be dishonoured, comprises a single member: the author, and the process of identifying and evaluating eligible improprieties is subject to the idle whims and fancies of that office-holder. (Rumour has it that henceforth, the committee's decision-making is apt to be swayed by overtures from deep-pocketed lobby groups prone to gourmandising.) Which brings us back to the question of defining the guiding principle behind the bestowal of Black Plaques.

Returning to St Paul's Cathedral and the unfortunate fellow nursing a burning needle up his nostril, the reason that this saga became the inaugural and emblematic Black Plaque lies with the fact that it is not a straightforward one-dimensional tale of murder (again, a topic given more than adequate treatment elsewhere). The episode was – and its current obscurity implies it still is – a peculiarly awkward mix of circumstances that happen to swerve between tragedy and comedy. It also had profound consequences for the nation and were schoolchildren to study it their faces might light up at the prospect of pondering events leading up to the English Reformation. (It is deeply ironic that had the nose job taken place at the Tower of London, Yeoman Warders would leap at the chance to horrify young visitors with the grisly melodrama.) Not every Black Plaque can claim such historical significance but they all possess this piquant blend of qualities that, when laid bare, stick out like a thoroughly unwelcome spot. And crucial to the Black Plaques physiognomy is the wide variety of colour, texture and filling in those blemishes. Several inglorious episodes warrant inclusion purely because they illustrate behaviour of such flagrant audacity, ingenuity or absurdity it is difficult not to feel some misdirected admiration – in fact, protagonists (or perhaps better put: antagonists) of many Black Plaques more than adequately atone for their wayward moral compass through their gift of grotesque entertainment. Other uneasy incidents fulfil the definition of history proposed by eighteenth-century historian Edward Gibbon as 'little more than the register of the crimes, follies, and misfortunes of mankind'.

But while posterity forever enjoys the smug wisdom of hindsight, this does not infer that Black Plaques are a means to cast stones at our ancestors, because as I am about to suggest, the current herd of hairless apes is barely any better.

Without wishing to become high and mighty over the idiosyncratic gazetteer of mishaps, misdeeds and mischief that you hold in your riveted gaze, I was dismayed to discover that once Black Plaques had been conferred on the most deserving sites, the whole was found to be more foreboding than the sum of its unedifying parts. Collectively, in its own modest way this unrepentantly subjective miscellany of misadventure conjures up an encyclopaedic survey of humanity's frailties, flaws and foibles – a lengthy charge sheet that includes (deep breath): cowardice, cruelty, dishonesty, envy, greed, homophobia, hubris, hypocrisy, ignorance, incompetence, lust, narcissism, naivety, misogyny, prudery, schadenfreude, selfishness, snobbery, vengefulness and xenophobia. Present form suggests these to be ineradicable shortcomings of the human intellect (as is the unavoidability of our various inelegant bodily functions) and it became clear that in my self-indulgence I had unwittingly plumped for stories that enjoyed an exceptionally intoxicating cocktail of them, not only in events themselves but, just as importantly, in our reactions towards them today. Cowardice, hypocrisy and plain squeamishness have suppressed cringeworthy or unsettling stories such as the brutal force-feeding of suffragettes, the Victorian

Nowadays we have at our fingertips considerably more convenient forms of pillorying.

establishment's zest for female genital mutilation, or simply a Member of Parliament's memorable fart. (I trust that readers who have made it thus far are of sufficiently robust constitution not to label this work: 'I Didn't Want To Know That About London'). So while the substance of some Black Plaques can appear comfortably distant, this compendium holds a mirror to its audience and parallels with the present-day can also feel uncomfortably close.

As befits a metropolis that has long stood at an international crossroads, Black Plaques London does not merely highlight peculiarly British blemishes of character, but those of what might be styled *Homo londoniensis* – inhabitants of a city driven by its own singular imperatives. And reflecting on the roles played by women in the ensuing drama, this sorry behaviour materialises predominantly among the male of the species. Evidence presented here challenges the notion that mankind is somehow the pinnacle of creation because Exhibit A is *Homo insapiens* – and fingers crossed this does not become our eventual epitaph. But before we sink into cynicism and misanthropy, it is worth a gentle reminder that as a cure for The Great Forgetfulness, Black Plaques are merely a means to rebalance commemorative subject matter and such a damning indictment stems naturally from this in-built bias towards our dark side. Readers who wish to restore their faith in humanity may remind themselves of those do-gooders and noble pillars of society who merit blue plaques, or view

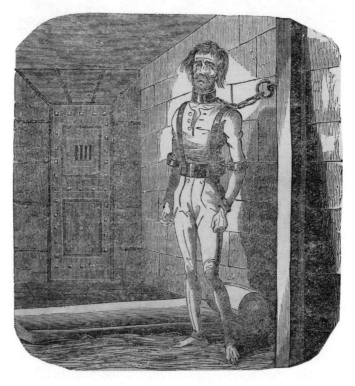

American James Norris found treatment at Bethlem Hospital especially wanting (see page 271).

Black Plaques through blue-tinted spectacles. To this end, one of several possible examples (beyond the comforting fact that we no longer proffer our piss to prophets) is the hospital of the Priory of St Mary of Bethlehem (a.k.a. the Bethlem/Bedlam lunatic asylum – yes, it crops up later), which should be widely celebrated as one of the first places on earth where people suffering the twin afflictions of mental illness and poverty were cared for, because that was the primary human impulse behind it. These pages recall moments when civilisation was not enjoying its finest hour, so focus is placed solely on the bad bits of Bedlam.

So while Black Plaques can be seen as a delicious serving of fresh anecdotes with which to regale one's drinking companions, they also provide food for sober reflection. I can assert with reasonable confidence that as well as being less cruel to animals and women, we are by and large cleaner and healthier than our predecessors. However, I hope the opportunity for a spell of retrospective rubbernecking prompts interesting thoughts on whether it would be asking too much of human nature to wish for anything more.

John Ambrose Hide

GRUBBY NICKER

As dawn was breaking one morning in December 1838, the night porter at Buckingham Palace was suddenly confronted by a ghostly face at his door. But when the apparition promptly vanished, he was left wondering whether it had been a figment of his imagination, so out of caution he alerted police who began a careful search of the building.

Smudges of a curious fatty, yet sooty substance was all that confronted constables until a figure was spotted lurking in the shadows of the Marble Hall. Quietly creeping up on the intruder, an officer lunged at them – but the mysterious dark form was daubed with grease so simply slipped from his clutches; it scurried across the room, leaped out of a window and sprinted across the lawn. When police finally caught up with it, the trespasser turned out to be 14-year-old Edward Jones, Britain's first royal stalker.

Jones was frogmarched to the kitchen, where the full extent of his filthiness became apparent, leading officers to believe that he had disguised himself as a chimney sweep. It later became clear that Jones was habitually this dirty, however his grubbiness had been cultivated by means of a bottle of bear's grease – a popular (though misguided) hair loss treatment that he had discovered in a state bedroom and, for reasons known only to him, chosen to smear over himself. But most appalling to onlookers was the conspicuous bulge in his trousers that, when forcibly slackened, caused the spilling out of several items of Queen Victoria's underwear.

Undergarments made no appearance on Jones's charge sheet and a prevailing desire to avoid airing intimate Royal laundry in public eased a jury towards a verdict of sending the youth on his way.

But two years later, despite an assassination attempt on the Queen and the birth of her first child, palace security was again found wanting. During a December night in 1840, the Queen's midwife heard something moving in the Royal dressing room, just a door away from the sleeping monarch. She summoned assistance and from beneath a sofa was dragged a creature of 'most repulsive appearance'; there was no mistaking that it was soap-shy Jones again. On this occasion he had none of the Queen's unmentionable apparel on his person, but there was an awkward feeling that he might have observed it being worn by its owner. Nothing more than a wry grin escaped Jones's lips, but were he to delight the press with the finer details of his escapade there would be acute embarrassment. Consequently the safest course of action was to deal with the scoundrel in a manner more befitting treasonous barons in medieval times: he would be interrogated in secret by the Privy Council.

Jones merrily informed the venerable assembly how he climbed a wall into the palace garden, hopped through an open window, then curled up for a snooze under one of the servant's beds. The following evening, he sauntered off to procure dinner and when suitably sated wandered between state rooms and private apartments. A trail of dirt confirmed his palace peregrinations and this time Jones was handed three months' hard labour.

Palace security was stepped up with a detachment of four-teen constables on twenty-four hour watch, yet on 16 March 1841, a midnight patrol of the Grand Staircase revealed a squat shadow lolling in a recess beside a pair of grimy shoes. With weary resignation, an officer called out: 'What, Jones is that you?' to which: 'Yes, it is me,' was the sheepish reply. Once again, Jones recounted his caper around the palace to the Privy Council – how he tried a throne for size, pulled out books in the library, then came upon a room with a crown and jewels to play with. Grubby stains again bore out the truth of his tale so 'In-I-Go Jones' returned to the treadmill.

When the scoundrel later emerged frail and sickly from what seemed a concerted effort by the authorities to break him, his family had an unexpected surprise – their landlord, Mr James, was suddenly expressing heartfelt concern for the delinquent boy's welfare. As luck would have it, a Captain acquaintance of his would shortly set sail from London so why didn't the lad sign up as an apprentice seaman? Jones declared no yearning for the sea but the promise of financial favour dulled any reasoning so he gaily set off – unaware that it was an emigrant ship bound for New Zealand. But the plan had an unexpected flaw: the boy's exploits had brought such notoriety, the captain recognised his cargo and immediately offloaded it; the rascal reached no further from Buckingham Palace than Gravesend. James was evidently not devoid of nous because he hurriedly bribed another boy to take the voyage and on arrival announce he was Jones, thus satisfying the shadowy figures behind the plot – but the deception lasted merely a few weeks.

Had this story been a work of fiction, it would now conclude with a dramatic last act, but regrettably, the final curtain is somewhat threadbare. After James spent several years making whistle-stop tours of Britain's docks with the boy, coaxing him aboard ships bound for far-flung regions, the scallywag's grimy trail finally loses its scent somewhere in Australia.

KENNINGTON PARK SE11

BATTLE LINES

The south field of Kennington Park bears a distinct series of bumps, which in summer become a pattern of brown lines in the grass; they are the ghostly outline of a vast underground air raid shelter dug in 1938 to accommodate up to 3,000 people. Towards one end the contours become fainter, and for tragic reasons.

Like many Second World War shelters in parks and commons across London, Kennington Park's was built by the local authority from pre-cast concrete slabs; wall panels slotted into floor and roof sections to form a warren of tunnels

buried 12in below ground. But even before war was declared, workers died while constructing shelters such as these due to their poor-quality materials and the speed at which they were built, and concerns were voiced over their grid layout because an explosion would funnel straight through them. While later versions adopted a zig-zag design or steel frame with reinforced brickwork, these early so-called trench shelters remained highly vulnerable.

The scale of its inadequacy became apparent at 8 p.m. on 15 October 1940 when a 250kg high-explosive bomb struck the southern end while several hundred men, women and children were taking refuge from an air raid. Not only was the impact zone obliterated, but the huge blast lifted the shelter's roof so its walls caved in under the weight of soil; an area of almost 10,000 sq ft collapsed and amid a scene of utter horror; those not blown to pieces were buried alive.

Messages relayed to the Air Raid Precautions post offer a dreadful glimpse into the tragedy that night. Rescuers arrived with shovels to dig out survivors in the darkness but five hours after the bomb landed, it was estimated that at least 100 people were still trapped underground – their condition perhaps hollowly described as 'fairly calm', despite the fact that further bombs had landed in the vicinity. A couple of hours later, those who had not been recovered were declared dead and rescue attempts were called off. Screens were erected around the devastation, quicklime scattered to hasten decomposition, and all memories of the disaster erased for the rest of the war and some time afterwards.

An official death toll has never – or perhaps will never – be given, not least because numbers entering the shelter were not recorded and bereaved families may have kept their grief private. Although the bodies of forty-eight victims were recovered, it is generally declared that 104 people lost their lives; the remains of those unrecovered individuals still lie beneath the grass.

An easily overlooked memorial in the adjacent sunken garden commemorates 'over 50' men, women and children who died in the tragedy.

DUDMASTON MEWS SW3

COTTAGE SPY

In 1953, male homosexuality was causing moral panic and the Government acknowledged its duty to halt the spread of what Home Secretary Sir David Maxwell Fyfe labelled 'this plague'. Answering urgent Parliamentary questions about the sharp rise in sexual delinquency, Fyfe fulminated: 'Homosexuals in general are exhibitionists and proselytisers and are a danger to others, especially the young', and expressed confidence that male perversion could be curbed through custodial sentencing: sodomy and bestiality warranted life imprisonment, attempt to commit unnatural offence or indecent assault on a male person: ten years, gross indecency: two years, and importuning: six months on summary conviction, or two years on conviction on indictment. One parliamentarian urged the adoption of medical procedures because the conviction rate was such it necessitated two or three men to a prison cell – which could only exacerbate the epidemic.

It was while walking home at about 11 p.m. on 21 October 1953 that the newly knighted Sir John Gielgud visited the gentleman's lavatory on Dudmaston Mews. As the actor made his exit, an attractive young man sauntered in and smiled at him. A particular glance or wink was sufficient for gay men to discreetly identify each other and because this particular lavatory was a well-known 'cottage' for homosexual liaisons, Gielgud turned around and followed him back in. Despite being an immensely private man, Gielgud evidently derived a thrill from both the fruits and hazards of cruising.

What happened next remains unspecified, but at a timely moment when an act of intimacy was perhaps on the cards, the man revealed himself to be a plain-clothes officer from Metropolitan Police B Division – one of the so-called 'pretty police' who lurked in men's toilets to entrap homosexuals. Dudmaston Mews was one of at least thirteen gents' lavatories across the West End known to be 'notorious for perverts', so the Home Office arranged that they were staked out by pairs of undercover officers working four-week shifts as agents provocateurs. It is uncertain exactly what form training took for those alluring members of the constabulary chosen to adopt the role, but it was by far their most unpopular duty.

Whatever Gielgud's endeavours in meriting the withdrawal of police notebooks, he was arrested for 'persistently importuning male persons for immoral purposes' – a charge that reveals how this was not his first brush with lavatory-dwelling law enforcement. His only response was: 'I am so terribly sorry,' which, while not exactly Shakespearean, was a line he no doubt delivered with impeccable pathos.

At Chelsea police station the actor informed officers that he was a single man named Arthur Gielgud – perhaps in a fumbled attempt to hide his identity (something Alec Guinness had successfully pulled off when in a similar predicament a few years earlier, giving the name of a Dickens character, Herbert Pocket). Gielgud had, in fact, been christened Arthur but when asked his profession stated that he was a self-employed clerk earning £1,000 a year. While the story may have grated with his refined enunciation, it conformed with the working man's cap he donned to blend in on his forays; Gielgud was bound over to appear at West London Magistrates' Court at 10.30 the following morning.

Many among the police and judiciary were uncomfortable with the witch-hunt of homosexuals for little more than tactile or suggestive behaviour – especially when caught by entrapment – and at 8 the next morning Gielgud's telephone rang. The caller was a police sergeant, who informed the actor that a magistrate was prepared to hear the case before the court opened to the public – and more importantly the press – thereby letting him slip away before he was spotted. Through luck or design, the magistrate turned out to be of a sympathetic persuasion and showed no outward sign that he recognised the renowned Knight Bachelor and star of a triumphant run of *Venice Preserv'd* stood before him. Gielgud pleaded guilty following advice that the case would not be reported if he did so, and fumbled an explanation for his situation, declaring that he had been tired and drunk. Rather than face six months in prison, he was fined £10, told to seek immediate treatment from his doctor and warned how his conduct imperilled young men and was a scourge in the neighbourhood.

But his fortune was short-lived. As the actor hurriedly exited the scene, a sharp-eyed reporter was arriving for the first hearing and immediately recognised him; by afternoon the story was front-page news. A Tory peer called for Gielgud to be stripped of his knighthood, taken into the street and horsewhipped, but the proposition drew less support than he hoped because in the court of public opinion attitudes were beginning to soften. When Sir John returned to the stage he found himself greeted with a standing ovation – a reaction he thought would have been inconceivable only twenty years earlier (though he noted with bitterness how newspapers were less cruel in those times). But despite popular indifference to his sexuality, he later wrote how his arrest led him to contemplate suicide, until on reflection he resolved that such a course of action was unnecessarily 'melodramatic'.

SHEEN GATE, RICHMOND PARK SW14

SHREWD OPERATOR

Folklore attributes mystical qualities to ash trees, and a revered specimen known as the Shrew Ash once stood in open ground near Adam's Pond at Sheen Gate. However, in contrast to the cherished tree, our forefathers invested the humble shrew with the most malignant character. Should the creature cross your path, crawl over you, or more ominously, sink its teeth into you, the prognosis was bleak. Lameness in livestock was one of several conditions commonly triggered by the velvety fiends.

To arm the parish against such evil, the tree was imbued with magical healing properties; a hole was bored in its trunk, a live shrew pushed inside it and the opening plugged – an operation perhaps embellished with mystical incantations now long forgotten. Twigs or leaves from the tree were then caressed over the person or beast's afflicted region and their malady miraculously transferred itself to the unfortunate shrew – as could be witnessed for oneself on inspection of the wretched creature. And locals need not wait for a varmint to strike because branches also acted as a deterrent, so were hung in cattle sheds at calving time as protection against shrewish mischief.

But should immured critters fail to work, all was not lost; this particular tree possessed another therapeutic quality by dint of being cloven, or split in two down the trunk. Before dawn, sickly infants were brought to it for a ritual superintended by a 'shrew mother', who passed them nine times around a witchbar – a wooden stake wedged between the divided trunk – while muttering mysterious and likely incomprehensible verses, timed so that a specific 'word' coincided with the first ray of sun. If going through such motions subsequently proved of little purpose, blame could be laid on flawed timekeeping, though as with all similar methodologies, one success quickly blotted out 100 failures.

In all likelihood, the tree was cloven owing to earlier service curing 'weak, rickety or ruptured' children. Young ash trees were split in two down the trunk and the sections held apart while the naked youngster was drawn through the gap as many times as seemed fit. The tree was then tightly bound back together and as it healed, so did the poorly child.

Warty folk also flocked to the Shrew Ash. Pins were pushed in its bark, jabbed into the wart then back in the tree, and with a few verses of 'Ashen tree, ashen tree, pray buy these warts off me', the growths were expected to deflate. (In the event that unsightly scabbing was the only outcome, the next thing to try was rubbing them with a piece of stolen beef.)

The ancient tree was still a focus for rituals in 1875 when the greater part of it was blown down, and though its magic powers waned thereafter, it survived until the storm of 1987.

ST PAUL'S CATHEDRAL EC4

CLERICAL ERROR

Guidebooks to St Paul's omit to mention that the medieval cathedral (which was destroyed in the fire of 1666) contained a prison cell, and the experiences of one inmate were exceptionally ungodly.

In 1511, at the funeral of his newborn baby in Whitechapel, prosperous tailor Richard Hunne refused the priest's demand for the infant's christening robe as payment. Ecclesiastical law permitted the church to claim a possession belonging to the deceased, so the priest sued Hunne in the church court. The grieving father was unperturbed; civil law indicated that a corpse could not own property, so Hunne boldly raised the stakes: he issued a writ in the King's court under a law entitled the Statute of Praemunire, cautioning church authorities that it was treason to appeal to a power higher than the King – in this case, a foreign jurisdiction under the Pope. From a trivial squabble, church and state were now on a collision course.

Hunne's impudence did him no favours with the Bishop of London, who accused him of heresy and condemned him to the prison cell in the Cathedral's south-west tower. And when the prisoner was found hanging from the ceiling shortly afterwards, his captors revealed that a guilty conscience had driven him to suicide.

Hunne's demise was no impediment to the progress of his trial and the former tailor was summoned to court in the Lady Chapel before three bishops, the Lord Mayor, city officials and a concourse of churchmen. The not insignificant burden of evidence had been resolved when, just in the nick of time, a Bible printed in English complete with heretical annotations attributed to the dead defendant fell into the hands of the prosecution, and following four days of proceedings with silence throughout from the accused, it came as no surprise that Hunne was found guilty. As was customary, the condemned heretic was removed to Smithfield, tied to a stake and burned – though because this act was wholly incompatible with Christian principles, the sentence was effected by secular authorities.

That might have been the end of the affair were it not for the City of London Coroner Thomas Barnewell, who examined the prison cell shortly after the grisly discovery. Puzzlingly, he found Hunne's body hanging 'with fair countenance, his head fair combed and his bonnet right sitting upon his head, his eyes and mouth closed without any staring, gaping or frowning. Also without any drooling or spurging in any place.' Furthermore, he noted 'the skin both of his neck and throat fret away' and 'out of his nostrils two small streams of blood to the quantity of four drops. Save only these the face, lips, chin, doublet, collar and shirt was clean.' In contrast however, Hunne's jacket lay in the opposite corner of the cell with a 'cluster of blood' staining its front, alongside a 'great parcel' of bloodiness on the floor. It was not to be the coroner's most challenging case because, along with the litany of suspicious detail, someone had left behind a luxurious fur-lined gown; 'Wherefore we find that Richard Hunne was murdered.'

Barnewell soon discovered that a church official, Charles Joseph, had fled to Essex and claimed sanctuary, so he was duly apprehended and robust interrogation at the Tower of London prompted a confession: the Bishop's Chancellor, Dr Horsey, had instructed him to kill Hunne and then contrive the illusion of suicide. (In truth, Hunne may have been tortured to disclose his associates, but in the circumstances an admission of murder was expedient.) Drafting in muscle in the shape of the bell-ringer, they had pinned Hunne down, heated a long needle in a candle until red hot, then thrust it up his nose and into his brain to kill him cleanly. Alas, as churchmen not hitmen, the lynching went horribly wrong – Hunne struggled, suffered a catastrophic nasal haemorrhage and in the scuffle his neck was broken.

However, all was not lost. With Horsey's assistance they washed Hunne's body, dressed it a clean shirt and, warming to the deception, closed his eyes, combed his hair and arranged his nightcap before stringing him up from a hook in the ceiling. Blind to the fact that the stool Hunne supposedly jumped from was on the other side of the cell and Horsey's gown lay over the stocks, they snuffed out the candle and departed.

While the evidence was compromising, it not a calamity because, as members of the clergy, all three were immune from prosecution. Public outrage was another matter, however, and the affair became a source of great embarrassment to the young Henry VIII – not least because Hunne's property had been forfeited to the Crown. The royal solution was an exemplary fudge: Horsey waived his immunity to appear before the King's court charged with murder, and under written instructions from Henry, the Attorney General accepted his not guilty plea and dismissed the case; the three perpetrators were then obliged to make themselves decidedly scarce.

It was only sometime later that Henry resolved whether he or the Pope wielded more authority, and doubtless recalling the legal manoeuvre employed by the obstinate tailor, indicted the entire English clergy under the very same law.

OLD BILLINGSGATE MARKET EC3

SWEAR TO COD

Selling fish spawned such deplorable language that Billingsgate, the name of fish market on the site from the sixteenth to the twentieth century, became a synonym for swearing.

Fishermen have long been noted for their command of the more colourful corners of the English tongue and the circumstances of their profession stimulated their wives to follow suit. Responsibility for selling the catch originally fell to the womenfolk and this was not to be done through meek chinwagging; to tout their wares in the busy market they bellowed and shrieked at the top of their lungs – their salty vocabulary further enriched by the urgency of shifting a perishable stock. (Should it fail to sell, the reeking remains were carefully set aside to be peddled beside the pillory.) Although these women were more liberated than many of their gender, it was their unsparing profanities that led 'fishwife' to become another term for someone with a coarse tongue.

Thus, there was an element of truth to writer Ned Ward's account of the Billingsgate Surly Club, which was dedicated to advancing the art of abusive discourse among the piscatorial labouring class. Members convened at a local watering hole to exercise their powers of denigration by insulting each other in ever more impudent terms, though should a participant become corrupted with good manners or utter a civil expression, they were summarily expelled – no doubt with a cacophony of eloquent expletives ringing in their ears. His story may have been sardonic, but were one to venture into a Billingsgate alehouse, the lively exchange of vernacular would certainly foster such an impression.

Ward offers a flavour of the robust local phraseology when he paints a scene at Billingsgate in 1700, shortly after somebody has scooped a turd from the Thames and flung it at his lady friend. He graciously disposes of it – though only as far as a waterman's forehead, provoking some highly disobliging remarks:

You shiten-skulled son of a turd, that has spit your brains in my face, who was begot in buggery, born in a house of office and delivered at the fundament, fit for nothing but to be cast into a gold-finders ditch, there lie till you're rotten, and then be sold out to gardeners for a hot bed to raise pumpkins to feed the Devil withall. And as for you, you brandy-faced, bottle-nosed, bawdy, brimstone whore, every time you conjobble together may he beget your belly full of live crabs and crawfish, that as you strive to pluck 'em out they may hang by the sides of your tu quoque, and make you squeak nine times louder than a woman frighted into labour a month before her reckoning.

PEACOCK THEATRE WC2

ANATOMY THEATRE

In 1737, George II's foul temper was further inflamed when his widely known difficulties with piles became aggravated by an adjoining anal fistula. Matters were not eased when news reached him of plans for a stage play in which he was depicted submitting to magical unctions administered by rectal syringe. Small wonder that a bill to license and regulate theatres received Royal assent.

It was 1968 before this censorship was finally shaken off, though in later years it was less concerned with protecting those in power than shielding the public from pornography. Full advantage of these new freedoms was seized in 1970 when what was then named the Royalty Theatre staged a production of *Oh! Calcutta!* whose themes had no connection with the subcontinent. Cognoscenti recognised that its unusual title was a pun on *quel cul tu as* – a Gallic way of expressing admiration for someone's derrière. Scripted by provocateur Kenneth Tynan and bankrolled by the theatre's colourful new leaseholder, Paul Raymond, the 'Revue with Music' contained nudity, swearing, fetishism, simulated sex and masturbation. (Pifco Ltd was graciously acknowledged for facilitating dramaturgy through the loan of its 'vibro massager'.) The production received a welcome publicity boost when establishment figures loudly proclaimed it pornographic, and following a minor hiccup when the cast defied the direction to disrobe because the theatre was too cold, it proved box-office gold.

PAUL RAYMOND's

Royalty Folies

ROYALTY THEATRE

Such lucre made it another notch on the bedpost for Raymond, who was diligently laying the groundwork for the flesh trade stereotype: the caramel tan, louche mane of hair, and full length fur coat accessorised with Champagne flute and meagrely attired females. Buoyed by the show's success and absence of police raids, Raymond set about planning his next production: Royalty Folies – a big budget affair blending lavish Las Vegas glamour with Parisian cabaret, along with an artificial ice rink and two giant water tanks that would rise from beneath the stage to reveal bottlenose dolphins. Unsurprisingly, they were not the only mammalian features unveiled.

The curtain went up in March 1974 and perhaps to make plain its subject matter, the spectacle was also billed The Great International Nude Show because twice nightly, audiences enjoyed a phalanx of forty dancing showgirls in various states of undress – high kicking in a chorus line, gyrating in giant birdcages, pirouetting on the ice or careering through the air from specially designed trapdoors. Two lithe and curvaceous specimens flitted in the water and these graceful creatures had been painstakingly trained to separate 'Miss Nude International' from the confines of her bikini. Raymond's pre-show publicity lifted the lid on this unique piece of stagecraft by divulging how the skimpy garments were soaked overnight in liquidised fishmeal, then under the tutelage of marine biologist Dr Frederick Finn, the water nymph had been trained how to acquit herself alongside cetaceans by practising with a stunt double. This came in the shape of retired Navy diver Chief Petty Officer Perkins, who stood in as the nibbling dolphin; the gallant frogman had been selected from a shortlist of several thousand because prior to rehearsals the pensioner could remove his teeth. Irreverent humour was not found wanting in Raymond's public relations.

In truth, the bikini feat was pulled off through the judicious placement of tasty morsels of fish alongside strips of double-sided sticky-back plastic, and in a gift to headline writers the cavorting mermaid's name was Lindy Salmon.

Royalty Folies was also a family show because Raymond's daughter, Debbie, took a leading role, despite notable short-comings in her singing voice. No one thought to mention this to the proprietor, perhaps because it was overshadowed by a more fundamental snag – Debbie refused to perform *au naturel*. While this would gravely hamper the job prospects of any other girl in the company, her father arranged that, like the token smattering of 'Royalty Boy Dancers', she retained the use of costume throughout.

Female nudity was also sporadically interrupted by light entertainment from speciality acts including two tap-dancing brothers, a ventriloquist and puppet troupe. After a turn in which 'The Nude Showgirls and The Fabulous Royalty Dancers' entered 'The Exotic Palace of Love', the heady atmosphere was cooled by magician Luxor Gali-Gali, whose routine included producing a live duckling from the jacket of one audience member and cheeping chicks from the trousers of another.

Cheap was not how such extravagant razzmatazz was hatched, however. Ironically for a nude show, its costume budget was colossal to cover thousands of feathers and sequins as well as forty fur coats – and what with hydraulic lifting gear to raise the water tanks and an ice rink imported from America, Royalty Folies came close to becoming the most costly production ever staged in the country.

And folly was how Raymond's pet project turned out. After twelve weeks when losses topped £400,000, he had no option but to abort it; perhaps theatregoers did not appreciate someone interfering with their trousers.

Raymond's monetary woes were not eased by a spot of bother over his magazine *Men Only* – half a million copies of which were seized by police after a High Court judge had flicked through its bumper Christmas special and deemed it indecent, presenting him with another censorship battle.

BEATING THE SYSTEM

Picture the scene: a boat crammed with choirboys robed in cassocks and pleated ruffs is bobbing about on the Thames beside the Tower of London. One of the boys is called forward then dangled over the side, and as a clergyman sternly commands 'Whack it boy, whack it!' the hapless youth thrashes at the water with a limp stick. Supplementary colour and pageantry may be visualised by witnessing the latest incarnation of this entertaining but absurd annual spectacle for oneself.

The idea of pitting a poorly armed minor against the river did not materialise fully formed from nought, but as a twist in the ancient custom of Beating the Bounds – a peculiar agglomeration of pagan, Roman Catholic, Protestant and secular endeavours.

The Romans honoured Terminus, deity of boundary stones, through neighbourly rituals at markers between fields, and made appeals to a host of other gods for auspicious weather and fertility in crops and livestock; even Robigus, revered god of grain mildew, demanded appeasement through the expedient of a sacrificed puppy. The early Christian church, eager to foster the notion of its magical agency, brought fruits of the earth and their preferred superabundance under the auspices of saints who were petitioned in a schedule of outdoor ceremonies. These included the St John's Eve bone-fire, whose stench repelled dragons that discourteously 'spermatise in the wells'. It was also provident to pace the parish boundary to inspect its marker stones and ensure that conniving neighbours were not encroaching, and while a priest bellowed a curse on anyone who stooped to such a thing, frantic beating encouraged His Infernal Majesty to slope off elsewhere.

The Church of England promptly jettisoned such conjuring, but though discouraging lustful dragons from tainting the drinking water ceased, walking the perimeter with willow wands while praying for a bountiful harvest crept back into the church calendar during springtime Rogationtide. In the absence of accurate maps it was useful for reasons territorial and parochial, and in some parishes – particularly metropolitan – the procession became entirely secular and various improvements were made to it, such as the introduction of cake and alcohol, and permitting the Mayor to kiss the prettiest maiden at each marker.

Youngsters were necessarily involved because it was formerly not boundaries that were beaten, but boys. The clergy reasoned that thrashing a juvenile in front of a marker was an efficient means to reinforce its location in his youthful, receptive mind – in fact, a simple knock of his head on the stone also left a lasting impression.

The parish of All Hallows by the Tower requires a boat for the ceremony because its boundary lies halfway across the river – which is no reason to forgo a thorough whacking.

16 WELBECK STREET W1

CREATE A BUZZ

It is immensely ironic that the inventor of the electric vibrator, Joseph Mortimer Granville, flinched at the notion of aiming his contraption at women – to say nothing of it falling into their trembling hands.

Granville lived and worked at Welbeck Street, where he proudly unveiled his electro-mechanical tool to the world in 1883. The unwieldy appliance was energised by a bulky external battery and bristled with an armoury of interchangeable rubber and ivory attachments called vibratodes, including pointed and flat-headed hammers and both soft and hard brushes. Manufactured by the reputable medical instrument makers Weiss & Sons, the apparatus offered both a speed control that reached the heights of '2,000 blows per minute' and means to vary the length of stroke.

Medical men had long employed massage techniques on various regions of the sickly frame, so Granville's Hammer (or 'Percuteur') was a welcome improvement on its hand-cranked and clockwork forerunners, saving doctors' both time and wrist muscles. Patients proved less eager to submit to the throbbing head of the newfangled contrivance, so its creator found it necessary to clarify that 'no current passes through the hammer of my instrument'.

As Granville anticipated, his invention proved beneficial at relieving pain, nervous tension and even the common cold, so he began investigating its efficacy on other ailments. Directing a pointed ivory hammer at a patient's perineum and pounding firmly, he declared: 'I have in no instance failed to produce activity of the bowels, even in the case of previously obstinate constipation.' With it presumably targeted elsewhere, he made a singularly bold claim: 'I have now under treatment the case of a child who was six weeks ago to all appearance an idiot, but who has already developed so much cerebral activity and growing intelligence under the influence of specific centre and nerve vibration that I entertain the strongest hope of his ultimate awakening.' But whatever the condition, in Granville's treatment room it was strictly only men who benefitted: 'I have avoided, and shall continue to avoid, the treatment of women by percussion.'

Exactly what happened to Granville's creation after it jumped from his unsullied hands into the wider world is mired in mythology. His contemporaries were undoubtedly less reticent about applying the instrument to womankind, however the exact manner in which they did so is the subject of much speculation. While doctors certainly reached for vibrators to relieve symptoms to which nuns, spinsters and widows were especially vulnerable such as irritability, headaches and chronic anxiety – a condition they vaguely defined as hysteria – the burning question is whether their *modus operandi* entailed wheeling the instrument between the patient's legs. If they did so, the journals of both parties are disappointingly anticlimactic.

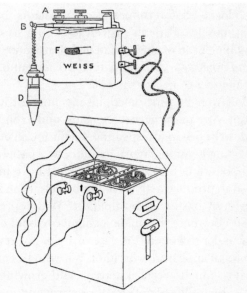

The Percuteur worked by electro-magnetism, and the *Bunsen's
Battery,* as supplied by Messrs. Weiss & Sons.

So while the image of hysterical Victorian gentlewomen
visiting their physician to be massaged/masturbated to par-
oxysm/orgasm with neither party thinking it in any way
inappropriate might be enticing (and forms the storyline to
a feature film about Granville 'based on true events'), there is
no evidence that it ever came to pass; the device was almost
certainly aimed anywhere but the genitalia. The medical
profession considered 'self-pollution' highly dangerous to
health, causing disorders ranging from bed-wetting to imbe-
cility – some even believing hysteria itself to be triggered by
masturbation, so doctors were hardly predisposed to re-ori-
entating the latest medical instrument to finesse the practice.

Granville did power up his vibrator to treat gentlemen who
presented the exclusively Victorian malady Spermatorrhoea
(excessive loss of semen, through whatever agency), though

precisely which portion of the patient he vibrated is unclear. He also brandished it on men who displayed symptoms of hysteria, noting that patients were 'generally of a feminine character', but remained sceptical of the condition: 'I do not want to be hoodwinked and help to mislead others by the vagaries of the hysterical state.'

Granville's tool was grasped with the greatest gusto in the US where anything a Brit could do an American could do better, so a panoply of new models appeared including the Victor Vibrator, which achieved a blistering 6,000 strokes per minute and boasted an array of twenty-three vibratodes as well as 12in rectal probe on special order. (Experience showed that this last attachment was best employed on a short, well-lubricated crank for no longer than three minutes.) One doctor fanatical about curbing masturbation was John Harvey Kellogg, who pummelled patients with Granville's gadget before developing devices of his own – something he certainly would not have done had the instrument possessed the whiff of sex about it.

The potential of vibrators became explicit when domestic versions appeared alongside the electric sewing machine and kettle in the years following 1900 (housewives had to wait another decade for the electric vacuum cleaner and iron), which perhaps fittingly was the year Granville died. In the privacy of the home, the debilitated willingly took matters into their own hands, particularly when mains electricity remedied a frustrating drawback: the battery petering out halfway through the job. The 'personal massager' spent the best part of the next century camouflaged in euphemism or touted as a miracle cure for wrinkles or headaches, but liberated from the hands of doctors the potency of its ultimate misapplication had been recognised.

LEATHERMARKET, MOROCCO
& TANNER STREET SE1

STICKY BUSINESS

Definitions of the adjective 'pure' include: unsoiled, faultless, and of unmixed ancestry: a pure breed of dog, etc. Meanwhile, the noun denotes dog faeces used in the production of leather.

Leathermarket, Morocco and Tanner Street recall Bermondsey's once prevalent leather industry – a trade banished to the outer reaches of the city on account of its pernicious assault on the olfactory system, even by the standards of our ancestors' noses (although plague victims considered the area's stench a salubrious countermeasure to the disease).

Tanners stripped raw hides of hair, fat and any portions of rotting animal still clinging to them – a process aided by lime (or in earlier times, human urine) then cleaned them with a soak and massage in a warm infusion of dog shit: 'For every four dozen of skins they add one bucket of dog's excrement, which is worked up with their hands into a kind of pap.' History does not record who first applied a dog poo gravy to animal pelts but its purifying qualities, which modern science assigns to digestive enzymes, meant that it became known, unexpectedly, as 'pure'. (An alternative etymology suggests that it derives from the French *puer* – to stink.) It was only after this repugnant preamble that the tanning process proper could begin.

Bermondsey's innumerable tan yards required a steady stream of pure and an army of up to 300 workers scoured streets across London on the scent of their valuable brown spoil. Pure pickers were generally elderly women known as 'bunters' (also the term for a destitute whore) who without poop scoops, plastic bags, disinfectant, deodorants or even gloves (which experience showed were impossible to keep fit for use), harvested droppings with their bare hands and plopped them in a pail.

Not all excrement was equal. Bunters with contacts in the kennel trade accumulated shite by the bucketload, but it was less desirable than the street article because the dogs were fed poor-quality food. Most sought-after and commanding the highest prices were dry, limey-looking specimens that had turned white by exposure to air. These antique turds were even dignified with the scholarly sounding denomination: *album graecum*: literally 'white Greek' from the days when they were used to cure a sore throat. In order to exploit this disparity, bunters were not afraid to employ deception and the vintage look could be carefully cultivated by hand-rolling a freshly moist and sticky dropping in crumbled mortar picked from a wall.

A fruitful day's stool gathering would yield about a bucket-
ful, which at 1840s prices raised three or four shillings – not
to be sniffed at. But the commodity was not immune to economic forces and a decade later when the bottom had fallen
out of the dog muck market the same quantity fetched a
meagre shilling.

Lesser quality leathers were purified not with dog defeca-
tion but pigeon guano – which was imported rather than
plucked from the pavement.

6–8 KENSINGTON PALACE GARDENS W8

CAMP OUTED

Kensington Palace Gardens may contain some of the
most magnificent houses in London, but certain residents found the surroundings singularly unpleasant.

In 1940, buildings at Nos. 6/7 and 8/8a were secretly com-
mandeered by MI9 (from 1941 MI19) – the division of Military
Intelligence responsible for obtaining information from enemy
prisoners of war. The site, known as London Cage, became
its principal interrogation centre and although it could accommodate just sixty detainees, more than 3,000 passed through it
during the war and another 3,500 after hostilities ended. That
its existence is not more widely known is the result of careful
national amnesia – and not without reason.

The camp's somewhat maverick commander, Lieutenant
Colonel Alexander Scotland, was altogether suited to his
posting thanks to an unusual set of circumstances. In 1904 he
worked for a distribution business in the Cape Colony whose
principal customer was the German military in neighbouring

German South-West Africa. To overcome a requirement
that the German army trade only with members of its own
forces, Scotland was invited to join up and later claimed that
he took part in several battles. However, on the outbreak
of the First World War, Herr Schottland of the Kaiserliche
Schutztruppe had no sooner begun supplying information to
the British when he was arrested by German military police,
interrogated, and held in solitary confinement for a year.
After the war, he continued to work for British intelligence
and when visiting Munich in 1937 found himself face to
face with Adolf Hitler, who was keen to meet the mysterious
figure who loomed large in intelligence files. Scotland's deep
understanding of Germans, their language, history, culture
and even Führer confounded and unnerved many of his
prisoners at Kensington, with devastatingly effective results.

But such expertise, along with the utility of secret bugging
devices, was not always sufficient; London Cage held the
Allies' most stubborn yet potentially most valuable prisoners
– high-ranking officers and diehard Nazis, rich in information but particularly hard to crack. However, the precise
methods used to acquire intelligence are difficult to determine for several reasons: the camp did not exist – at least
officially – so was concealed from the Red Cross, documents
are still withheld under the Official Secrets Act, resentful
inmates spouted likely exaggerated accusations, and relevant
files have been destroyed – apparently due to asbestos contamination. But there is no doubt that prisoners were subjected
to ill-treatment – some might say torture.

The worst abuse is thought to have occurred in the
unsalutary surroundings of the basement at No. 8, where
prisoners claimed they were starved, whipped, beaten
around the head, confined in cramped cubicles that sprayed
ice-cold water, forced to stand for up to twenty-six hours and
threatened with execution. Four inmates died at the camp –
the cause officially recorded as suicide.

After the war, the site became headquarters for the War
Crimes Investigation Unit – also commanded by Scotland,
who was responsible for obtaining statements (or preferably
confessions) from suspected war criminals, then standing as
prosecution witness at their trials, and it is during this period
that more can be gleaned about interrogation techniques.

SS officer Fritz Knöchlein arrived at Kensington Gardens
in 1946 and claimed that he was starved, kicked, deprived
of sleep, and required to perform continuous exercise; he
even overheard a fellow officer begging to be killed. After
complaining to Scotland, he alleged that his treatment
then worsened: he was beaten over the back, subjected to
extremes of heat and cold, forced to run around the garden
carrying barrels of oil and on one occasion was screaming so
much that local police knocked on the door wondering what
all the noise was. But after making the allegations, Knöchlein
was found guilty of ordering the cold-blooded massacre of
ninety-nine British soldiers, and subsequent to his execution
the substance of his claims was probed little further.

Also appearing on the doorstep in 1946 was a Red Cross
inspector but he was refused entry, and in a letter to the War
Office shortly afterwards Scotland warned how it would
take a month to remove the 'secret gear' used to check the
reliability of prisoners' statements. This is thought to have
included electric shock equipment and medical apparatus
for administering barbiturates or 'truth drugs' under the
guise of a blood test. When the inspection finally took place
shortly before the Cage closed, the official suspected that
prisoners had been recently moved elsewhere and was not
informed that No. 8 was part of the prison.

Scotland wrote candidly about the camp in his memoirs,
which he hoped to publish in 1954 but Government officials
who read of his breaching the Geneva Convention thought
otherwise. Special Branch officers raided Scotland's home,
the offices of his literary agent and publisher, and threatened

him with prosecution; when the book appeared in 1957, it was in heavily expurgated form.

After the Cage closed in 1948, Nos 8/8a fell into disrepair and, no doubt with relief in certain quarters, the building was demolished to make way for luxury flats. Nos. 6/7 most likely still hold secrets as they now house the Russian Embassy.

GRAND AVENUE,
SMITHFIELD MARKET EC1

FROM ALTAR TO HALTER

On 25 February 1832, *The Times* was, as usual, reporting newsworthy events of the day, including one at Smithfield: 'About 2 o'clock in the afternoon a fellow came into the market leading his wife by a halter and gave her to a drover, desiring him to tie her up to the pens and sell her to the best bidder.' Sold alongside cows, pigs and sheep in the world's most civilised nation was a woman.

Since at least the sixteenth century, popular belief held that a man could sell his wife if the transaction conformed to certain principles: the sale had to be performed in front of witnesses in a marketplace (and livestock markets were thought most appropriate), a collar signified that the woman could be legally sold like cattle, and a simple dress was favoured to display the goods to their best effect. The notion was in fact entirely erroneous – this species of divorce and remarriage had no foundation in law and selling one's wife was a misdemeanour punishable by a fine and imprisonment. However, the delusion was deeply rooted and ambivalence from both church and public officials did little to quell the practice.

However, women were generally willing commodities; as hostages to a legal system derived from the understanding that patriarchal authority was divinely mandated, a new de facto husband might be less objectionable than the current one de jure – or divorce, the cost of which was beyond the means of the labouring class. And because a married woman was not, legally speaking, a person, the situation for an estranged one was even worse – 'homeless, helpless, hopeless' as one legislator put it. Perhaps in recognition of this, tradition permitted the penned up merchandise the concession of a veto on her sale – so buyers were invariably prearranged. The keen-eyed reporter continued:

The woman who did not appear to be above 25 years of age and not bad looking, suffered herself to be tied up very quietly. A crowd of persons soon gathered round and a man of rather respectable appearance entered into a negotiation with the drover for the purchase of the wife and after some haggling she was finally knocked down to him for the sum of ten shillings. The money was paid but the drover refused to release her except on the payment of two shillings as his commission.

The receipt for the dealer's cut served as a mock marriage certificate: 'Some confusion took place about the demand but it was eventually paid and she was released from the pens opposite the Half-Moon public house' (now the site of West Market Building). Transaction complete, the goods were 'delivered to her purchaser, who appeared highly pleased with his bargain. The parties adjourned to a neighbouring public house, where the late husband spent the greater part of the money in brandy.'

WEMBLEY STADIUM HA9

TORMENT AT THE TOWER

In 1889 Sir Edward Watkin, Chairman of the Metropolitan Railway Company, dreamed up a scheme to sell more train tickets. Watkin had visited the newly completed Eiffel Tower, which at 984ft (or in French, 300m) was the world's tallest building, and returned home lamenting that his native country was somehow diminished, so resolved to remedy the situation. On an elevated plot of land owned by the company near the village of Wembley (which, as fortune would have it, gloried in a gleaming new Metropolitan Railway station) he would let Britain stand proud by building something taller.

However, Watkin's first move was to look to France and invite Gustave Eiffel to design the tower, but the Frenchman flatly refused, no doubt mindful of what his countrymen might think. Undeterred, he instead launched a competition whose only proviso stipulated a structure 'not less than 1,200 feet in height' and which prompted sixty-eight entries to land on his desk from around the world and across the stylistic spectrum. Mr Baillairge of Quebec proposed a 'Circumferentially, Radially and Diagonally Bound' tower of 1,600ft that resembled a ten-tiered wedding cake; Mr S. Fisher suggested a whopping 2,000ft 'Monument of Hieroglyphics Emblematical of Queen Victoria's Reign' that featured a railway snaking in a spiral around the outside (at a cost of more than £3 million); Mr Wilkins of Poland Street proposed a tower of steel and glass boasting a library, patent office, courtrooms, stock exchange, scientific institutions, fireproof document chambers, pipes to supply pure air to houses in the neighbourhood and 'other measures tending to civilise and educate the human race' – though in case of war he highlighted how it was ideally suited to signalling. A design submitted by Mr Arnold Hills of the London Vegetarian Society (and proprietor of a shipbuilding business) perched an ironwork obelisk on a set of Eiffel Tower legs to incorporate a garden on the first stage 'in which might be held flower and fruit shows', a temple on the fourth floor, an observation level at the summit inside a one-twelfth scale replica of the Great Pyramid, and elsewhere facilities 'to provide for an aerial colony'.

It is perhaps not surprising that Watkin rejected these flights of fancy in favour of a conservative, practical and sensibly priced eight-legged structure by Messrs. A.D. Stewart, J.M. McLaren and W. Dunn of London. Constructed from steel, it stood a modest but acceptable 1,200ft tall and offered

on its first stage a vast octagonal hall, balcony and ninety-bed hotel, on its second 'other accommodation such as restaurants etc.' and, perhaps running thin on selling points, 'a sufficient variety of light and shade on its faces'. The builders of the Blackpool Tower were duly called upon, as was a supervising engineer who had overseen the construction of Forth Bridge and Aswan Dam – as well as Watkin's railway. As to the cost of this new London landmark, its designers estimated the precise sum of £352,222 but Watkin had no intention of paying such monies himself so appealed to the public for subscriptions. By the time construction began in 1893, funds raised through donations totalled next to nothing, so Messrs. Stewart et al. were hastily instructed to modify their design into a less expensive one; four legs were unceremoniously amputated to leave a ham-fisted impersonation of the Eiffel Tower.

By 1894, the structure had reached 155ft and surrounding fields were landscaped into pleasure grounds including an artificial lake, and pitches for cricket and football. Some 120,000 visitors flocked to the site during 1895 and the following year the first level opened to sightseers; the prospects were looking good.

But, there was a snag: Watkin was horrified to discover that the 'Great Tower for London' was sinking into the soft Wembley clay. (One wonders how this news would have been received had he opted for a design by Albert Brunel of Rouen – a 2,296ft solid granite reproduction of the famous tower at Pisa.) Construction was halted and visitor numbers dwindled; Watkin had run out of cash and in 1899 had no alternative but to call a halt to the enterprise. It cannot have helped that his attentions were distracted by a less lofty vision because Watkin's Submarine Railway Company was busy digging a train tunnel to France – a project that raised eyebrows among military top brass who feared hordes of foreign invaders charging through it, so its designer promised a fail-safe means to blow it up. As for what was now dubbed Watkin's Stump or Watkin's Folly, it attracted a trickle of voyeurs until 1902 when, it being a respectable period after Watkin's death in 1901, the structure was declared unsafe and cordoned off. It was dynamited from the skyline in 1907.

Watkin might be gladdened to learn that during the 1920s, the abandoned site was thought ideally suited to a national football stadium thanks to its excellent transport links. In 2003 when the original Wembley stadium was demolished to make way for the present building, the ill-fated tower's shoddy foundations were discovered directly beneath the pitch.

DRUGS OF CHOICE

The luxury apartment block at No.8 was formerly the Westminster Hospital, which opened in 1939 and aided the recovery of tens of thousands before it closed in 1992. But one of its patients wished to be harmed.

In 1944, the hospital hosted an unsettling instance of that noble yet often foolhardy tradition whereby medical research-ers use themselves as guinea pigs. Dr Frederick Prescott, Clinical Research Director at the Wellcome Research Institution, was investigating muscle relaxants for use during surgery based on curare, the poison extracted from tree bark and used on arrow-tips by Amazonian tribespeople. Prescott had tested the drug on animals and now required a human volunteer but, regrettably, the chemical possessed a frighten-ing reputation – if pure curare penetrated the skin, rapid death ensued – so he reasoned that his subject would have to be himself. The scientist did at least have a track record in self-experimentation following a stimulating encounter with a cocktail of morphine and speed (for the purposes of assess-ing blood pressure) and although he chose to perform the trial at home, hospital promptly followed.

This may go some way to explain why Prescott was in the controlled environment of a hospital operating theatre where his pulse, breathing and blood pressure were closely monitored by a team of doctors, when 10mg of tubocurar-ine was injected intravenously into his arm. Within a short time he reported numbness in his face and neck, drooping eyelids and hazy vision, which began to wear off after fif-teen minutes. One week later, a 20mg dose left him unable to speak and paralysis of his eye muscles caused everything to appear double. So far, so good, and it seemed that he was nearing the ideal dosage.

The following week, 30mg was injected. Its effect was potent to say the least: within two minutes Prescott was fully conscious but completely paralysed – unable to speak, cough, swallow or open his eyelids. Worse still, he was struggling to breathe and could feel himself gradually drowning as saliva and mucus collected at the back of his throat; with no means to communicate his distress, he was utterly terrified.

His shallow breathing was noted by doctors but because he had not turned blue they proceeded to a second aspect of the experiment: whether the drug offered any pain relief properties. Blithely unaware of Prescott's panicked state, they spent the next few minutes sticking adhesive strips to the hair on his chest and legs, then forcefully tearing them off. As a depilated Prescott was on the point of losing consciousness, artificial respiration was applied and several doses of antidote injected; it was another seven minutes before Prescott could breathe for himself again.

Sometime later, Prescott informed his colleagues that curare has no effect on pain.

430 KING'S ROAD SW10

UNSAFE SEX

The name King's Road might evoke overtones of majesty but it played a part in an ungracious rendering of 'God Save the Queen' – because it was the birthplace of punk.

In 1971, Vivienne Westwood and Malcolm McLaren opened a fashion boutique at No. 430 in the Chelsea district rejoicing in the suitably apocalyptic appellation World's End. Called Let it Rock, the shop sold 1950s-style clobber such as teddy boy drapes, drainpipes and brothel creepers, but it was not long before the duo opted not to follow fashion but forge it, so in 1974 a bold new aesthetic was adopted – fetish. Available for purchase was rubber, vinyl and leather gear from masks to full body suits, thigh-high stiletto boots, dog collars (canine, not clerical), chains, whips, and crudely slashed T-shirts bearing anarchist slogans. Nothing was taboo and shock factor obligatory – one T-shirt stimulated comment for its boiled chicken bones painstakingly appliquéd with miniature chains to spell out the word 'Perv'; another presented Disney characters enjoying sexual relations with each other – and something that particularly disgruntled the mums and dads was liberal use of the swastika. Early visitors to the refitted shop included former clientele who did not take the makeover kindly so stormed it for some punk-bashing, and police who had their knickers in a twist over a T-shirt adorned with two cowboys whose trousers and underwear were notably absent.

McLaren daubed the signboard with the maxim 'Craft must have clothes, but truth loves to go naked', but made the schoolboy error of starting too large so the lettering ended

up cramped at one end – and although it happily complemented the anarchic ambiance, it was soon obscured by the
proprietors' more concise denomination for the boutique.
Spelled out for all to see in king-size pink lettering was: SEX.
And all this beside Chelsea Conservative Club.

One breed of shopper undaunted by venturing within was
the 'rubber men' – solitary older gentlemen with a peculiar
fondness for latex, who included among their number a well-
known newsreader. But another bunch – young, rebellious
and drawn by the danger and iconoclasm – saw it more as a
social hangout than shop and this meeting of minds was to
light a fuse. Key actors in the volatile drama that ensued confess rueful lapses of memory, but the gist of those portentous
events is as follows.

Guitarist and self-confessed wastrel Steve Jones wanted to form a band, and hampered by a deficiency of equipment, took the practical step of pilfering some. Setting his sights high, he liberated as much gear rigged for a David Bowie gig at the Hammersmith Odeon as his stolen van could accommodate, and with an eye on bagging suitable apparel, started hanging around the shop with drummer schoolmate Paul Cook. Foiling shoplifters at SEX was the job of Saturday boy, art student and bass player Glen Matlock, and it was not long before it dawned on McLaren that the perfect vehicle to promote the shop and its wares was a band – ideally a car crash of one. But the weakest link in 'Kutie Jones and his Sex Pistols' was the singing of Jones himself.

Other SEX lovers included singers Siouxsie Sioux, Adam Ant and Chrissie Hynde but it was John Lydon who attracted particular attention for his unique sartorial sensibilities – a Pink Floyd T-shirt on which he had clumsily scrawled a supplementary 'I Hate'. With his spiky green hair, demented stare and rictus grin, here was what looked like a potential frontman and despite his candid claims to tone deafness, Lydon (later dubbed Johnny Rotten on account of his teeth) was coerced into auditioning for the job. With Alice Cooper's 'I'm Eighteen' blaring on the shop's jukebox, Lydon was handed a broken shower head and instructed to sing along into it – a performance, aided by a couple of pints to steady his nerves, that his audience found excruciatingly maniacal. In fact, the band thoroughly hated him – which was music to McLaren's ears because hostility was to underpin the Sex Pistols' chaotic creativity, so Lydon was duly signed up. Following two years of antagonism, Matlock's professed love for The Beatles put the kibosh on his punk career and he was replaced with another SEX maniac and high priest of insouciance, Sid Vicious.

McLaren and Westwood did indeed sell an abundance of T-shirts off the back of the Sex Pistols, in particular those designs featuring Her Majesty with eyes and mouth torn away, or with a safety pin through her lip – yet the furore that permanently surrounded the band obscured its original purpose as a shop window of shambolic mannequins.

Another of McLaren's ideas for remodelling the shop was to encourage the impression that a bomb had hit it so he ripped down the ceiling to create precisely that effect. He was unaware that it contained asbestos, which perhaps contributed to his premature death from the cancer meso-thelioma in 2010.

GEORGIAN ORTHODOX CHURCH, ROOKWOOD ROAD N16

A BROAD CHURCH

The handsome church on Rookwood Road owes its exist-ence to a vicar's quest for a promiscuous sex life.

Rev. Henry James Prince founded the Agapemonite sect in 1846 following a theological spat with the Church of England arising from his insistence that he was the Messiah. Blessed with the power to redeem humanity or condemn it to a fiery apocalypse, Prince persuaded wide-eyed acolytes to hand over worldly possessions and live communally in a high-walled estate purchased with their money in the village of Spaxton, Somerset.

Agapemone means Abode of Love and it was no coinci-dence that Prince's converts were predominantly affluent women – as an impecunious womaniser they amply fulfilled both his needs, and safely away from prying eyes his benefac-tors discovered that the path to salvation passed through their redeemer's bedroom. No one thought to question why Prince shared the grand house with a bevy of younger, more attractive women while the remainder lived in surrounding cottages and performed menial chores, and little objection arose – even from his wife – when Prince led services in which he selected a 'favoured one' from a parade of young virgins clad in white robes in the chapel-cum-billiard room. A few months after his congregation meekly witnessed one such 'mystical union' with a 16-year-old, telltale signs indicated that the connection included a carnal dimension because the girl was pregnant. Prince denounced her condition as the cunning work of Satan, but showed great compassion by not punishing her.

It was natural that Prince extend his ministry to London and the £15,000 required to build the Clapton church was soon procured through the generosity of two elderly ladies, who were pleased to bequeath no less than £80,000. Called The Ark of the Covenant, the unusually decorated building was designed by Joseph Morris (who, as a convert, did not call for payment) and completed in 1896. With pews for 400, the metropolitan mission was a highly visible statement of Agapemonite influence and would serve as headquarters for its global evangelising – though during its early years under an ageing leader it witnessed only sporadic, poorly attended fellowship. However in 1899, that was all to change. As immortal Messiah, Prince very much surprised his followers by dying – but they had the good fortune to have another saviour waiting in the wings.

Rev. John Hugh Smyth-Pigott shared Prince's qualities of a well-developed sense of self-importance, a knack for holding mesmeric influence over people, and a rabid propensity to defrock his female flock. Seeing a wealthy, womanly throng in desperate need of a leader, he declared himself 'The Heavenly Bridegroom' and immediately impressed disciples by demanding absolute obedience. Newly invigorated, Agapemonites assembled on Clapton Common

in anticipation of their ascent into heaven, and although God made it apparent that He was not yet ready for them, followers conscientiously paid the milkman weekly to forestall any debts when the time came. And cometh the hour, cometh the Son of Man because a more auspicious sign materialised during Sunday worship on 7 September 1902; Smyth-Pigott installed himself on a throne that stood in place of an altar and wasted no time in declaring himself Messiah – a recently granted revelation that left his audience weeping for joy.

Word of the King of Kings' coming to Clapton was not slow to spread and the following Sunday, a congress of 6,000 assembled outside the church as witness. But when Smyth-Pigott appeared, it became apparent that doubting Thomases were among the gathering because he was greeted with universal jeering and hissing, and when he used the service to reprise his messianic status, it only made the situation worse. Mounted police escorted him from the church and his carriage was chased along Clapton Common by an indignant mob, interested to see how he fared walking across Clapton Pond. A somewhat chastened Christ was warned of the consequences should there be further disturbance – no hollow threat because others who had been inspired to announce themselves Messiah were promptly re-accommodated in mental asylums.

Smyth-Pigott led a few more services for his female congregants (men were now actively discouraged) and worship typically took place in the more intimate surroundings of the crypt; however, the lure of Spaxton proved too great and he relocated to Somerset in 1906. With the exception of an incident in which disgruntled intruders tarred and feathered an Agapemonite in the belief he was the Clapton Messiah, Smyth-Pigott enjoyed the attentions of spiritual brides undisturbed until his death in 1927.

With no one stepping forward to fill the great redeemer's sandals, and both Prince and Smyth-Pigott proving reluctant to rise from the dead, Agapemonites waned into obscurity – yet the building was maintained at great expense until the 1950s. It was then adopted by a Christian sect led by a former waiter at the Savoy Hotel who conducted divine healing, clairvoyance and ministering to pets, and since 2005 has been used in a more orthodox manner by the Georgian Orthodox Church.

LILLIE BRIDGE DEPOT,
BEAUMONT AVENUE W14

WHEEL OF MISFORTUNE

A conspicuous attraction of the 1895 India and Ceylon Exhibition at Earl's Court was the world's largest Ferris wheel, standing 308ft high with a capacity of 1,200 passengers in forty carriages – ten handsomely furnished for first-class customers, five for smokers (the exact site is inaccessible today). However, the prospect of panoramic views from 'The Great Wheel' failed to excite everyone, including *The Builder* magazine, which sniffily carped: 'It is only a pity that all the ability and cost expended in its construction should not be devoted to some more useful end than carrying coachloads of fools round in a vertical circle.'

But at 8.30 on the evening of 21 May 1896, those merry dupes suddenly ceased their transit. Initially, this appeared perfectly routine because the wheel paused so that every carriage could enjoy the views from its summit, and as time passed and spectators gathered beneath, the episode was thought rather jocular, with droll banter about spending 'a night in the air'.

However, it was not the wheel that inexorably turned, but the joke. As closing time neared and darkness fell, passengers' worst fears played out – as did the Band of the Grenadier Guards, which mustered at its base to blast out jolly tunes in an attempt to lighten the mood. 'Many belonging to the fair sex gave unmistakeable evidence of alarm,' a reporter circuitously noted, and as the screams wafted on the evening breeze they blended with the cheerful strains of 'Her Golden Hair was Hanging Down her Back'. Anxious captives

dropped messages to friends and family, and spent sixpence to peer through opera glasses in the hope of seeing help arrive. They could indeed watch rescuers free those in the lowest carriages with ropes and ladders, but when the band packed up and the exhibition ground lights were switched off, the seventy-three who remained prepared themselves for a long and uncomfortable night.

As morning dawned, two former sailors were drafted in and the brave tars climbed to each carriage and hauled up a basket of iced buns, coffee, whisky, water and the morning papers for its weary occupants. One of the daredevils was later interviewed by the press who were especially pleased to thrill readers with his account of a lady and gentleman who had enjoyed a carriage *all to themselves* near its peak, along with reports that one couple had announced their engagement on the wheel, and a gentleman whose wife was trapped had launched divorce proceedings.

At about 11.30 – fifteen hours after it had ground to a halt – the wheel finally sprang into life, and as 'the fools' completed their vertical arc back to terra firma, the directors of the Great Wheel Company felt obliged to compensate each of its prisoners with a crisp £5 note. Over the following weeks, tens of thousands took to the wheel in the hope of another breakdown.

FINSBURY SQUARE EC2

BRUISING FOR CRUISING

During the eighteenth century, the marshy expanse of Moorfields was found unsuited to building and instead tree-lined avenues in its southern field (today's Finsbury Circus) attracted 'a great concourse of well-dressed citizens of both sexes walking there, particularly every Sunday noon in fine weather, and on evenings'. Meanwhile, recreational pursuits on the less salubrious terrain to the north were somewhat analogous; it served as a cruising ground known as Sodomite's Walk.

But among perambulating menfolk in July 1726 were Constables Willis and Stephenson, who had been dispatched to collar anyone engaged in 'sodomitical practices'. In order that they might delegate their dirty work they were accompanied by one Thomas Newton, a notorious police informer who was drafted in to play agent provocateur. Newton's subsequent testimony at the Old Bailey debriefed the court on the threesome's sortie into the field that day and deserves recounting at length. The action took place along south side of Finsbury Square.

'There's a walk in the Upper Moorfields by the side of the wall that parts the Upper Field from the Middle Field. I knew that this walk was frequented by sodomites and was no stranger to the methods they used in picking one another up. So I takes a turn that way and leans over the wall.' Meanwhile, the queer-bait's intrepid support team took up position at a conveniently distant observation point.

'In a little time the prisoner passes by and looks hard at me and, at a small distance from me, stands up against the wall as if he was going to make water. Then by degrees he sidles nearer and nearer to where I stood 'till at last he comes close to me.'

The suspect made his overtures in time-honoured meteorological terms: ''Tis a very fine night says he; Aye says I, and so it is,' but briskly assumed a less temperate air: 'Then he takes me by the hand and after squeezing and playing with it a little (to which I showed no dislike) he conveys it to his breeches and puts his **** into it.' (The asterisks are eighteenth century.) Newton grasped his opportunity: 'I took fast hold and called out to Willis and Stephenson, who coming up to my assistance, we carried him to the watch-house.'

The owner of the tightly clutched genitalia, William Brown, boldly declared (regrettably, centuries too early): 'I think there is no crime in making what use I please of my own body', and his wife of twelve years testified to his honesty, kindness and sobriety, but such petitions were in vain. The jury found him

guilty of 'sodomitical intentions' – a misdemeanour for which
he was fined, sentenced to twelve months in prison and treated
to a trip back to Moorfields for a spell in its pillory.

FORMERLY HOLLOWAY PRISON
PARKHURST ROAD N7

FED UP

The gothic revival decorations of St Stephen's Hall at the
Palace of Westminster were given further ornamentation
on 24 July 1909 when Marion Wallace Dunlop surreptitiously
wielded a large rubber stamp to adorn a wall with the words:
'It is the right of the subjects to petition the King and all
commitments and prosecutions for such petitioning are
illegal.' Dunlop was a member of the Women's Social and
Political Union – a militant organisation that arose from the
frustration that peaceful, legal campaigning for women's right
to vote was proving futile. As a consequence of her wilful
damage, two men armed with soap and pumice stone were
obliged to spend more than two hours patiently scrubbing
off her purposeful quotation from the 1689 Bill of Rights.
Dunlop, meanwhile, was subject to a one-month sojourn at
Holloway prison for women.

But just a few days later she was out. Dunlop had been
horrified to discover that her crime was not acknowledged
as politically motivated and she was instead classified as a
common criminal. In protest, she refused all food and in so
doing, invoked a radical new method of resistance. After
ninety-one hours, the authorities were so concerned that
Dunlop might die as a martyr to her cause, they released her.

As might be expected, other imprisoned suffragettes immediately followed her lead, but rather than allow them to make a mockery of the justice system, the Government responded in a different way; their detention would continue and they would be force-fed. For the next five years, hunger-striking women were subjected to this brutal and dangerous procedure, while officials reasoned that the consequent pain and suffering was self-inflicted because they violently resisted.

Sylvia Pankhurst described the manner in which staff at Holloway went about superintending mealtimes: she was pinned to a bed by six women officers while two men attempted to prise open her mouth, first with their fingers then failing that, with a metal instrument, causing grievous injuries as they did so. A steel clamp was inserted in her jaw and screwed tight to hold her mouth open while a greased rubber tube was forced down her throat. Into a funnel at the other end was poured two pints of milk mixed with raw eggs; no sooner was the tube withdrawn, she involuntarily retched it all up. This she endured on numerous occasions and later wrote how she considered the pain more bearable than the overwhelming sense of degradation. Unknown to her, the Home Secretary received twice daily bulletins on her condition, most of which informed him that her vomiting was expertly 'wilful'.

If staff were unable to push a tube down the women's throat, it was instead rammed up their nose, running the risk of entering the windpipe. Kitty Marion recalled how over a period of fourteen weeks at Holloway she was force-fed this way more than 200 times, and on one occasion the tube twisted and emerged from her mouth – something she described as so excruciating it felt as if her nose was being wrenched off. It later became apparent that as well as Bovril and brandy on the menu, she was given bromide to unwittingly subdue her.

Another technique was to tie a prisoner to a chair and tip it back, wedge open her jaw with a steel plug, pour the liquid directly into the mouth, then pinch her nose and hold her tongue, thus forcing the victim to swallow. A hand was then quickly clamped over the mouth to impede the egress of vomit. It was obvious to all that force-feeding was not being employed as a means to keep the women alive, but vengeful punishment.

Lady Constance Bulwer-Lytton found imprisonment at Holloway an entirely benign experience but quickly realised that it was by virtue of her aristocratic status, and in protest used a hairpin to carve the letter V into her chest. When later arrested in Liverpool posing as working class seamstress 'Jane Wharton', she was handed two weeks hard labour and force-fed eight times. In an bid to draw attention to the inhumanity of force-feeding, Emily Wilding Davison inflicted considerable injuries on herself by twice leaping from a landing at Holloway and later achieved martyrdom when trampled to death beneath the King's horse at the 1913 Derby.

Such desperate measures bore fruit; growing public sympathy for suffragettes prompted the Government to change tack and pass the Prisoners (Temporary Discharge for Ill Health) Act, which released hunger-striking women when they were in a medically perilous condition, then rearrested them when sufficiently recovered to continue their sentence. It was soon dubbed the 'Cat and Mouse Act' and Sylvia Pankhurst found herself in and out of Holloway no fewer than eight times as a result.

In 1914, as the Government contemplated using lunatic asylums to confine suffragettes, the outbreak of the First World War brought about an amnesty; the conflict also drew attention away from the revelation that a hunger-striker in Perth had been force-fed through the rectum and vagina – blatantly not a means of nourishment, but torture and sexual abuse.

The prison closed in 2016 and the land earmarked for redevelopment; 1,000 new homes will soon grace the contaminated site.

WALBROOK EC4

TACKLE THE SUBJECT

In the 1840s, workmen constructing a sewer along Walbrook were a little taken aback when a shiny phallus popped up out of the ground. Blushes were not spared when other risqué relics were hesitantly uncovered – bowls ornamented with couples copulating in various imaginative ways, earthenware oil lamps whose primary feature was a prodigious penis, and other artefacts exhibiting 'vices contrary to nature'. Although a conventional helmet was among the objects discovered, providing antiquarians with a welcome distraction, those troubling items bearing 'delineations of an indelicate character' provoked an uncomfortable clash between Classical and Victorian cultures.

In Roman times, Walbrook was a small river – somewhere to both make offerings and throw rubbish – and the discoveries were declared 'proof of a great amount of dissoluteness in the morals of Roman society in Britain'. Not wishing to risk the collapse of civilisation, the obscene *objets d'art* were promptly hidden from view, and when donated to the British Museum in 1865, similar concerns about corrupting impressionable minds saw them safely locked away in the basement – where many still linger.

'It is hardly likely,' mused one of the less timid Victorian archaeologists, 'that such objects could be in common use at the family table,' however his assumption could not be more mistaken. Although excessive modesty still hampers straight-faced discussion of the subject, Romans were phalloholics; the phallus found universal favour as a symbol of good luck and a potent tool with which to protect one's person and property – certainly not an object of embarrassed giggling. Bronze phallic charms called fascinum were commonly worn as jewellery – something a father might hang around his daughter's neck so that the penis could magically discharge a bewitching spell (from which the word fascinate originates) and avert the gaze of the evil eye. The enchanting properties of a standalone membrum virile could be heightened if the tumescent organ was endowed with supplementary male generative apparatus as well as feet, wings and even ears to become an autonomous, if sightless being that might be festooned with dainty little bells. Called tintinnabula, these phallic clusters were dangled above a front door or erected in a garden to frighten away harmful forces by tinkling in the wind.

Phallic charms have also pricked the interest of modern scholars, the more undaunted of whom speculate that the female genitalia seen on artefacts granted similar safeguarding powers to the man, woman and child in the Roman street but appear less frequently because they do not lend themselves to such unambiguous artistic representation. The comparative scarcity of the vulva might also be explained by the fact that it was viewed as dangerous and threatening not to evil forces, but to Roman men.

BARBER-SURGEON'S HALL EC2

DEAD HEAT

The Company of Barbers built a hall on the site during the 1440s and its members' dexterity with sharp blades saw them called upon for minor procedures such as blood-letting or boil-lancing. But as surgical procedures became more sophisticated, the notion of a sole practitioner delivering both competent coiffure and couching of cataracts became unrealistic, so the professions of barbery and surgery remained uneasy bedfellows until eventually parting ways in 1745.

The company enjoyed an annual allowance of four hanged felons, who were dissected at the hall over the course of several days, and by the 1630s there was a consensus that dedicated facilities would be welcome: 'Bodies have been a great annoyance in our upper kitchen by reason of the blood, filth and entrails of these anatomies, and for preserving the kitchen to its own proper use do now order that there shall be a fair convenient room built.' The upshot was the country's first purpose-built anatomy theatre, and, with the body count rising to six annually, modest advance in understanding the mysteries of the human body. Except on one occasion.

24 November 1740 went down as one of the company's more memorable days. The Beadle was despatched to Tyburn (near today's Marble Arch) to assess whether any of the condemned – three men and two women – were suited to dissection, and he plumped for 16-year-old William Duell, who was convicted of gang rape, robbery and murder. Duell hanged for twenty-two minutes before his body was cut down and carried to the waiting coach; half an hour later it arrived at Barber-Surgeon's Hall and

as the body was hauled to the dissection table, porters were surprised to hear a groan. No sooner had they dismissed it, there was another. To their consternation, the corpse felt warmer than was customary, so a surgeon was hastily summoned to slice it open – in so much as to bleed Duell's arm in an effort to revive him.

No signs of life were forthcoming so the surgeon wondered whether drawing blood from under the tongue might prompt a response. His judgement was spot on because as he was poised with lancet in position, the corpse raised its arm, struck the blade away and it came to rest in the surgeon's lip. Duell then favoured his startled audience with conclusive proof that he was very much alive 'by his most violent screamings and was often in strong convulsions in his bowels which he then expressed by applying his hands to those parts'. Meanwhile, a message was dispatched to the sheriff at Newgate Gaol to inform him that his services were still required.

A draught of hot wine was sufficient to calm the unexpected guest, but Duell remained obstinately mute and 'behaved very artfully, insomuch that it remained a doubt with some of the spectators whether he had fully recovered his senses or not'. This prompted the question 'whether he was indeed incapable of speaking or would not be induced so to do through a false apprehension of being again conveyed back directly to the place of execution'. Amid the awkward atmosphere, attempts were made to spark conversation and observers noted how Duell reacted especially forcefully when touched: 'Whensoever anyone offered to stir his neck or mentioned that he would in all probability be hanged up a second time, he would fetch deeper groans than ordinary.' Duell's uncommunicative attitude was frustrating because everyone was itching to know whether he had seen the gates of Hell – or perhaps even endured a taste of the fiery furnace beyond them.

The concerns of the sheriff were less for infernal abyss than the more earthly duty of accomplishing the sentence before the day's end, but by the time he arrived to take charge of his unforeseen prisoner, word of Duell's resurrection had spread and a noisy horde convened outside the hall. Rather than call for him to cruelly hang, the mob now demanded his freedom, so to pre-empt a riot, the sheriff waited until after midnight to cart his prisoner back to Newgate.

A few days of prison hospitality helped Duell recover his powers of speech, but he emphatically denied any memory of his death – something that did not hinder publication of his extraordinary journey to nightmarish worlds: 'A thousand dreadful spectres the one more terrible than the other presented themselves … Hell with all its terrors opened to his view and numberless fiends seemed to stand ready to catch at his departing soul and hurry it to that place of endless torment.' And should that blast of sulphur not be sufficient, some readers were offered a morality tale: 'Nothing so exquisitely dreadful presented itself to his terrified fancy as the image of the unfortunate woman whom he had robbed, ravished and murdered, standing ready to appear against him at the tribunal of divine justice,' while a more compassionate title described his transport to paradise, where his sins were forgiven by an angel.

In fact, Duell experienced transportation of a different kind, as a convict to North America, and we must assume that in compensation the Barber-Surgeons demanded a corpse that remained dead.

WALBROOK WHARF EC4

AT EARLIEST CONVENIENCE

W hen the Romans departed these shores they took with them the notion of cleanliness, and a millennium passed before someone bravely faced London's rising tide of filth. That august citizen was its mayor and future panto-mime star, Sir Richard Whittington.

Dramatists who around the year 1600 dreamed up the rags to riches fable of feline-loving 'Dick' Whittington would have been familiar with one of his tangible legacies because it was still a London landmark. Erected beside the riverbank during the 1420s was the House of Easement – a public lavatory built courtesy of a bequest by Whittington, and a generous and practical act that provided Londoners with more comfort than any other civic project, yet it is almost entirely forgotten. (The nearby Whittington Gardens is so named not due to the privy, but because its patron was buried in the adjoining St Michael Paternoster Royal.)

But those who beheld this edifice did not find it forget-table. A formidable structure amid the medieval city, it also went by the designation The Long House because this was no Lilliputian latrine; 130ft from end to end, it was the most cavernous of its kind in Britain, if not Europe, and could seat up to 128 simultaneous users. A bench running along its length with sixty-four holes served men and a partition separated them from a similar arrangement for women (London's earliest known instance of gender segrega-tion, although additional privacy was still centuries away). Teetering on timber stilts over a dock dug in the riverbank, the capacious crapper benefited from an elegant flush system

whereby twice a day the tide sloshed in to pick up droppings for their voyage out to sea. Whittington also endowed funds for its upkeep, which thoughtfully included a lantern for nocturnal evacuations, and granted relief to London's needy in another way: directly above the privy were five rooms to accommodate the poor of the parish.

Another concept not yet fixed in the medieval convenience was the role of toilet paper, although in the eighteenth century, by which time the rebuilt longhouse was a piddling twelve-holer, boys paced up and down hawking torn up printed matter. As one wit observed: 'He that writes an abundance of books … may in some sense be said to be benefactor to the publick, because he furnishes it with

Bumfodder' (from which the word 'bumf' originates); in the case of official handbills it offered a gratifying way to express one's feelings towards them. But for much of the House of Easement's existence, the medium of choice was either a wad of leaves or straw, a mussel or oyster shell, or, if this operation was indeed performed at all, a finger or two.

The last vestige of the longhouse was wiped away sometime in the nineteenth century.

GORDON GROVE SE5

NURSERY CRIME

Dead infants dumped in the street were a distressing but not uncommon sight in Victorian London; during 1870, police recovered no fewer than 276 rotting remains and, although they were unaware at the time, many originated from the home of Margaret Waters and Sarah Ellis on Gordon Grove.

The sisters were in the adoption business – taking in newborns from mothers unwilling or unable to look after them, along with payments for their care. What with the shame attached to children born outside marriage, most were illegitimate and 'baby farms' such as theirs offered an invaluable public service to those wishing to preserve their reputation following an indiscretion. If either parent came from a comfortable background, perhaps a respectable gentleman who had suffered a moment of weakness with his young housemaid, the infants might command reasonable fees, along with the opportunity for further funds through extortion or guilt money. However, in truth, all parties tacitly acknowledged that such remuneration was too meagre for its supposed purpose and baby farmers such as Waters and Ellis, who were also unwilling or unable to look after children, offered the same outcome as abortion or infanticide, without the attendant complications.

To dispose of her livestock, Waters' favoured method was to take a train for a stop or two then leave the baby in the hands of any children she came across; if lucky it might end up in Lambeth Workhouse. In one ruse she would ask a child outside a sweetshop to hold the infant in return for a few pence for sweets, then as the child happily entered the shop she scarpered. On other occasions, unavoidably if her charge was already dead, Waters saved the cost and inconvenience of burial by simply discarding it on the street at night.

When the carcasses of eighteen infants were found across Brixton and Camberwell in May 1870, police stepped up investigations. Midwives were a valuable source of information and inquiries led them to a Mr Cowan, who had answered an advertisement in *Lloyd's Newspaper* written, it later transpired, under one of Waters' many pseudonyms: 'Adoption. A respectable couple desire the entire charge of a child to bring up as their own. They are in a position to offer every comfort. Premium required, £4. Letter only. Mrs Willis, P.O., Southampton Street, Camberwell.' Cowan explained that when his 16-year-old daughter was about to give birth, 'Mrs Willis' had happily offered the newborn a home because she and her husband of thirteen years had no children of their own – but in order that he had no further contact, she declined to give her address. They had arranged to meet at Walworth Road Station, where Cowan handed over the 2-day-old boy; Waters remarked how beautiful and healthy he was, Cowan admitted he had never looked.

Someone else who replied to Waters' advertisements was police sergeant Richard Relf and after meeting 'Mrs Oliver' at Camberwell Station, ostensibly to arrange adoption,

secretly followed her home. The following morning, Relf and Cowan paid a visit to No. 4 Frederick Terrace (by coincidence, now the site of a playground). Inside the stinking and flyblown house were six infants aged under 4 weeks – barely alive and huddled on the sofa in soaked and soiled blankets. The fact none were crying was accounted for by a bottle on the kitchen table labelled 'Paregoric Elixir' – an impactful cocktail of alcohol and opium. Five toddlers were playing in the yard and Waters explained that they were healthier because she had weekly payments for their care (and consequently greater incentive to sustain them). Cowan was horrified at the state of his filthy, emaciated grandson and a doctor and wet nurse were hastily summoned, but despite their best efforts the boy died two weeks later – circumstances that proved no barrier to charging the sisters with his murder.

During their trial, the simple tale of mercenary child abuse became clouded; a doctor frequently called to examine the children and Ellis, who was mother to one of the babies, regularly fed the Cowan boy 'a drop of titty' – hardly the actions of murderers. In fact, the doctor's recommendation that the sisters feed the children cow's milk diluted with water probably gave them cholera, and his prescription of mercury was the likely cause of Cowan's grandson's death. But such considerations held no sway against the weight of moral outrage – pitiful decomposing corpses had been directly linked back to Waters, including one wrapped in a scrap of brown paper bearing her name.

There was insufficient evidence to convict Ellis and she was instead found guilty of obtaining money through false pretences and sentenced to eighteen months' hard labour – customary comeuppance for a baby farmer. Waters admitted that about forty children had passed through her hands during the last four years – no doubt an expedient underestimation – and following a guilty verdict she went to the gallows.

Such a harsh sentence was later vindicated by the conclusions of a phrenologist, who examined a cast of Waters' head and helpfully confirmed: 'Her nature was radically evil and covert practices were her delight.'

THE WINDMILL,
TABERNACLE STREET EC2

ON THE GAME

Chuck-farthing was a popular tavern game in which players tossed coins across a room, aiming for a hole in a
bench or table, but during the late 1650s, patrons of the
Jack-a-Newberry in Upper Moorfields enjoyed the pastime
along somewhat different lines.

The establishment stood near six windmills on the edge
of rising open ground – made up in a great measure from
accumulated rubbish shot from the city, and although its
exact location is impossible to verify, the pub on Tabernacle
(formerly Windmill) Street seems most appropriate for the
plaque. Proprietors of the alehouse were Edmund and
Priscilla Fotheringham, who, as pimp and bawd respectively,
enjoyed a marriage of professional convenience imperilled
only when 'Priss' became scarred with smallpox and Edmund
shared his syphilis with her – neither affliction especially
advantageous to her trade. However, by applying her knowledge of clients' various predilections she hit upon a lucrative
novelty act; dispensing with undergarments 'Priss stood
upon her head with naked breech and belly whilst four cully-
rumpers chucked in sixteen half-crowns into her commodity'.
This ribald new sport aroused considerable interest among
London's libertines and the watering hole soon gloried in the
name 'Priscilla Fotheringham's Chuck Office', while 'chuck
office' became yet another euphemism for the coins' intended
destination. Priss spotted this gap in the market when probably in her forties and much pocked, so whether or not she
anointed her face with strategically placed beauty spots, she

could be certain that the principal object of participants'
attention lay elsewhere. And although she would adopt the
resplendent posture several times a day for as long as her customers' supply of projectiles lasted, should she wish to ease
her burdensome situation there was no shortage of volunteers willing to grab her legs.

Priss alone could not satisfy demand for such a money-
spinning enterprise and her acrobatic artistry still afforded
no long-term career prospects, so she nurtured fresh talent
including a girl from Holland who styled herself 'Mrs
Cupid'. Coins were not the only articles lobbed in their
direction: 'French dollars, Spanish pistolles, English half-
crowns are as plentifully poured in as the Rhenish wine was

into the Dutch wench's two holes till she roared again, as she was showing tricks upon her head with naked buttocks and spread legs in a round ring, like those at wrestling.' German white wine was not a beverage Mrs Fotheringham wished to have directed at her commodity so she permitted only fortified Spanish sack (sherry) to be ministered, because it was less 'smarting'.

The athleticism of Priss's labours must have kept her in good shape but she was not long overtaken by the effects of disease and died sometime around 1668.

69–71 REGENT STREET W1

HAIRS AND GRACES

Nowadays, it would breach every principle of decency to which modern society aspires to gawp at human oddities in any way other than through an electronic screen. Yet nineteenth-century voyeurs had no compunctions about not only viewing nature's aberrations in the flesh, but also manhandling them.

For a brief spell during the 1850s, the Regent Gallery behind 69–71 Regent Street (now demolished) catered to the thriving market for curiosities, and its greatest sensation by far was the presentation in 1857 of 23-year-old Mexican, Julia Pastrana.

Pastrana suffered from what is now diagnosed as hypertrichosis – a rare disorder that covered her body with thick, black hair. She also happened to possess both an unusually projecting jaw and swollen lips – a combination of features that warranted her various billings as The Bearded

Lady, Baboon Lady, or Mexican Bear Woman. For London audiences, Pastrana's impresario handler Theodore Lent favoured the title: 'The Nondescript ... a hybrid wherein the nature of woman predominates over the ourang-outangs' – a condition that he did not consider an impediment to their marriage. 'Her ideas of making money are limited,' Lent lamented, but she was fortunate that he more than compensated for her shortcomings: 'Levees from Eleven to One, Three to Five and Eight to Ten daily ... Admission, 1*s* and 2*s*, Stalls 3*s*. Miss Julia is pleased when the ladies and gentlemen ask her questions, and examine her pretty whiskers, of which she is very proud.'

Pastrana's hairiness confounded Victorian expectations because it in no way diminished her intelligence or femininity. Just 4ft 6in tall, the slender and graceful young lady wore pretty knee-length dresses, spoke three languages fluently, sang romances with a fine voice and danced the Bolero and Highland Fling to a packed house of ogling onlookers. She appeared proof that if there were indeed tribes of hairy, pint-sized people running around remote lands, then the British Empire could civilise them in such matters as where to place an oyster fork at the dinner table.

The press eagerly puffed her attractions: 'The appearance she presents is hardly conceivable, and not easily forgotten,' raved *Court Circular*; 'We are undoubtedly astonished at the intelligence and aptitude displayed by this extraordinary creature,' *Era* enthused; 'Physiologists and those curious in such matters will doubtless visit this specimen of an uncommon variation in our species,' noted *Morning Advertiser*; 'She has decidedly the prettiest little hands, feet and ankles in London,' deemed *Saturday Review* – a comely detail about which *Illustrated News* concurred: 'The legs and feet are pretty.'

For those whose curiosity was not sated solely by renditions of The Last Rose of Summer or leering at her legs from afar, Lent granted private viewings. Upon presentation of

appropriate coinage, 'scientifically interested' gentlemen were at liberty to probe Pastrana more intimately than was seemly during public recitals; 'Exceedingly well proportioned in the trunk and limbs,' observed one eminent clinician, musing how 'her breasts are remarkably full and well developed' and 'she menstruates regularly'. There was also much scrutiny of her posterior; 'From her uncouth gait it may be conjectured that the mysterious animal moves as if an elongation of the spinal column should have taken place producing a tail, which in consequence of humanity predominating, has been denied.'

Audiences took great umbrage when claims about freaks were overstated, so such inspections enabled Lent to demon-strate that there was no deception – Pastrana was indeed hairy. However, the integrity of his expansive pamphlet (available for a modest fee at the door) was more questionable. He informed readers that Pastrana's mother had strayed into Mexico's Sierra Madre Mountains, a region uninhabited by humans but 'abounding in monkeys, baboons and bears', where mother and suckling child had been discovered in a cave. The inference regarding bestial paternity was hard to miss and no one was suf-ficiently enlightened to call attention to the fact that baboons were not native to the continent, let alone the impossibility of any such union.

Five years later, Julia visited London again to appear at the Burlington Gallery in Piccadilly, but her repertory differed because she was dead. She had suffered complications while giving birth to a son (who was also richly hirsute) and both died within days of delivery. But this did not spell curtains for her career; Lent's busy touring schedule remained unaffected by the death of his wife and son because he instead displayed them embalmed: 'This unprecedented triumph of taxidermic skill was executed by Professor Suckaloff of Moscow.' Ticket prices were lowered on account of the necessarily mute and static entertainment, but on the up side, Lent and his new hairy wife, Zenora, could keep the exhibition open all day without breaks.

Lent's death in the 1880s afforded no let-up in the mummies' exploitation as they spent the next century in the hands of several more showmen. Mother and son travelled across America as recently as 1972 and the following year toured Sweden and Norway – still billed as a hybrid between human and ape. In 2013, Pastrana was finally returned to Mexico for burial but her son was not so fortunate; during a bungled attempt to hijack the pair in 1976, his remains ended up in a ditch as a meal for some mice.

CENTRAL CRIMINAL COURT,
OLD BAILEY EC4

PRESSING MATTER

Central Criminal Court stands on the site of Newgate Gaol, which served the city from the twelfth century until 1902 and for much of that time featured a small, dark cell called the Press Room – which was unconnected with newspapers.

It was once mandatory for defendants to plead innocent or guilty before their trial could proceed and should they obstinately refuse to do so, this was their next destination. Prisoners were stripped naked, laid on their back with arms and legs tied, and a board placed on their chest. Iron or masonry blocks were then stacked on top and if no plea was forthcoming, further weight was added until an inevitable result one way or the other.

It might take several days for due legal process to take effect, so it was greatly accelerated by the careful placement of sharp objects next to the body – and should the subject attempt to hasten his demise by cracking his skull on the

floor, a soft bandage was wound around his head. Remaining mute had its attractions: defendants died without the shame of conviction, a public execution became unnecessary, and there was no forfeiture of personal property.

But silence also had appreciable drawbacks. The mere threat of pressing was sometimes sufficient to provoke fluent pleading, but in 1721 after William Spiggott was arraigned for highway robbery, he found himself beneath 350lb and 'complained that they had laid a cruel weight on his face, though it was covered with nothing but a thin cloth ... which might be caused by the blood being forced up thither and pressing the veins as violently'. A further 50lb persuaded him to gasp his way to the courtroom, where a swig of brandy cleared his throat sufficiently to voice 'not guilty'; he was convicted and hanged at Tyburn.

Major Strangways was put under pressure at Newgate following a murder charge in 1658. 'He was denied what is usual in these cases, to have a sharp piece of timber under his back to hasten execution,' but luckily he had friends in attendance and implored them to contribute their own weight to his burden in an act of ghastly mercy; 'His groans were loud and doleful and it was eight or ten minutes before he died.' Pressing also achieved decisive results when defendants pretended to be (or perhaps genuinely were) deaf or dumb.

Although weights were last employed in 1726, their memory was immortalised in the name of a prison courtyard, the Press Yard, where in a less barbaric age, pleas were instead obtained by squeezing the thumbs with a twisted whip cord; silence was considered a guilty plea – later amended to not guilty.

VIRGIN TERRITORY

It is just after midnight on 4 June 1885 and in a brothel above a ham and beef shop at 32 Poland Street, Eliza Armstrong is being prepared for her client. A few weeks earlier she reached the age of consent, and the nervous 13-year-old is a virgin – something confirmed at the customer's request earlier in the day by a backstreet abortionist. In the room overlooking the street, Eliza is told to undress by brothel madam Rebecca Jarrett, who procured the girl from her family in a Marylebone slum. Though Eliza at first resists, she is persuaded by the promise of a picture book and climbs into the four-poster bed while Jarrett draws the curtains around it, then attempts to render the girl unconscious by holding a chloroform-soaked handkerchief over her face. This is also at the request of the client, who has paid a princely £5 for the encounter and detailed his every requirement; in an adjoining room he delights in telling the brothel owner exactly what he intends to do with the girl. Eliza is now quite anxious and recoils at the unpleasant smell, doubting Jarrett's assertion that it is merely perfume. The woman persists and Eliza becomes even more distressed when she hears the door open and someone enter the room; Jarrett murmurs something to the visitor and at the sound of a man's voice, Eliza starts screaming.

The client was devout Christian and pacifist W.T. Stead, who had set up the encounter to expose the legal trafficking of young girls into the sex trade; he also happened to be editor of the *Pall Mall Gazette* and was thus busy creating his own headlines. Stead had likely not considered how the girl might react to her role in the melodrama and briskly quit the room while Jarrett helped her dress. Eliza was then conveyed to a reputable medical practitioner, who successfully applied chloroform and certified her virgo intacta; in this regard Stead clearly felt the need to prove that he acted respectably.

But he was not yet finished with Eliza. Next morning, she was taken to Charing Cross Station and escorted to southern France where she was to toil as a housemaid, thereby allowing the journalist to demonstrate the ease with which it was possible to abduct a child.

Stead was mindful that his actions bordered on illegality but blithely assumed that guilt required prior criminal intent, so had shared his grand scheme with prominent churchmen and lawyers. A lone dissenting voice was the Archbishop of Canterbury, but Stead felt justified by public duty; for years, Parliament had debated measures to outlaw the 'white slave trade' but failed to act, leaving the impression that lawmakers wished to protect only the interests of those who engaged juvenile prostitutes. As one peer conceded in a debate on the matter: 'There were very few of their Lordships who had not, when young men, been guilty of immorality.'

Two days before his article 'The Maiden Tribute of Modern Babylon' hit the news stands, Stead issued a frank warning imploring squeamish or prudish readers to steer well clear of it; newsagents W.H. Smith went a step further and declined to stock the paper. The hype stoked precisely the reaction he hoped for and publication caused a sensation. This was not surprising when readers were fed 'trade' titbits such as the existence of soundproof subterranean rooms for 'lust and brutality', although they were not essential 'to enjoy to the full the exclusive luxury of revelling in the cries of the immature child'. So great was the demand for moral outrage and titillation, one and a half million unauthorised copies found their way into circulation and the pandemonium continued for days as Stead artfully spread his salacious hyperbole across several instalments.

But while Stead revelled in the notoriety of his exposé, the *Pall Mall Gazette* enjoyed new readership among the Marylebone slums. Despite the anonymous and embellished storytelling, incidental details led Eliza's mother to suspect that 'Lily' was her missing daughter and she reported her abduction to the authorities. Stead remained steadfast, however, because public opinion had been swayed and Parliament, spurred on by his threat to reveal the Royal and aristocratic regulars at brothels ('we might subpoena almost half the Legislature in order to prove the accuracy of our revelations'), hastily upped the age of consent to 16.

Yet in highlighting the iniquity of one law, Stead had indeed fallen foul of another. He had paid Jarrett to procure a girl and she omitted to inform Eliza's mother what was intended for her daughter beyond the offer of work in service – and her father was never consulted. Furthermore, Stead never thought it pertinent to ensure that the girl was already 'in the market' – circumstances that somewhat spoiled his assertion that disreputable, alcoholic parents willingly sold their virginal daughters into prostitution. He was found guilty of abduction and physical assault, but a three-month prison sentence provided both welcome publicity and further material for his cause célèbre.

In later years, Stead's campaigning led to six nominations for the Nobel Peace Prize, but he met a premature end amid appropriately dramatic circumstances in 1912, as will be recounted later.

LAVENDER PARK, MITCHAM CR4

DRUG CULTURE

During the early nineteenth century, the opium of the people was ... opium. As an ingredient in hundreds of patent medicines, it was the go-to drug of choice; it cured ailments from toothache to diarrhoea, brewers laced beer with it, a significant proportion of the nation's children were put to bed with a dose of Godfrey's Cordial (a tempting blend of opium and treacle), both Wilberforce and Gladstone took it to calm nerves before speeches, and others enjoyed it merely for recreation. Dire warnings from the East concerning its addictive properties were scornfully dismissed because drugs posed no threat to the well-adjusted British character and constitution.

The highest-quality opium originated from Turkey, which regrettably was not part of the Empire, so Britain found itself at the mercy of unscrupulous foreigners, apt to adulterating consignments. What was needed was honest home-grown produce, so the Royal Society for the Encouragement of Arts, Manufactures and Commerce offered prize money to anyone who demonstrated successful domestic production. In 1800, fifty guineas went to a grower who harvested 21lb of raw opium following 'herculean labour' on fields in Enfield, employing local boys to perform the art of slicing the half-ripe seed head at sunset, then gathering the exuded latex in a tin cup come morning. However, the roots of Victorian drug culture lie beneath twentieth-century housing developments around Mitcham.

The village lay at the heart of vast swathes of land dedi-cated to cultivating a cornucopia of pharmaceutical flora – from liquorice and rhubarb to wormwood, aconite and belladonna – and it was the obvious locale for intensive pro-duction. The area soon fluttered with the flowers of *Papaver somniferum* and by the 1830s, the majority of London's opium originated from Mitcham, where the area's principal nurse-ryman was James Moore, who set aside at least 2 acres for the crop in the rich black loam of the West Field (centred on today's Lavender Park). Traditional harvesting methods proved futile, what with the vagaries of British weather, so seed capsules were collected into bags of 3,000 and sold to druggists, who extracted their narcotic virtues by boiling

them down into cakes of 'English Opium' with a respectable 5 per cent morphine.

But in the 1840s, poppy fields were complemented by the dense foliage of *Cannabis sativa* after it was recognised that hemp could treat opium withdrawal; the wonder drug's star was waning. Untold numbers of teething children had died from injudicious draughts of opium and the realisation that Britain was not immune to its harmful effects put paid to Mitcham's status as the nation's drug capital.

Nowadays, the local authority prefer to highlight the district's historic connection with peppermint and lavender.

BERWICK STREET W1

PISS ARTIST

FFresh urine has offered an instructive index to health since ancient times, but during the seventeenth and eighteenth centuries – an era when anyone could set themselves up in medicine – its potency reached saturation point. Opportunists were not slow to glimpse gold at the bottom of a chamber pot.

Where conventional medicine failed (and because purgatives and leeches were standard treatment, it regularly did), was too expensive, or simply held no appeal, quack medicine flourished. In the hands of a bogus practitioner, the reputable procedure of uroscopy became 'water conjuring', in which no ailment was too complex or indeterminate to be diagnosed from the shade and bouquet of urine. And to truly impress clients, flavour might be added to that analysis – because as well as take the piss, some even tasted it.

A high water mark was reached during the 1770s with the arrival in London of Theodor Myersbach. A post office clerk in his native Germany, he came to London to join an equestrian circus but when informed that he was of insufficient stature, modified his ambitions. Encyclopaedic ignorance of medicine did not dissuade Myersbach from opening a consulting room at a handsome house in Berwick Street (the exact address remains unknown – and regrettably we have no picture of the piss doctor), where he built up a wealthy and influential clientele willing to pay his reassuringly high fees. Patients ranged from the naive and unsuspecting, such as ennobled hypochondriacs, to the desperate, including actor David Garrick, who was near death when he staggered to Myersbach's door; in no time, piss-pots of cash flowed in.

How favourably the diminutive doctor's enterprise affected his coffers may be imagined from his turnover of up to two hundred patients a day – each one benefiting from his uncanny knack for instantly discerning their health complaint, purely by perusing their piss. Those sat in his waiting room remained oblivious to the fact that Myersbach's minions were extraordinarily adept at striking up conversations and encouraging the sick to eagerly gabble about themselves and their ailments. The less loquacious found themselves waiting two or three hours, then perhaps informed that the doctor was unavailable.

After rendering invalids dumbstruck with his unnerving perspicacity, the doctor would gravely announce in broken English how the specimen denoted a worrying case of 'slime in de kidneys' or some such spurious pathology sufficient to terrify them, but thankfully, he could prescribe special nostrums to effect a cure. In reality, whatever the diagnosis, treatment involved a seemingly random choice of either 'red powder', 'silver pills', 'green drops' or 'sweet essence', which patients swallowed as readily as his pantomime. The precise formulae of these potions was deemed too complex

QUACK·DOCTOR·

to be entrusted to laypersons, but they might bring about a drastic transformation in health because their pharmacology ranged from harmless, such as water imbued with toast crumbs, through narcotic, for example a cocktail of opium and brandy – certain to numb any pain and foster feelings of well-being (and likely account for his steady stream of repeat custom), to poisonous, such as lead acetate or mercury, which provided permanent pain relief through death.

When physician John Coakley Lettsom noticed that many of his patients laboured under symptoms brought about by quack remedies, he soon traced the source to the failed equestrian. Exasperated by public gullibility, Lettsom published pamphlets to vividly demonstrate the dangers of Myersbach's methods: 'In August 1775 I was desired to visit T.W. of Thames Street, about 54 years old; he had laboured under a cough and a slight difficulty in breathing and restlessness for which he had consulted Dr Myersbach about a fortnight before. When I entered the sick chamber the patient was so near his end and the family in such distress

that I could not collect a very accurate account of the process
he had been under.' But it quickly became evident that the
cough had likely been attributed to kidney slime: 'I found
however in the room the green drops, red powder and some
pills.' The medication cost Mr W. a fortune, and shortly
afterwards, his life: 'He opened his eyes two or three times
and I think uttered a few words before he expired.'

But Myersbach's pretensions to medicine flowed beyond
urine because he was blessed with another arcane gift for
diagnoses. By hovering his hands over a patient's body and
rapidly lurching them about while intoning: 'De pain is here,
de pain is here!', he could magically reveal the source of a
condition by the locality in which his hands stopped. There
then followed likely pronouncement of 'sickness in the stomach', 'disorder of the womb' or doubtless, that pernicious
kidney ailment, and by this means, Myersbach identified a
liver complaint in a patient suffering pain at the extremity
of his penis. A two-month course of Myersbach's pills consigned the man to such agony and violent inflammation he
sensibly sought a second opinion; a surgeon immediately
extracted a formidable bladder stone and he was restored to
perfect health.

Such was Myersbach's prowess he could even diagnose
patients without seeing them. One man brought the urine
of his sick wife to the doctor, who readily identified the perennial renal sludge as well as pain in the limbs, head and
stomach, a womb disorder and a cough. The husband later
informed the newspapers that the sample originated from
a horse.

SLEEPING DOGS LIE

Just visible through a privet hedge on Bayswater Road is an unexpected sight – hundreds of miniature headstones solemnly mourning the loss of beloved Fattie, Titsey, Freeky, Runty, Bogie, Smut, Drag, Scum, Nigger, Gyp, Wee and Muff. It would be quite something to hear the Victorians calling after their dogs.

The bestial necropolis came about by chance in 1881 after a Maltese terrier named Cherry succumbed to the infirmities of old age. Naturally, his owners believed the mutt not merely special but 'graceful, elegant and dandified … an accomplished dog of the world' who delighted in giving drawing room entertainments. When Cherry was 'dressed up as a soldier in a little uniform coat, a helmet and a musket he was an inimitable sentinel. But as a sick baby carefully tucked up in a perambulator, he always brought down the house' – this latter amusement presumably much favoured during the dog's dotage. The family were regulars in Hyde Park and knew the gatekeeper Mr Winbridge because he sold lollipops and gingerbread to children, and they had no qualms asking whether he might bury Cherry in his very small garden. Evidently, Mr Winbridge was of too benevolent a persuasion to object, because 'so intelligent and so amiable a dog assuredly deserved a Christian burial'.

Sometime after Cherry's demise, Yorkshire terrier Prince suffered a fatal mishap with a carriage wheel outside the lodge, much to the dismay of his owner, Mrs Sarah Fairbrother. The popular actress, who had secretly married the Duke of Cambridge, was denied a royal title and

her existence ignored by Queen Victoria, but she could take advantage of her husband's position when it came to Prince's funeral arrangements. As well as Commander in Chief of the British Army, the Duke was Park Ranger, so the genial gatekeeper duly committed another pooch to his garden-cum-graveyard.

What with the opportunity for one's hound to enjoy a resting place beside that of royalty in Hyde Park rather than the traditional dustheap or river, a tide of dead dogs duly washed up at the lodge: 'The burial ceremony is generally performed by Mr Winbridge himself, but only rarely in the presence of the bereaved owners of the lamented pet, who are mostly too much overcome with grief to be able to face this last cruel parting.' But although mourning owners were otherwise engaged when the long-suffering gatekeeper administered last rites, several headstones express hope for an eventual reunion.

Burials at this first pet cemetery in Britain came to an abrupt halt in 1903 when the meagre garden was chock-full with in excess of 300 composting pets. Not one for sentimentality, George Orwell considered it one of the most horrible sights in England.

32 AMBLESIDE AVENUE SW16

STORM IN A D CUP

Streatham police were no strangers to shutting down rowdy house parties but after bursting through the door of No. 32 Ambleside Avenue on 6 December 1978, they came upon a great deal more than over-exuberant merriment.

In fact, local constabulary had been keeping a close eye on activities at Cynthia Payne's unremarkable four-bedroom residence on the quiet, tree-lined street for some time, and one of their more noteworthy observations was what appeared to be a man dressed as a woman putting out the weekly rubbish. When on that December evening they counted no fewer than fifty-three men and sixteen women enter the premises, they decided to pounce, and the *mise-en-scène* that confronted them from the front doorstep – two

startled young women, one sporting merely a bra and knickers, the other, nothing – confirmed their suspicions. This was
no vicarage tea party but an orgy in full swing.

But perhaps the distinction was blurred. Partygoers were a
mix of middle age and elderly barristers, company directors,
accountants and clergymen – as well as an Irish MP and a
peer of the realm. When not fussing over cigarette burns in
her chintz upholstery, Payne kept convivial company in the
kitchen, from where she dispensed cups of tea and poached
eggs on well-buttered toast – her fortifying remedy for veterans drained by their amatory exploits. Police arrived too late
to witness the blue movie lapped up by sherry-sipping guests
in the lounge (exactly what example of the cinematic art featured on the bill has been lost to history, though *Casanova and
the Nuns* and *Naughty Girl Guides* were among items confiscated
as evidence) and missed the live floor show executed with
amateurish aplomb by two young ladies, so were instead
confronted by a gentlemanly queue snaking up the stairs.

Officers were at a loss to understand why each guest was
excitedly clutching an out of date luncheon voucher, so
Payne kindly enlightened them: partygoers paid £25 to enjoy
cucumber sandwiches and drinks in the conservatory, entertainments in the lounge and, in exchange for the voucher
they were given, girls who gave every satisfaction in the bed-
rooms. Any would-be Don Juans with sufficient stamina for
further adventures between the pink polyester sheets availed
themselves of additional copulatory coupons at the going
rate. Meanwhile, the girls accumulated a pile of the house
currency on the bedside table as proof of their labours, and
at the end of the evening, returned the vouchers to Payne
in exchange for either £8 or £10 each – the precise figure
being a matter for the madam of the house. (Payne later
explained that she had originally employed a system based
on badges from a high street stationers, but quickly realised
that her girls were also patronising the shop.) To guests' great

disappointment, they were obliged to dress for a brief sojourn at Streatham police station to assist officers with their enquiries, where even in their flustered state, many had the presence of mind to offer false names and addresses.

In April 1980, Payne stood in the dock charged with keeping a disorderly house and controlling three prostitutes (other girls were perhaps ignominiously considered mere amateurs hoping to pocket some cash for Christmas). She was found guilty, fined £1,950 with £2,000 costs, and sentenced to eighteen months in prison. The judgement provoked instant outrage; there had been no coercion, no illegal substances, all involved were consenting adults and the house was run in a safe and respectable manner – in fact it was scrupulously clean courtesy of Payne's slaves – two submissive men who delighted in being chastised by the domesticatrix for their wholly unsatisfactory housework. It was hardly a realm of hardened criminality and many applauded Payne for supplying an innocuous service to kinky men in their twilight years (needless to say, none of whom were ever charged or their names made public). On appeal, the sentence was reduced to six months, and perhaps as a result of her tightly sealed lips, she was out after four.

Payne basked in her new-found celebrity, but was propelled to national treasure status in 1987 courtesy of the movie *Personal Services* – a thinly veiled biopic of her bawdy life. To celebrate the film's release, Payne did what she knew best – host a party at Ambleside Avenue. But unbeknownst to the retired chief superintendent who was intently focused on the live lesbian entertainments, police had the foresight to send in two undercover officers, one of whom chose to bolster his disguise with effeminate dress and eye shadow. At a prearranged moment, Payne's front door again felt the full force of the law and merrymaking was abruptly curtailed.

Back in court, the prosecution's dry depiction of kinky sexual antics studied by the not entirely plain clothes officers was met with an atmosphere of barely subdued mirth, and this became outright hilarity when a sack brimming with sex toys was lugged into the courtroom – an assortment that took a week of police time to sift through. Payne's defence suggested that the undercover policemen enjoyed her hospitality more than professional duty permitted – chronicling an unfortunate misunderstanding between one of them and a gentleman dressed as a French maid, and when 'Madam Cyn' was finally acquitted much of the nation erupted in applause.

DRAYCOTT AVENUE SW3

ROYAL FLUSH

In the field of lavatorial progress there is no doubt that the contribution made by Thomas Crapper has been inflated at the expense of other pioneers of sanitary technology who bore less memorable surnames (Bramah, Jennings, Twyford et al.). Contrary to popular belief, Crapper did not invent the flushing toilet and held only seventeen of the thousands of Victorian patents and registered designs for lavatories and their associated equipage, but he could comfortably settle himself on the throne for discharging another business function with honours. Despite living in an age of strict propriety in which the WC was secreted away and great lengths taken to avoid mentioning it, in 1872 he boldly opened what is now termed a bathroom showroom.

Crapper's premises at 50–54 Marlborough Road (now Draycott Avenue – the site covered by the Wiltshire Close Estate) featured plate glass windows brimming with the most recognisable object of his trade – toilet pedestals.

It was (unreliably) reported that ladies were overcome as they passed the shop and glimpsed his range of pans proudly lined up like an orchestra of gleaming white tubas. The senses were further confounded because this chamber of secrets was dominated by a gilded royal crest, reminding onlookers that Royalty crapped and Crapper supplied them with the hardware to do so.

Those fearless enough to venture inside this sanitary sanctum sanctorum enjoyed theatrical demonstrations of the merchandise: an apple or two were plopped into a pan and with one tug of a shiny brass chain – its handle exhorting users to 'Pull and Let Go', customers peered into the bowl to witness the consignment vanish amid gurgling pipework and a frothing torrent of water. (Crapper's powerful Valveless Water Waste Preventer cistern grievously impaired any attempt to disguise the completion of a trip to the lavatory – though its designer was alert to public discomfort and later developed a silent version.) Much store was set on the motive power behind a flush and gold medals were up for grabs for the quantity of fruit purged from a toilet pan; in 1884 one of Crapper's competitors triumphantly dispatched one flat sponge, four sheets of paper closely adhered to the pan with smearings of plumber's smudge, and no fewer than ten apples.

When the deluge subsided, customers who were trialling the popular willow pattern pedestal could begin to make out Windsor Castle at the bottom of the pan – an unexpected subject placement for a royal warrant holder.

As to the sticky subject of the proprietor's surname, mopping up the etymological mess will not attempted here, but 'crap' in its excretive sense was already in use by the 1850s after a spell as a term of indignation – as attested by a charming line of poetry from 1801: '… Crap! … crap! … 'twas a moist one! A right brewer's ****!' (the preceding line closes with the word 'part').

OLD PARADISE GARDENS,
LAMBETH SE11

STIFF COMPETITION

A s may be deduced from the headstones lining its walls, the park is a former graveyard that in 1817 had 'for a considerable time past been the scene of transactions of the most daring and horrid description'. Specifically, 'the depositories of the dead have been nightly invaded, and the feelings of surviving relatives exceedingly harrowed, by the depredations upon their deceased friends of that callous gang of wretches known by the name of Body Snatchers'.

In the second half of the eighteenth century, the Barber-Surgeons' long-held monopoly on teaching anatomical science was challenged by private anatomy schools. Numbers aspiring to enter the medical profession had burgeoned and lucrative sums were commanded by classes that laid on plenty of morbid flesh for carving up. But lecturers could not sully their reputation by direct involvement in the acquisition of teaching materials, so a new underworld profession arose.

While most reasonably minded people considered that stealing a dead body was an abominable crime, the law perceived it quite differently. A deceased human belonged to no one – or rather, its owner had ceased to exist, so it could not be stolen, unlike a dead pig or sheep. The best the law could offer was a charge of unlawful disinterment – a minor misdemeanour punishable with a paltry fine or prison sentence, and a wholly ineffectual deterrent if a fresh corpse fetched £10 while more conventional, law-abiding employment garnered just a few shillings a week. In 1828 it was estimated that ten Londoners lived solely from the profits of corpse-mongering and at least 200 toiled part-time, supplying about 800 anatomy students with a similar number of corpses per year – a significant and burdensome body of work.

A body snatcher's modus operandi was as follows: after dark and with minimal torchlight, a sloping trench was dug to the head end of a recently buried coffin. Wooden tools prevented the telltale noise of metal hitting stones and the task was less taxing than might be supposed because the soil was still loose and the perpetrator probably much the better

for drink. Two curved chisels were employed to prise open the coffin lid and a rope was threaded under the corpse's armpits to drag it to the surface. Any clothing or shroud were stripped from the body to avoid the charge of theft, the soil was returned to the grave, and a seasoned practitioner could be staggering away with his booty within an hour.

Grieving relatives were less pleased with the results of body-snatching and one way to prevent mourning over an empty grave was to postpone burial until a loved one was sufficiently putrefied to be unappealing to anatomists. Another, less troublesome method was to simply guard the grave, so at Lambeth a watch-house was built and parish sexton Mr Seagar employed former gravedigger Thomas Duffin and his sidekick George Marshall as night watchmen. Their presence brought about negligible benefit, however, so the pair laid man-traps across God's acre but 'still the ground was robbed; scarcely a night passed without a body being stolen'. On Sunday, 30 November 1817, the sexton decided to take matters into his own hands and following a busy day with five burials, he hid in the graveyard after dark accompanied by his son and a young man named John Sharp, and waited to see what happened.

They did not linger for long; at about ten o'clock, they glimpsed 'two men passing over the graves. They first proceeded to that part of the ground where there were man-traps set, which they let off.' The intruders were evidently well prepared and 'commenced their operations upon a grave wherein a body had been deposited the preceding day'. Seagar patiently watched their exertions until the coffin was struck by their spade 'then came from his concealment and called out to these men to desist and surrender themselves'. But he was in for a shock: 'He then discovered, to his astonishment, that they were the very identical persons whom he had hired and paid to protect the ground.' And his employees were not intending to follow orders:

Marshall sprung from the grave, and with dreadful impre-
cations swore that he would murder Mr Seagar, and at the
same time made a desperate blow at him with a spade, and
knocked him down; he was about repeating the blow, when
Mr Seagar's son flew to the protection of his father, fired a
pistol at Marshall, and wounded him in the left arm; he then
thought proper to surrender.

Meanwhile, 'Duffin attacked John Sharp with a drawn sabre
and cut him dangerously in the forehead. Sharp had armed
himself with a poker, with which he maintained a conflict of
several minutes and at last brought his adversary to the ground.'

The episode was the final nail in the coffin for both their
employments and though a magistrate urged that the men
be excommunicated and have an ear cut off, they instead
received two years behind bars. Sometime later, both
returned to the graveyard to be buried.

ST STEPHEN'S HALL, PALACE
OF WESTMINSTER SW1

HOT AIR

Until 1834, when fire destroyed the old Palace of
Westminster, the House of Commons sat in the Chapel
of St Stephen, whose two sets of choir stalls still informs the
seating arrangement of Parliament today. (St Stephen's Hall,
which is closed to the public, now stands on the site.)

One of the chamber's more memorable days turned out
to be 4 March 1607 when a highly charged debate took place

about the naturalisation of Scots in a united England and Scotland, and whether it was sensible to grant the hordes north of the border free run of the rich south. No sooner had the King's Serjeant, Sir John Crooke, concluded an important announcement from the Lords than a sudden kerfuffle arose. To the great indignation of those in the room, somebody had pushed out a full-bodied fart. An earwitness noted how it originated, appropriately enough, from 'the nether end of the House' and those nearby rapidly got wind that the seat responsible for the malodorous outburst belonged to young Henry Ludlow, member for the Wiltshire borough of Ludgershall. A noticeably different atmosphere now permeated through the chamber; however, a clerk tactfully confided in his diary that he did not think the noisy intervention constituted Ludlow's informed judgement on the debate. Apparently, his father Sir Edward Ludlow, had fallen asleep before a committee and (resorting to Latin for the unseemly details) *sonitum ventre emisit* – emitted belly noise, so instead of malice, sonorous involuntary wind was merely a family infirmity. That may be guff, however.

But Ludlow's noteworthy nay-vote left a permanent mark on the fabric of history by inspiring a hugely popular ode: The Parliament Fart. The poem, to which no one chose to attach their name, begins: 'Puffing down comes grave ancient Sir John Crooke/And reads his message promptly without book/Very well, quoth Sir William Morris, so/But Henry Ludlow's foysting arse cry'd no.'

The doggerel continues in a similar scatological vein ad nauseam, and more than twenty-five different versions exist after a plethora of poetic wits jumped on the bandwagon and delighted in ever more jocular couplets for each member of the house. One long-winded rendering puffs its way through in excess of 200 lines, while others kept member's names updated to ensure the butt of the joke remained fresh; 'Nay, by my faith quoth Sir Henry Jenkin/The motion were good, were it not for the stinking/Quoth Sir Henry Poole 'tis

an audacious trick/To fart in the face of the body politic/
Now without doubt, quoth Sir Edward Grevill/I must
confess, it was very uncivil/Thank God, quoth Sir Edward
Hungerford/That this fart proved not a turd.'

Historical records make no mention of Henry Ludlow
offering any further contribution to the work of Parliament.

RIVER THAMES/ST MAGNUS
THE MARTYR EC3

CUT TO THE CHASTE

In 1840 dredging work on the Thames dragged up a
curious item from the riverbank beside St Magnus the
Martyr church: an ornate bronze tool bearing the head of
Roman cult deity Cybele and believed to date from around
200 CE. However, it was not thought appropriate to edify the
Victorian public that the gadget facilitated castration, so
the British Museum chose to label it: 'A pair of pincers for
the nose of a victim,' while other antiquarians were at least
partly correct in calling it a set of nutcrackers.

Besides Cybele, the tool bears the head of her consort,
Attis, and the eight deities associated with the days of the
Roman week. Its two shanks were originally hinged at one
end and a threaded bolt passed between the other ends
so that the tightening of a nut clamped its serrated edges
around the scrotum. But this was no veterinary or surgical
instrument because, without medical assistance, men were
expected to employ a sword or knife to detach themselves
from their gonads. And a blade was not always necessary

because hacking with a flint or broken potsherd also amply served the purpose.

The cult of Cybele originated in Phrygia, now part of Turkey, and spread throughout both the Greek and Roman world including, it would appear, Londinium. Statues of Cybele and Attis have been unearthed in London (as perhaps was an ornate stone box-cum-altar now at the Fitzwilliam Museum, Cambridge) and a temple dedicated to her may have stood nearby. As a mother goddess figure, Cybele was associated with nature's regenerative cycle – perhaps not the obvious deity to inspire castration – and as is customary among mythical figures, fables about her are laden with discrepancies. However, a common thread tells how she discovered her handsome young lover Attis (sources are uncertain whether he was a prince, a shepherd, or her son) being unfaithful and in a fit of guilt-ridden madness he grabbed a sharp stone and emasculated himself, thereafter adopting the dress and manners of a woman. Cybele's more zealous devotees were prepared to make a similar lifestyle choice and should they survive any haemorrhaging or subsequent complications, became priests known as Galli, which, paradoxically, probably derived from *gallus* – Latin for cock (in the poultry sense, that is).

Self-castration took place outside the temple during springtime on 24 March, the 'Day of Blood' when amid crowds of spectators and a noisy, fevered atmosphere, men whipped themselves into an ecstatic frenzy, then sliced or bit into their skin to spill blood on the altar to Cybele and effigies of Attis. Then: 'A young man seized with this fury instantly tears off his clothes from his back, leaps into the middle among the Galli, snatches up one of the short swords that probably has been kept many years in readiness for the same use, [and] castrates himself'. The freshly fashioned eunuch likely benefitted from cauterisation or stitches to staunch the flow of blood because he was then expected to hotfoot it through the streets: 'He runs with what he has cut off in his hand round about the city, and goes into whatever house the fancy takes him to throw it, from which house he must be provided with a complete suit of woman's apparel, and all the ornaments becoming a lady' (homeowners' feelings

towards this contract went unrecorded). The tossed testicles were retrieved from whichever household they unexpectedly graced, deposited in a box at the temple and, in consideration for the fruits of this harvest, Cybele granted the land bounteous fertility (happily, it is entirely unnecessary to make any of this up). Archaeologists uncomfortably noted that the tool bore signs of heavy use.

Relieved of both male attire and organs, Galli wore their hair long and bleached, were partial to extravagant make-up and jewellery, and relied on charity to survive – often obtaining alms by telling fortunes or performing dances. But that might not have been all; certain sources, perhaps wishing to denigrate cult worship, disdainfully referred to them as *mollis* (soft) and suggested that they swelled their purses by granting sexual favours to all comers.

The clamp had been expertly repaired but also appeared to have been intentionally broken, perhaps by Christian iconoclasts when any unacceptably pagan temple was destroyed around the year 300 CE. However, Galli were still sashaying around the Roman Empire during the early fifth century after Christianity had become its favoured faith, prompting theologian Augustine to harrumph: 'These effeminates no later than yesterday were going through the streets and places of Carthage with anointed hair, whitened faces, languid bodies and feminine gait, extracting from the people the means of maintaining their ignominious lives.' Evidence of Cybele worship has been found at other sites in England and, in 2002, archaeological excavations in North Yorkshire uncovered the grave of a young man thought to be a Gallus. His body was dripping with jewellery and in his mouth were two pebbles – perhaps representing something he lacked in life.

By curious coincidence, the name for a temple dedicated to Cybele, *sedes Magna Mater*, Seat of the Great Mother, is strikingly similar to the church beside which the clamp was found – St Magnus the Martyr.

PRINCE HARMING

When Prince Albert died unexpectedly in 1861 following a short illness, national mourning was swiftly followed by calls for a fitting way in which to memorialise Queen Victoria's consort, who found himself fêted more in death than life. But it was Albert himself who made the undertaking acutely challenging: 'I can say with perfect absence of humbug that I would rather not be made the prominent feature of such a monument,' he once wrote in response to the suggestion that a statue of him be erected in Hyde Park, 'as it would both disturb my quiet rides in Rotten Row to see my own face staring at me, and if, (as is very likely) it became an artistic monstrosity like most of our monuments, it would upset my equanimity to be permanently ridiculed and laughed at in effigy.' Unfortunately, his words proved difficult to misinterpret.

A committee of the great and good wrestled with all manner of schemes that would not fall foul of his wishes, a task further complicated by the fact that the customary method of dodging an awkward decision – a competition – was also something of which the Prince disapproved. Proposals for ways in which to perpetuate his memory included the installation of commemorative stained glass windows up and down the country, an 'Albert University' at South Kensington offering degrees in the sciences and arts, the construction of cottages across London for poverty-stricken artisans, an international exchange programme, and a sprucing up of the shabby Brompton Road. However, what found most support was an oversize obelisk.

Queen Victoria had invariably deferred to her husband with regard to artistic matters, but when her opinion was delicately solicited, she expressed satisfaction with such a monolith, provided it was of sufficient grandeur. Cleopatra's Needle still languished in Egypt four decades after it had been gifted to Britain so was eyed up for the job, but the considerable cost and logistical obstacles involved prompted the committee to instead favour the fashioning of a new granite obelisk, and the hunt began for suitable stone. Although this extended as far as Russian Finland, a 100ft length of Scottish granite was earmarked, until the committee learned that merely assessing its feasibility would swallow most of its funds. Plans for a needle were thus discreetly dropped – a turnaround welcomed with relief among the artistic community, who sought an opportunity for creativity, and the church, who viewed obelisks as alarmingly pagan.

The only way out of the predicament was to quietly forget Albert's objection to statues and competitions and execute both, resulting in a gilded effigy inside a monument of the highest Gothic that triumphantly embodies the Prince's foreboding.

SOUTHBANK CENTRE,
BELVEDERE ROAD SE1

TEXTBOOK MURDER

At two o'clock in the morning on 17 February 1872, the streets around Belvedere Road echoed to the sound of gunfire. George Merritt was making his way to work at the Lion Brewery, on the site of the Southbank Centre, when a man suddenly appeared and began angrily shouting at him; Merritt started to run, but the shadowy figure pulled out a revolver and began firing in his direction. Of the three or four shots, one struck Merritt in the neck and another, his spine; either injury alone was fatal. Police were rapidly on the scene to discover the victim lying beside the brewery gates, face down in a pool of blood (in today's geography, just in front of al fresco diners at the Southbank Centre's ground-floor restaurant). The murderer still stood where he had fired the gun and a constable approached the well-dressed figure to ask who he had shot. 'A man,' he replied calmly. 'I should not be such a coward as to shoot a woman.'

The gunman was William Chester Minor, an American who had arrived in London a few months earlier and though relatively wealthy, settled in insalubrious Lambeth for the convenience of its proximity to prostitutes. A police doctor made note of the prisoner's gonorrhoea and its host explained to startled officers how he was treating it by injecting German white wine into his urethra. His inquisitors were equally surprised to hear that Minor had been a medic in the US Army – and shot Merritt by mistake. This cultured but extremely odd man was patently not a typical murderer.

Born in 1834 to missionaries living in Ceylon, Minor was sent back to America in disgrace aged 14 when his parents became aware of his lascivious interest in girls – an over-developed appetite that demanded the attention of his libido throughout his life. Minor majored in medicine at Yale, joined the Union Army as a surgeon and found his training put to the test treating hideously maimed casualties of the Civil War.

But nothing could have prepared him for another of his responsibilities. The penalty for desertion was branding and Minor found himself duty bound to sear the letter D into an Irish soldier's cheek with a red hot iron; the act was to haunt him for the rest of his life and provoke paranoid delusions that his victim's countrymen were out to wreak revenge on him. In fact, London police already knew of Minor's anxieties because three months earlier he informed them that Irish Nationalists were sneaking into his bedroom at night to poison him; alas, it was during one of these delusions that George Merritt innocently became the embodiment of Minor's Celtic persecutors.

The peculiar circumstances of the crime persuaded a jury to agree with Minor's lawyer that his client was insane, and despite his acquittal he would be indefinitely detained at Her Majesty's pleasure. But safely locked inside the new Asylum for the Criminally Insane at Broadmoor, Minor was still tormented by poisoners sneaking into his cell at night – hallucinations interspersed with episodes in which he was forced to commit immodest acts on young girls. Yet what ended up a lengthy stay at Broadmoor for events on Belvedere Road had significant consequences in an unexpected quarter.

Minor struck up an unlikely friendship with Merritt's widow, who visited regularly with supplies of books for him. Inside one, Minor spotted an advertisement calling for volunteers to work on what would become the Oxford English

Dictionary – a project that had started in 1857 and though it was now the 1880s, was still years away from publishing definitions for a to ant. Its editor, James Murray, sought quotations from historic texts to illustrate the first known use of each word and Minor, perhaps recognising an intellectual activity that might keep his mind from young maidens and Irishmen, offered to help. He was ideally suited to the task – he had built up an impressive library, possessed the enthusiasm and attention to detail required for such an unimaginably vast project, and most importantly, he had time on his hands. In 1885, his first sheaf of neatly handwritten notes was despatched to Oxford and in no time Murray was inundated, something that continued uninterrupted for almost twenty years and ran to tens of thousands of letters about words. It was several years before Murray learned that perhaps the greatest single contributor to the dictionary was a patient at Broadmoor.

But despite the dictionary, Minor's demons – particularly his sexual fantasies – still persecuted him and in 1902 he attempted a cure of his own making; grasping his freshly sharpened penknife in one hand and his penis in the other, he sliced off the offending organ and tossed it on the fire. His training served him well because beforehand he applied a ligature to staunch the bloodloss and the operation went with reasonable success, but Minor's health continued to deteriorate and, thanks to a campaign led by Murray, he was permitted to return to America where he died in 1920.

The first edition of the complete dictionary was published in 1928; the word auto-penectomy was defined some years later.

CORINTHIA HOTEL,
WHITEHALL PLACE SW1

PIE IN THE SKY

Although the building opened as a hotel in 1885, for much of its existence since the Second World War it housed Government offices, including perhaps the most mysterious and secretive of all, and one whose existence was only revealed in 2001 following repeated Freedom of Information requests. From 1950, this was where officials investigated unidentified flying objects.

After an American pilot spied something moving 'like a saucer skipping on water' above Washington State in 1947, the British Government established the magnificently appointed Flying Saucer Working Party to investigate home-grown sightings. The committee's findings make encouraging reading for the conspiracy theorist because it concluded that UFOs could be explained through reasons meteorological, astronomical or delusional.

But no sooner had it done so, UFOs staged a show of defiance during a 1952 NATO exercise to simulate Soviet invasion. The Government was suddenly less sceptical and five of Britain's finest scientific and military minds began to meet regularly in a top secret garret room on the ninth floor to analyse reports, while the public was assisted in the identification of alien craft courtesy of movies such as *The Day the Earth Stood Still* and *Flying Disc Man from Mars*.

For the next five decades, sightings of UAPs (Unexplained Aerial Phenomena, as Whitehall preferred to dignify them) were analysed and 'credible witnesses', a euphemism for anyone who wore uniform, interviewed and sworn to secrecy.

Dealings with the public were kept, in the words of one civil servant, 'politely unhelpful' yet every report, however unyielding its disregard for common sense, was scrutinised and placed on file. As a result, the nation's 'X-Files' include voluminous correspondence between Whitehall and a psychiatric home in the West Country (much of which is barely legible but concerns aliens disguised as human children inhabiting the Mendip Hills, although they occasionally stray into Tesco), myriad sightings of colourful lights erupting from a neighbour's garden (presumably accompanied by a deafening bang) and, following exhaustive analysis of every sighting between 1988 and 2009, a statistically anomalous number of UFOs floating over the sleepy village of West Kilbride, Ayrshire, around pub closing time.

The files lay bare how over the years UFO aeronautics has masterfully mimicked human enterprise – both real and fictional. Invaders from space have adopted disguises ranging from sky tracker searchlights and Chinese lanterns to weather balloons and stealth bombers, while 1978 (the year *Close Encounters of the Third Kind* was released) proved to be a record-breaking year with more than 700 extraterrestrial visits, closely followed by 1997 (when *Men in Black* landed in the cinemas).

The UK's UFO desk, which was latterly housed in the MOD building on Whitehall, was finally jettisoned in 2009 after the Government concluded that in more than fifty years of sightings, not one posed a credible threat to national security. There is, however, no obligation to believe that.

1 GILTSPUR STREET EC1

BAPTISM OF FIRE

Inscriptions beneath the Golden Boy monument on the junction with Cock Lane announce (in charmingly archaic language) how it was: 'In Memmory Put up for the late FIRE of LONDON Occasion'd by the Sin of Gluttony 1666' at the place of the inferno's 'staying'. The unusual charge of immoderate gourmandising rests on the fact that the locale was known as Pye (or Pie) Corner and the fire began in Pudding Lane. (Pudding was indeed edible at that time but referred to stuffed animal intestine; Pudding Lane may have conspicuously harboured a baker but it was primarily the domain of butchers.) These gastronomic references were no mere coincidence but unambiguous proof that the conflagration was God's punishment for overeating, so concerned residents erected the portly wooden figure to highlight that danger.

But do not be fooled by this quaint fable; unquestionably, it is first-rate drivel yet no one offers a sensible explanation of how it became literally set in stone.

It seems hardly necessary to point out that contemporary reports of the fire and its aftermath make no reference to a singling out of the overweight. Blame was laid squarely at the door of foreigners or Catholics (or better still, persons fulfilling both criteria) until the more humdrum explanation of a neglected baker's oven was eventually settled upon. Admittedly, such sober reasoning did not discourage the king and everyone beneath him from also concluding that the fire was God's judgement for whichever of society's ills the individual wished to berate – but gluttony was never one of them.

Mention is made of Pye Corner in the records because the flames did indeed stop at this site, but it was by no means the fire's furthest reach. Fetter Lane held that distinction and because its denominative 'faitours' were idle loafers, the opportunity was missed for admonishing the sin of sloth. And neither was Pye Corner the last area to be extinguished; such a widespread inferno with embers frequently fanned back into flame did nothing to favour easy pinpointing of

a single location as its final realm, and a ferocious blaze at St Paul's took days to bring under control, hampering claims that the conflagration signalled punishment for 'Forgetfulness of God'. So although Pye Corner was on the boundary of destruction, the site held no other significance; in fact, one local householder handed workmen £50 to blow up his neighbours' houses to create a firebreak to save his own – suggesting a monument to greed or envy more fitting.

It also cannot be overlooked that although the designation Pye Corner is thought to originate from the sign of a tavern, in all likelihood the hostelry's name or symbol was not a pie but a magpie, which perhaps reveals that the fire was caused by thieving.

Another snag with the monument is that although current norms might not identify gluttony in the boy's physique, even to our ancestor's eyes he was no more portly than the cherubic figures that grace the city's ecclesiastical architecture. Earliest images of the figure (which are no older than the 1790s) show wings on his back, hardly an appropriate appendage for someone supposed to be unduly plump, and to further contradict his corpulence, the unclad whippersnapper originally graced the wall of a watering hole named not The Fat Boy but The Naked Boy – indeed, the fact he was erected on a tavern brings into question the sincerity of the original gesture.

It is almost certain that the carving, which best estimates date to the late seventeenth century, was originally the sign of a shop, and because nakedness would draw attention to the necessity of clothing, such a figure was often adopted by tailors. (Alternatively, though more speculatively, he perhaps represented Cupid and therefore signified another trade known to flourish in the vicinity, prostitution, echoed in the helpfully descriptive name of the adjoining street.) So how did Londoners come to swallow the gluttony story?

A century after the inferno, churchmen were still exploiting the event to bolster their apocalyptic preaching and a satirical epigram appeared, poking fun at their sermonising. Putting words into their mouths, it suggested that the fire, 'could not be occasioned by the sin of blasphemy for in that case it would have begun at Billingsgate; nor lewdness for then Drury Lane would have been first on fire; nor lying for then the flames had reached from Westminster Hall – no, my beloved, it was occasioned by the sin of gluttony for it began at Pudding Lane, and ended at Pie Corner.' Alas, it was not entirely clear to God-fearing citizens that its author's tongue was planted firmly in cheek, and this comic reasoning was meekly accepted as the genuine cause of the conflagration. The misunderstanding then latched itself onto a former shop sign at Pye Corner whose subject's truculent demeanour could be interpreted as gluttonous, was gilded by those loathers of overindulgence, the Victorians (who tastefully garnished it with a fig leaf), and the chubby cherub now has protected status.

In an effort to lend credence to the absurd monument, there is a quaintly garbled inscription at ground level – though it is no older than the 1890 guide book from which it has been crudely lifted.

CUTLERS' HALL, WARWICK LANE EC4

SPARK OF LIFE

B etween 1679 and 1866 the Royal College of Physicians' anatomy theatre stood on the site, and its proximity to Newgate Gaol on Old Bailey had distinct advantages.

On 17 January 1803, George Foster spent an hour dangling from the end of a rope outside the prison for drowning his wife and child in the Paddington Canal. His body was then swiftly conveyed around the corner, where a distinguished audience expectantly awaited a demonstration by Italian professor Giovanni Aldini. A nephew of Luigi Galvani, Aldini was touring Europe to promote the medical use of galvanism – his uncle's theory of 'animal electricity'. At home in Bologna, Aldini enjoyed free rein to experiment on living specimens at the city's lunatic asylum, where he claimed 'the complete cure of two who had laboured under melancholy madness', but the largesse of London's medical establishment cautiously extended no further than a corpse. However, apart from being dead, 26-year-old Foster was otherwise young and healthy, and happily, had evacuated his bowels just before he arrived.

Aldini began by moistening his subject's mouth and ear with salt water, then grasping two electrodes connected to a powerful battery, introduced them to each orifice. At once, 'the jaw began to quiver, the adjoining muscles were horribly contorted, and the left eye actually opened'. After a pause for the assembled gentlemen to recover from that startling spectacle, Aldini withdrew the electrode from Foster's mouth and thrust it up his moistened

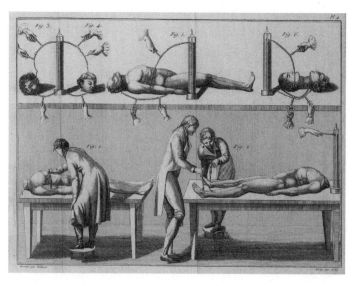

rectum; again, the convulsions were instantaneous: 'The action even of those muscles furthest distant from the points of contact was so much increased as almost to give an appearance of reanimation.' As the probes were relocated from ear to nostril and anus back into mouth, Foster grimaced abominably: 'The effect in this case surpassed our most sanguine expectations and vitality might, perhaps, have been restored.'

It was this idea of reanimation that had everyone on the edge of their seats – could Aldini's 'peculiar fluid' bring the dead back to life? The professor professed so, and his methods were ideally suited to Britain because as a maritime nation, countless victims of drowning could be resuscitated – though in the same breath he enthused about reviving 'unhappy creatures who labouring under a temporary privation of reason, form the horrible resolve of self-destruction'.

Even after Aldini had sliced open Foster's frame to expose muscles, nerves and the heart for shock treatment, some of those present remained convinced that the murderer's frenetic *danse macabre* signalled his imminent resurrection: 'Mr Pass, the beadle of the Surgeon's Company having been officially present during this experiment was so alarmed that he died soon after his return home of the fright.'

Aldini later demonstrated animal electricity at Guy's and St Thomas's Hospital, on which occasion he was supplied only with dead animals.

84–94 HALLAM STREET W1

WHORES RIDING

At Newgate Gaol in the 1820s and '30s, recalcitrant prisoners were stripped, their wrists and ankles secured to a specially designed 'horse', then flogged. Meanwhile, at No. 28 Charlotte Street (as the address then was – now the doorway to 84–94 Hallam Street), victims eagerly shelled out for similar punishment because the building was a brothel specialising in whipping the backsides of the wealthy.

No other country produced as many givers, takers, readers or spectators of the application of the whip or rod, and flogging became such a national pastime among the upper class, even the French honoured it with the designation: *le vice anglais*. London in the 1830s gloried in no fewer than twenty establishments whose sole line of business was flagellation, and mainstream brothels were prudent to equip themselves for wielding the birch when called upon. According to Pisanus Fraxi (of whom, more later), King George IV was known to have frequented 'noted whipper' Mrs Collet in Covent Garden and was perhaps also welcomed by the queen of the profession, Theresa Berkeley, at Charlotte Street.

Although Mrs Berkeley made her mark on countless posteriors, her discretion – no doubt a quality of particular importance to her clientele – ensured that she left little impression in historical records. However, the preface to an 1830 book of 'birchen sports' pornography offers rare insight in relation to her methodologies – and could even originate from the firm hand of the madam herself because it does not hold back from touting her services:

Her instruments of torture were more numerous than those of any other governess. Her supply of birch was extensive and kept in water so that it was always green and pliant; she had shafts with a dozen whip thongs on each of them; a dozen different sizes of cat-o'-nine tails, some with needle points worked into them; various kinds of thin bending canes; leather straps like coach traces; battledoors made of thick sole-leather with inch nails run through to docket, and currycomb tough hides rendered callous by many years flagellation.

And that was not the sum total of her formidable arsenal: 'Holly brushes, furze brushes, a prickly evergreen called butchers bush and during the summer, glass and China vases filled with a constant supply of green nettles with which she often restored the dead to life.' Urtication (flogging with stinging nettles) was a house speciality and a hook and pulley system attached to her ceiling enabled a gentleman to be conveniently drawn up for treatment: 'Thus at her shop, whoever went with plenty of money could be birched, whipped, fustigated, scourged, needle-pricked, half-hung, holly-brushed, furze-brushed, butcher-brushed, stinging-nettled, curry-combed, phlebotomized and tortured till he had a belly full.'

Should a client wish to assume a more dominant role, Berkeley would submit to an extent, 'but if they were gluttons at it she had women in attendance who would take any number of lashes the flogger pleased, provided he forked out'. Among recipients were: 'Miss Ring, Hannah Jones, Sally Taylor, One-eyed Peg, Bauld-cunted Poll and a black girl, called Ebony Bet.'

The tools of Berkeley's trade were undoubtedly ancient and established technologies but no business was immune to the effects of the Industrial Revolution and in 1828 the governess refined her modus operandi by designing a piece of apparatus that she christened the Chevalet or Berkeley Horse. By buckling a gentleman's limbs to the device he could be rendered fully immobile and arranged at whatever angle was most conducive; padding ensured that discomfort arose only in specific areas courtesy of an operator at the rear, while the agency of another at the front brought forth pleasure in a different region. The machine gave Berkeley's enterprise the whip hand and sparked its own revolution:

It is a great drawback on the business of any governess at this day not to possess a Berkeley Horse. Mrs Brown was the first to have one made, next Mrs Stewart, then Mrs Pryce and lastly Mesdames Collet and Beverley; but there is no doubt in the course of time they will find their way, not only into the boudoir of every flogging establishment, but will form a part of the furniture of every house of accommodation and entertainment in London.

Although Berkeley was scrupulously discreet during her years of public service, she had no qualms about posthumous publication of her blow-by-blow memoirs, and in preparation amassed a significant hoard of papers. As London's doyenne of discipline she also accumulated tremendous wealth and on her death in 1836 her brother, a missionary in Australia, travelled to England to learn of his £12,500 inheritance. But he was less agreeably disposed when he discovered how such riches came about, so renounced his claim and briskly returned home. The estate passed to Berkeley's executor, Dr Vance, who was alert to how hotly her memoirs were anticipated, but baulked at publishing, perhaps for fear of bringing the British establishment to its knees – a pose it amply rehearsed at Charlotte Street. He also shunned Berkeley's money, so it passed to the Crown, which showed no such scruples. The papers vanished following Vance's death and the Berkeley Horse was presented to the Royal Society of Arts – though the organisation today claims no knowledge of it.

105-109 OXFORD STREET W1

BEAVER AWAY

Those who pass the terracotta-fronted building are largely unaware of the creatures that inhabit its roof; four beaver perch on its gables – an unlikely situation as any for the nocturnal, semi-aquatic, tree-chewing, dam-building rodent.

Such an architectural flourish was entirely appropriate for hat makers Henry Heath Ltd when it built the emporium in 1887 because fashion had long dictated that the finest hats were made from beaver fur – the raw material par excellence for felting. Heath started his business on the site in 1822 and hundreds of thousands of pelts were shipped from North America to its factory (whose later facade can be seen in Hollen Street) until the creature found itself on the edge of extinction. But beaver were not the only victims of fashion.

When felting first developed in Turkey, it was recognised that camel hair matted best when rubbed with the animal's urine. Seventeenth-century French hatters overcame the scarcity of camel urine by using their own and developed a secret technique, thought to have arisen because one particular worker crafted felt of exceptionally luxuriant quality. He might not have wished it to be common knowledge but he suffered with syphilis and was treating it by injecting a compound of mercury into his urethra. (Mercury's utility in felting is also said to have been recognised after a British doctor treated a woman's breast cancer with a poultice of rabbit pelt spread with mercury; a hatter was later pleasantly surprised by the calibre of headgear it produced.)

By the time Heath opened what was one of the largest hat factories in London, the use of mercury was widespread, despite the fact that it had long been known to cause drooling, trembling, bouts of severe paranoia and a relentless pouring forth of gibberish (symptoms characterised by the expression 'mad as a hatter') as well as give rise to loose, blackened teeth and the coughing up of viscous slime. But health concerns were outweighed by economic utility because the chemical could transform cheap furs into lustrous felts – a sumptuous hat could be magically pulled out of a rabbit (or, more specifically, about five rabbits). Beaver could breathe a sigh of relief.

Mercury was still in use during the twentieth century, when it may have affected the founder's grandson, George Heath, who was managing the business in 1910. 'His health was quite deranged. He was vacant and always in thought and would stand and look without moving for a long time.' Heath locked himself in his upstairs office and when gunfire was heard, a director burst in to find him lying on the floor with bullet wounds to the chest. The inquest returned a verdict of 'suicide during temporary insanity'.

LAST TRAIN

In 1854, just six years after trains for the living began operating at Waterloo, services commenced for the dead.

London was suffering grave difficulties; God held a controlling interest in death so cremation was an abomination
(and technically illegal until 1902) and population growth
had led to woefully overcrowded churchyards that nutrified
the water supply in a most adverse fashion. Yet annually
upwards of 50,000 bodies sought a burial plot; the authorities
had met their Waterloo. However, a radical solution came in
the form of the world's largest cemetery at Brookwood in
Surrey – a city of the dead occupying more than 2,000 acres,
25 miles outside the metropolis. And the obvious way to dis-
patch Londoners to their final destination was by train.

But the scheme was not without opponents. Many wor-
ried whether a train journey was an appropriate prelude to
Christian burial. Should the living travel alongside the dead?
What was a respectable speed for a railway cortège? Would
long tunnels perturb mourners? The Bishop of London
voiced disquiet that 'persons of opposite characters might be
carried in the same conveyance' such that:

> The body of some profligate spendthrift might be placed in
> a conveyance with the body of some respectable member
> of the church, which would shock the feelings of his friends;
> and however poor they might be, I think they would feel
> a pride that their relations should not be conveyed to the
> place of interment in the same carriage with the body of
> such a man.

In fact, the solution was already in operation on the railways; in exactly the same way as the ordinary travelling public, funeral parties would be segregated according to class: first, second and third (or 'pauper' – those buried in unmarked graves at parish expense). Furthermore, passengers would be divided by denomination – Anglican or otherwise, as well as health – the living would not journey beside the dead. Thus, the bishop could rest assured that the corpse of a wealthy and virtuous Anglican was not unnecessarily inconvenienced by its proximity to a deceased penniless Methodist, or for that matter, an animate Roman Catholic. All that they would share, as with all train services, were any unforeseen delays.

A terminus called London Necropolis was built adjoining Waterloo Station (the site now covered by tracks just beyond Platforms 1 to 6) and discreetly screened off to curb inquisitive stares. Steam-driven lifts raised coffins to platform level, where funeral parties boarded the train in turn to prevent unsettling encounters between mourners of different status, while first-class ticket-holders could watch the coffin being loaded into the specially adapted hearse carriages. (After it had been securely strapped in a private compartment, it is not clear whether its occupant enjoyed further perks while on board.) The Necropolis service broke with one Victorian funeral custom in that the train departed without the departed at its head, and hearse carriages might be coupled anywhere along its length – a compromise necessary to minimise the burden of undignified shunting.

A return service operated daily and typically carried about fifteen parties on the fifty-minute journey to Brookwood. Once there, a track branched off the main line and trains ran directly into the cemetery. However, steam locomotives were not conducive to consecrated ground so the engine was uncoupled and black horses hauled carriages at walking pace to the two termini; South Station for Church of England, North Station for everyone else, and nearby chapels and burial plots served each denomination. Those journeying on a one-way ticket were carried on biers to a chapel of rest, or directly to the grave, at a respectable distance from the tracks. No mere train operator, the London Necropolis Company laid on every possible convenience to the bereaved including embalming, organist and choir, horse-drawn carriages, monumental masonry, floristry, maintenance of the grave and – long before their time – patented wicker and wood pulp coffins for accelerated decomposition.

One service not advertised by the company was its night trains. Brookwood also provided ample space to rebury the long dead occupants of London's ancient church vaults and burial grounds, which had become both a health hazard and obstacle to development. Graves were excavated and any uncorrupted contents placed wholesale into specially made packing cases lined with fresh charcoal to absorb the choking stench of liquid discharge. For less well-preserved graves, the soil was sprinkled with ground lime, then shaken through a $3/8$ inch sieve so that human remains could be picked out by hand. This way, tens of thousands of dead quietly vacated the city under cover of darkness.

The Necropolis station operated for fifty years until it became apparent that the dead were again blighting the living; Waterloo was in urgent need of expansion so the terminus was demolished in 1902 and a new one built at 121 Westminster Bridge Road, where it can still be seen today. Tracks and rolling stock were bombed beyond repair in 1941 and the service never reopened.

2 WILLOW ROAD NW3

NAMES BOND MOVIE

Ernö Goldfinger might wish to be best remembered as architect of Trellick Tower, thirty-one storeys of concrete brutalism in North Kensington that opened in 1972 and was for many years considered London's ugliest building. Or alternatively, Nos 1–3 Willow Road – the more modest, modernist terrace he designed in 1939 and where he lived at No. 2. But Goldfinger is more commonly remembered for less constructive reasons.

Ian Fleming, author of the James Bond novels, regularly found inspiration for his fictional characters in real people, and sometime during the 1950s he heard of the architect through a golfing friend. The surname struck Fleming as deliciously villainous so he appropriated it for Bond's nemesis in his latest novel, as well as the book title. In fact, the two Goldfingers shared more than their name – both turned up in London during the 1930s as Marxist émigrés (the architect from Hungary, the villain from Latvia), neither was deficient in ego, and while one possessed a passion for slabs of undressed concrete, the other exhibited a peculiar obsession with gold. However, there the similarities ended; fictional Goldfinger did not consider it excessive to murder the entire population of Fort Knox by poisoning the water supply with nerve agent, then blow open its gold vaults with an atomic warhead, while Ernö was known to be fastidious in following the letter of every statutory building regulation. And Fleming was not so unsubtle or uninspired to require further appropriation.

Nevertheless, in 1959 as *Goldfinger* was in press, Goldfinger learned of it and, perhaps fearing association with a meg-alomaniac attempting to destabilise the Western world, summoned his lawyers. Fleming's publisher, Jonathan Cape, suddenly found itself under threat of halting publication and pulping the print run – a precarious position in no way helped by its author, who suggested that the book be pub-lished regardless but with the addition of an erratum slip clarifying how throughout the novel, 'Goldfinger' should in fact read 'Goldprick'.

Matters were settled out of court when the publishers agreed to a number of Goldfinger's demands (which he made without recourse to imperilling his adversary's geni-talia with a laser beam), namely that wherever possible the villain would be referred to as 'Auric Goldfinger', advertising would make clear that the book was a work of fiction, and future print runs would include a statement to clarify that no reference was intended to persons living or dead (although recent printings appear to disregard this condition). And whether they were welcome or not, six complimentary copies were delivered to Willow Road.

But Goldfinger was perhaps the architect of his own mis-fortune because there was no happy Hollywood ending; following release of the feature film in 1964, Willow Road was plagued with phone calls from second-rate Sean Connery impersonators purring: 'Goldfinger? This is 007.'

259 WHITECHAPEL ROAD E1

CONTROL FREAK

Walk past No. 123 (now 259) Whitechapel Road in the 1870s and a bellowing doorman would leave no doubt as to the delights offered within; the premises was 'the best waxworks in London', where for one penny its Chamber of Horrors offered an encounter with 'all the celebrated murderers of many bygone years, including that beautiful piece of machinery of a man in the agonies of death'. But it was not long before wax monstrosities were superseded by living flesh.

In the 1880s, the address became Tom Norman's Penny Gaff, a makeshift theatre in which a motley assortment of performers pulled an equally motley crowd. Norman had among his roster giants, dwarves, strong men, fat ladies, savage Zulus (in truth, retired black sailors from East London extemporising tribal-sounding gobbledegook), performing fleas and a Mrs Baker, who bit the heads off live rats. The young showman operated as many as thirteen such premises in and around London, so was always on the lookout for fresh 'talent'.

Although Norman specialised in the exhibition of those to whom nature had not been kind, when he first met 22-year-old Joseph Merrick he was disappointed that such severe deformities made him too frightening to exhibit. Merrick's misshapen skull was three times normal proportions and his thick, lumpy skin with its warty, cauliflower-like growths exuded a nauseating, sour stench. But in November 1884, a banner draped from the front of the building, grotesquely depicting Merrick as half-man, half-elephant rampaging though an ill-imagined jungle, attested to Norman's change

of heart. The hoarding also served to block natural light and create a dingy atmosphere in which, at the back of the empty shop with its curious aroma wafting through the air, there hung a crude curtain.

After filling the room with expectant punters, Norman kicked off the show with some florid patter, firstly warning anyone in a delicate state of health to leave immediately. With appetites whetted, those who remained heard how the exhibit's pregnant mother had been frightened by a circus elephant, which accounted for its shocking condition; then with a flourish, he pulled back the curtain.

A gasp of horror arose as out of the gloom, spectators began to discern the source of the smell. Merrick was perched on a stool, naked but for a pair of threadbare trousers, and huddled over a gas burner that emitted the only light in the room; in contrast to the formidable, dynamic character on the canvas outside, the figure was small, motionless and fragile. Onlookers were invited to peer as close as they dared and when Norman barked the order to stand up, Merrick took his stick and did so, slowly and falteringly, while those at the front recoiled with revulsion.

For several weeks, the two lived rough at the shop, sharing the room as well as the satisfactory, though not especially substantial, takings. Merrick's condition compelled him to sleep sitting upright for fear that the weight of his head might break his neck, and Norman arranged for a basket-work frame to be crafted, which sat on his shoulders at night; unlike the popular portrayal, their relationship was not wholly exploitative.

Those spending tuppence to encounter the Elephant Man included students from the London Hospital Medical College on the opposite side of the street, and when word of the ghastly monster reached Lecturer in Anatomy Dr Frederick Treves, he came to see it for himself. Treves found the shop closed but on making inquiries, tracked Norman down in a nearby hostelry – the showman later claimed that he was drinking coffee in a café, Treves asserted that he was drunk in a pub; it was the beginning of a fierce animosity between the two, each claiming to be Merrick's better guardian. For a shilling, Norman agreed to a private viewing.

In later life, Treves wrote an account of this meeting and although several details are incorrect, most notably Merrick's name, which he mistakenly recorded as John (thus initiating a long-held confusion), his clinical recollections were less clouded and he diligently listed the extensive deformities presented by the 'disgusting specimen of humanity' – which, because no words emanated from his 'mere slobbering aperture', he assumed to be an imbecile.

Treves was eager to study 'the creature' in the more fitting environment of the hospital, and handed Merrick his calling card so he could make his own way there, but following three such visits, Merrick flatly refused further examination, and informed the doctor that he was willing to be scrutinised for payment but resented being treated like an animal. Treves was furious but within days, police shut down Norman's premises and the three men went their separate ways.

Merrick returned to a precarious life in a travelling show but eighteen months later found himself alone, weak, and hounded by a leering mob at Liverpool Street station. When police arrived, all that Merrick could do was reach into his pocket and pull out the doctor's calling card; Treves arranged for Merrick to live at the hospital until his death in 1890.

TEMPLE CHURCH EC4

KNIGHT'S TEMPER

Temple Church was built in the late twelfth century by the
Knights Templar, who have the dubious honour of two
kinds of history – one based on historical documents and artefacts, the other on best-selling novels. While there is no doubt
that candidates were not received into the secretive order lightly,
whether initiates underwent religio-military 'hazing' in which
they were compelled to spit on the cross, bestow 'obscene' kisses
on each other and worse, lies somewhere between the two.

Less hazy is that when it came to discipline, the order had
it whipped. Every aspect of a knight's existence was governed
by hundreds of regulations, from sleeping fully dressed in a lit
room, to the prohibition of 'laying with women', backgam-
mon, long hair and pointed shoes; much of Sunday worship
was taken up with corporal punishment for transgressors.

One brother, Adam de Valaincourt, made the foolish
error of quitting the order, then suffering a change of heart.
Before he could be readmitted, he was compelled to live
in the courtyard for a year eating bread and water off the
ground with the cats and dogs – though he was permitted to
chase them away if they stole his meagre rations. To further
prove his sincerity, the penitent presented himself naked at
the high altar every Sunday in front of his brothers to be vig-
orously whipped with a leather scourge at the hands of the
officiating priest; Templar rules permitted the use of a belt if
necessary. Eventually, he was led back into the order naked
to the breeches with a rope around his neck.

But flagellation was not the worst of it. Historic sources
refer to miscreants 'confined in chains and dungeons for a

longer or a shorter period, or perpetually, according as it might seem expedient', and one brother necessitating just such expedience was Sir Walter le Bachelor.

About halfway up a spiral staircase in the north-west corner of the chancel is a narrow opening in the stonework, roughly 4ft 6in by 2ft 6in – not generous enough for a man to even crouch comfortably. This was the penitential cell, reserved for the gravest sinners – though as a concession to its occupants' well-being it offered two narrow openings facing eastwards towards the high altar, affording them the consolation of religion; they also admitted air to the fetid niche. Bachelor was Master of the Temple in Ireland, where in 1301 he was caught pilfering Templar funds. Brought to London, he refused to confess his crime so was locked in irons and incarcerated in the cell without food and water until he died; it is thought that he survived for eight weeks. His body was then stripped of its Templar vestments and buried just outside the consecrated ground of the churchyard.

429 STRAND WC2

STATUES OF LIBERTY

Zimbabwe House, on the corner of Agar Street and the Strand, is adorned with a frieze of eighteen, 8ft statues – though they bear little resemblance to the sculptor's intentions.

In 1907, Jacob Epstein was commissioned to carve sculptures for the British Medical Association's new headquarters on the prominent corner site. The young artist was not enthralled by the prospect of turning out a parade of whiskered medical men, so urged the BMA to let him sculpt figures representing the ages of man and woman, from infancy to old age, and celebrating their bodies thoroughly unadorned. Members of the Association were no strangers to the presentation of human flesh and after Epstein's naturalistic designs had been approved, he carved the figures directly into the fabric of the building, two storeys up and shrouded in scaffolding.

Only when the first hoarding came down did it become apparent that across the street at eye level with the nudes was an office occupied by the National Vigilance Association. Unhappily for Epstein, this influential body, formed following W.T. Stead's exposé of child prostitution, was a self-proclaimed arbiter of public morality that had successfully campaigned to outlaw the poster of a female circus artist showing both her bare arms and legs, and burned 25,000 copies of Balzac's literary works, along with hundreds of thousands of 'bad photographs'. Unsurprisingly, its members were aghast when they craned their necks out of the window to be confronted by the spectacle of genitalia, breasts, buttocks and, perhaps most horrifyingly, a pregnant belly; it was the start of what Epstein later dubbed the Thirty Years' War.

The *Evening Standard* weighed in with its own indignation, pontificating how nudes were perfectly acceptable in an art gallery where educated viewers understood how to appreciate them, but to lay them bare to the gaze of all classes was beyond the bounds of propriety. Epstein's figures constituted 'a form of statuary which no careful father would wish his daughter, or no discriminating young man his fiancée, to see', prompting thousands to take a sudden interest in contemporary sculpture and flock to the Strand. A prominent clergyman suggested that Epstein had confused London with Fiji 'where there may be some excuse for want of drapery' and begged the BMA not to thrust them upon the public, many of whom would 'feast upon them with the hunger of a sensualist', adding: 'surely it is our duty not to feed but to starve that sort of appetite'.

Perched on his platform, the sculptor then received a visit from police; an officer undertook a comprehensive reconnaissance of the figures' nooks and crannies and Epstein mournfully observed him scribble the word 'rude' in his notebook. Next, the Bishop of Stepney (later Archbishop of Canterbury) ascended the scaffolding to scrutinise their contours at close quarters – though he conceded that nothing appeared overly intemperate. The BMA stood by Epstein, their resolve no doubt stiffened by the many voices in support of the embattled and now infamous artist, while a correspondent in *The Times* helpfully highlighted how no one objected to a hoarding in another main thoroughfare emblazoned with 'pot-bellied adipose ruffians' clad solely in the underwear they were advertising. The campaign to remove the sculptures or somehow make them decent reached as far as the Home Secretary, but he wisely declared that his remit did not extend to judging artistic matters, and the puritanical uproar fizzled out – though not before it emerged that the Protestant Association, which also overlooked the nudes, was charging sixpence to anyone wishing to view them from its windows.

Bare bodies caused no upset to the Government of the Dominion of New Zealand when it purchased the building in 1926; in fact they were re-interpreted as symbolic of the country's 'tremendous natural energy'. However, that view was not shared by new owners in 1934, the Government of the Crown colony of Southern Rhodesia. Impassive civil servants declared the nudes wholly unsuited to the dignity of a High Commission and speculated publicly about their removal. No statutory powers existed to protect the sculptures but after delicate negotiations, assurances were given that they would remain unharmed.

But privately, Rhodesian officials were itching to remove them and a golden opportunity came their way in 1937 when decorations for the coronation of George VI were taken down; by accident or design, a body part broke loose and injured a pedestrian below. While some sources gleefully identify the falling fragment as a penis (probably because Epstein had been obliged to downsize such an organ on one of his sculptures in St James's), it was somewhat more significantly an entire head, and further scrutiny of their anatomy revealed that the Portland stone was much the worse for acid rain. The sculptures now posed a markedly different threat to the public and the Rhodesian High Commissioner was scrupulous to ensure that London County Council issued an injunction against the building's owner, requiring it to make Rhodesia House safe. Ignoring pleas for the sculptures' removal or restoration, their protuberant parts were ineptly hacked off and the mutilated remains left in that sorry state ever since.

SANDERSON HOTEL,
BERNERS STREET W1

IMPRACTICAL JOKE

26 November 1810 began very early for Mrs Tottenham of No. 54 Berners Street (now the entrance to the Sanderson Hotel); at precisely five o'clock, she was rudely awoken by cries of 'Sweep!' from a pack of soot-smudged youths beneath her window. No sooner had the baffled widow sent the unwanted urchins packing, when out of the blue, a fleet of wagons laden with coal rolled up at her door, inexplicably accompanied by a dozen men, each of whom was carefully carrying a lavish wedding cake. In hot pursuit there then arrived a throng of boot-makers, upholsterers, tailors, carts loaded with barrels of beer and undertakers bearing coffins, all needing to reach her house on urgent business. By the time that twelve wedding carriages turned up, the neighbourhood was in gridlock, further exacerbated by crowds drawn to the delightful spectacle – and no doubt, the novelty of a traffic jam.

Mrs Tottenham was the innocent victim of perhaps the most spectacular prank ever staged in London, and one that inspired numerous pale imitations. It was the handiwork of inveterate wit and joker Theodore Hook, who wagered his companions that he could turn any address into the most famous in town, and as the plotters happened to be passing Mrs Tottenham's modest and unprepossessing abode at the time, they settled upon it as their chosen target. Come the climactic day, the conspirators took up position in a house opposite No. 54 to watch events unfold – and it had only just begun. There now appeared doctors seeking to amputate

a limb, solicitors engaged to draw up deeds, artists commissioned to paint portraits and clergymen summoned to minister to a weak mind, by now something Mrs Tottenham might indeed have need for.

And still the mischief continued; midday signalled the arrival of forty fishmongers bearing cod and lobsters, and hot on their heels, a comparable cadre of butchers wielding legs of mutton. Dentists, apothecaries, opticians and midwives jostled with deliveries of potatoes, feathers, cranberry tarts, furniture, wigs, pianos, hats and 'six stout men bearing an organ', while the local constabulary tried in vain to disperse crowds and curtail any further advances on the house. Finally, in Hook's *pièce de résistance*, VIPs put in an appearance – the Lord Mayor in his state carriage, the Chairman of the East India Company, the Governor of the Bank of England, and royalty in the full liveried form of the Duke of Gloucester.

Having won a mere guinea on the wager through the not insignificant effort of writing at least 1,000 letters, Hook found it convenient to be laid up for a week or two in the countryside.

BEULAH HILL, OPPOSITE
SPURGEON ROAD SE19

WON BY A NOSE

In 1966, suburban Norwood became the focus of world attention thanks to Pickles, a cheeky black and white mongrel with a fondness for chewing furniture.

As the country prepared to host the football World Cup, an exhibition of postage stamps at Methodist Central Hall Westminster enjoyed an improbable publicity boost when granted permission to display the tournament's Jules Rimet trophy. It was somewhat of a coup for the philatelic event because the solid silver and gilt cup had been seen publicly on only a few brief occasions and under the tightest security – after all, it would be acutely embarrassing if the host nation managed to mislay it. And so the trophy was exhibited inside a locked glass case with a security guard beside it, while four uniformed and two plainclothes guards patrolled the building.

The exhibition kicked off to much excitement on Saturday, 19 March, but while it was closed the following day and 300 Methodists were lustily putting voice to such sentiments as 'Purify our faith like gold, all the dross of sin remove', a burglar chose to forego the philately (resale value circa £3 million) and instead make off with the trophy (official value £3,000). In footballing terms, the tortured words 'we was robbed' never held more anguish.

That was certainly the sentiment among the Metropolitan Police, which set 100 of its finest detectives on the case, despite having few reliable leads to follow up; the enticement of a substantial reward left them swamped with wildly conflicting information on the trophy's whereabouts. However, they could make a substitution. On the evening of the theft, two officers accompanied the secretary of the Football Association to the premises of silversmith George Bird, who after being sworn to secrecy, was instructed to craft a trophy indistinguishable from the original.

Three days later, a parcel arrived at the house of FA chairman Joe Mears containing what appeared to be a gold ashtray, though on closer inspection was identified as the protective lining from the bowl of the cup. Accompanying it was a letter demanding £15,000 and threatening to melt the trophy if police were informed; Mears headed straight to Scotland Yard.

A suitcase of cash was hastily cobbled together (though anything more than a cursory glance would reveal bundles of blank paper with genuine banknotes at either end) and a couple of days later Mears received a telephone call from a man calling himself Jackson and claiming to be author of the ransom note. The caller agreed to meet one of Mears' associates in Battersea Park to make the exchange.

But when Jackson greeted an undercover police officer shortly afterwards he was without the trophy, and as the pair drove off towards Kennington to supposedly retrieve it, he laudably clocked the unmarked police van tailing them, so bounded out of the car and sprinted off. When eventually apprehended, he turned out to be Edward Betchley, a petty criminal known to police for receiving stolen goods, but Scotland Yard's optimism that they had clinched the prize was soon dashed. Betchley claimed that he was offered a mere £500 to act as intermediary for a man he knew only as 'The Pole', and knew nothing more about the trophy. It was back to square one.

Fortunately for the dignity of the nation, on the Sunday following the theft, Pickles was taken out to perform his essential business by owner David Corbett. As man and dog departed their flat at No. 50 Beulah Hill (now demolished), Pickles became distracted by a package that lay beside a parked car on the front drive. The dog's eager snuffling

persuaded Corbett to investigate further and discover that
inside the parcel, wrapped in newspaper and neatly tied up
with string, was the World Cup.

Pickles was instantly a national hero and made countless
TV appearances, starred in a feature film, was presented
with a year's supply of dinners, and received much patting
on the head. The fact that a dog sniffed out the trophy could
have been a humiliating own goal, but the jubilant media
frenzy served to deflect criticism from both police and the
private security firm responsible for losing it in the first place.
A relieved Scotland Yard quietly scaled back its investigations and the FA instructed George Bird to halt his labours
on the expensive replica and instead produce a gimcrack
copy from base metal – a task made easier because he was
now responsible for safeguarding the original in the company strongroom. Betchley was the only person charged in
connection with the theft and why the trophy ended up in
Corbett's drive remains a mystery.

The lucky streak continued when in July, England won the lost trophy, and no one was more pleased than the police, who quietly retrieved the original from the team dressing room and left behind the replica; few people were aware that it was this counterfeit cup that toured the country for the next four years. As for Pickles, he was unable to bask in the glory for long because a few months later he was garrotted by his own lead while in hot pursuit of the neighbour's tabby.

CANNON STREET STATION EC4

SLAVE AWAY

B ritish involvement in slavery has been made easier to downplay because its activities took place thousands of miles away, yet an enterprise run from the site of Cannon Street Station is also little acknowledged.

Following Britain's defeat by the newly independent American states in 1783, London's black population burgeoned; hundreds of slaves who had loyally served the Crown travelled to England expecting freedom and hospitality. They received neither and instead found themselves destitute and detested, particularly as a result of 'unnatural connections between black persons and white, the disagreeable consequences of which make their appearance but too frequently in our streets'.

A welcome plan to rid London of its black poor was proposed by would-be businessman Henry Smeathman; he would ship them to islands he knew off the coast of Sierra Leone and establish a self-sufficient free colony: 'Those who are desirous of profiting by this opportunity of settling in one of the most pleasant and fertile countries in the known world may apply to Mr Smeathman, the author of the plan and agent for the settlement, at the Office for Free Africans, No. 14 Cannon Street.' In what seemed a heaven-sent solution to the nuisance of begging black veterans, the Treasury was readily persuaded to bear the up-front costs of the exodus, offering Smeathman £14 for each person resettled, and providing three months' worth of food as well as clothes, bedding, tools, building materials and medicine.

But there was no throng eagerly beating a path to Cannon Street and only after concerted coaxing did numbers begin to sign up. Some were swayed by a certificate declaring them to be free citizens of the colony of Sierra Leone (in truth, a document of negligible worth), others by the threat of the scheme's withdrawal and the curtailment of charitable assistance; eventually in excess of 600 were reluctantly rounded up.

PRODUCTIVE FREE LABOUR IN SIERRA LEONE.

DRIVING THE BLACK MALE AT FREETOWN.

They were right to be wary; Smeathman omitted to mention that a promised land this was certainly not – in fact he had presented an entirely fantasy world; the terrain, seas, climate and natives were hostile, the islands were home to a British slave-trading post, and settlers would discover on arrival that they were indentured labour for his private business interests. Even Smeathman's sudden death from a tropical disease caught on the islands failed to expose his duplicity or halt the enterprise, and in 1787 approximately 300 blacks finally landed in Sierra Leone, accompanied by about sixty white wives. (To justify how these spouses ended up in such objectionable circumstances it was put about that they were prostitutes.)

Hunger, disease, conflict and widespread embezzlement soon took their toll and four years later just sixty-four were still alive, including 'seven of our countrywomen … so disguised with filth and dirt that I should never have supposed they were born white'.

88 REGENT STREET W1

LAST GASP

Sometime during the 1770s, musician and composer Frantisek Kotzwara moved to London from his native Prague and lodged in Bentinck (now Livonia) Street, Soho. His most memorable opus is 'The Battle of Prague', in which the music imitates the sounds of warfare, from cannon fire to cries of the wounded, and such was its popularity it merited mention in Mark Twain's Adventures of Huckleberry Finn a century later. But though the composition made his name,

Kotzwara's forte was composing music to which he did not append his signature. He was a dab hand at mimicking the styles of other composers, thus affording him a lucrative racket turning out tunes for unscrupulous publishers to sell under famous names. As a result, much of his oeuvre has had musicologists scratching their heads ever since. But however estimable Kotzwara's musical life, it was eclipsed by the clumsy manner of his death.

During the early afternoon of 2 September 1791, certain urges compelled the composer to call upon Susannah Hill, a lady of procurable virtue, at No. 5 Vine Street (an address obliterated in 1810 when the Regent Street Quadrant was constructed – and architect John Nash could not have sited its rounded sweep more centrally over Hill's whore-house). Susannah had not long been in her line of employment, a career brought about because she fell pregnant out of wedlock and the party responsible absconded, though 'being handsome rather than pretty, she found little difficulty of succeeding in this way of life'. Kotzwara meanwhile was no stranger to the ministrations of prostitutes, but was keen to first satisfy the hunger in his belly so instructed Susannah to procure brandy, ham and beef as well as her beverage of choice, which was porter beer. When hors d'oeuvres had been devoured, his attentions inexorably turned to the gratification of his other appetite and the pair withdrew from the front parlour to the privacy of a back room. There, the hostess was treated to the spectacle of scars inflicted at Kotzwara's behest by others among her profession before 'several acts of the grossest indecency passed, in particular he pressed her to cut off the means of generation and expressly wished to have it cut in two'.

Susannah had no doubt swiftly become proficient in catering to clients' peculiar peccadillos, but pocketing a guinea to cleave off Kotzwara's manhood was beyond the prostitutional pale. Undeterred by the rejection, the Bohemian rhapsodised that instead 'he should like to be hanged for five minutes'. Perhaps following some deliberations concerning the specifics involved, Susannah was more amenable to this demand but confessed that she was ill-equipped with the necessary hardware. Going by the testimonies of other prostitutes, Kotzwara was virtuosic at the practice and 'while he gave her money to buy a cord, observed that hanging would raise his passions – that it would produce all he wanted'. When Susannah returned, she had been unable to procure anything more than two paltry lengths of rope, but by crouching down, Kotzwara managed to satisfactorily suspend himself from the knob of the parlour door. By conincidence, the Marquis de Sade's novel, *Justine*, had been published only months earlier and there is a tantalising possibility that Kotzwara had studied its instructive account of how Thérèse assists Roland in his quest for sexual satisfaction through temporary asphyxiation.

But Kotzwara's endeavours failed to climax in the manner of Roland's exquisite ecstasy. Susannah noted that not long before the five minutes had expired, Kotzwara certainly had not because he flaunted a conspicuous clue that the enterprise was providing him with pleasure, but moments later observed that his enthusiasms were suddenly diminished, so hurriedly cut him down and summoned help. A surgeon arrived to perform the customary procedure of slicing open an arm to draw blood, but it was obvious that the musician had gasped his last; what with a strangled man laying in her parlour, Susannah was charged with murder.

The trial of Susannah Hill at the Old Bailey Sessions House on 16 September 1791 must have proven an enlightening experience for all involved. The judge decided that the finer particulars of the case were liable to discomfort to those of a gentle disposition, so ordered that all women should vacate the courtroom. It was also evident that the case would cause considerable excitement among the press, so he ensured that

the trial papers were burned. Thankfully, a public-spirited individual leaked pertinent details for the historical record and they appeared in an anonymous pamphlet, accompanied by an artist's impression of the tragic scene, tastefully adapted for publication. The murder charge was reduced to manslaughter but the bench was eager for conviction so that 'it might deter the depraved part of mankind from seeking indecent stimulatives to pervert the ordinary course of nature'. However, after nine hours of deliberations the jury chose to believe Susannah's testimony that Kotzwara's death was simply the result of an unfortunate self-inflicted accident; she was acquitted and told to lead a better life.

Frantisek Kotzwara was doubtless not the first person to suffer the indignity of ending up dead in such unbecoming circumstances but he deserves a modest fanfare to mark that on the now iconic Regent Street site, his was the earliest proven case of 'amorous strangulation'.

BEAR GARDENS SE1

CREATURE DISCOMFORTS

The street name recalls a popular entertainment on the site, described by a spectator in Elizabethan times:

> There is a place built in the form of a theatre which serves for the baiting of bulls and bears. They are fastened from behind and then worried by great English bulldogs, but not without great risk to the dogs, from the horns of the one and the teeth of the other and it sometimes happens they are killed on the spot. Fresh ones are immediately supplied.

All sections of society revelled in watching animals being tormented into a rage, fatally injured, then suffer an agonising death amid blood, shit and slobber, and the arena was one of several in London to offer the amusement. Bulls fought to the death not only for entertainment but also their meat, which was thought to improve through such a demise, whereas bears, which were generally too valuable to lose, had their claws and teeth sawn down to prolong their harassment. Crowds loved nothing more than when a dog with its jaws tightly clamped on its adversary's nose was frantically swung around by the beast until tossed high into the gallery – perhaps leaving its teeth behind, and to further enliven proceedings, pepper was blown up the creature's nose or dried peas pushed in its ears.

In 1614, when the neighbouring Globe Theatre was seen to be enjoying notable success with conventional drama, the venue was rebuilt with a stage and optimistically renamed The Hope, but there was meagre hope that theatricals would become exclusively human. Facilities were dual purpose so alongside dressing rooms were kennels and stabling, the stage was removable, and the name 'Bear Garden' stubbornly clung on.

In 1638 this corner of Southwark was home to a veritable menagerie of four bulls, including one called Goldilocks; seventeen brown bears, including Blind Robin and Rose of Bedlam; two polar bears named Will Tookey and Mad Besse; two apes and seventy mastiffs. Such a cast list lent itself to considerable dramatic potential, such as 'whipping a blinded bear which is performed by five or six men standing circularly with whips, which they exercise on him without any mercy as he cannot escape because of his chain'. Further variety was provided by dogs baiting either a pony with an ape tied to its back or a bull with a cat tied to its tail, or men baiting dogs that had been skilfully 'dressed up with fireworks'.

Numerous attempts were made to rein in the sport. In 1642, with the country on the brink of civil war, bear baiting was outlawed by Parliament – though more for reasons of keeping the peace and encouraging church-going than animal welfare. The ban was widely ignored and in 1655 a packed house delighted in a rare treat – the killing of a bear, which came about following a tragic accident. A boy aged 4 or 5 had found his way into the bear enclosure and, after stroking the beast, had his face bitten off; 'The bear ward came in at last and got away that of his body which was left,' by which time the child was long dead. Common law dictated that the animal was forfeited to the Crown and the bear keeper fined, in this case 50s, to recover then destroy it. 'They told the mother that the bear should be baited to death and she should have half the money and accordingly there were bills stuck up and down the City of it and a considerable sum of money gathered … some say above sixty pounds.' The keeper offered the bereaved mother £3 on condition that she did not prosecute.

It was not the first such incident because in 1609 another child had been mauled to death after it was inadvertently locked in the bear house. The animal was delivered to the Tower of London where James I wished to see it killed by lions, but they proved stubbornly reluctant and 'every one of them so soon as they espied the trap doors open, hastily ran into their dens'. The bear was conveyed back to Southwark and instead baited to death, though on this occasion, the grieving mother was compensated with 20 pence.

In 1656, the High Sheriff of Surrey, Colonel Pride, was so exasperated by the brazen flouting of the ban he dispatched troops to Bear Garden to seize the dogs (which were then shipped to Jamaica) and shoot six bears – though sentimentality may have got the better of him because he spared 'one white innocent cub'. But the sport continued nonetheless; in 1682 notice was given that an immense horse, nineteen hands high, would be baited to death by dogs. The animal proved invincible and as it was led away, spectators made plain their feelings about being denied the *pièce de résistance* with a riot; to appease them the horse was led back into the ring and stabbed with a sword.

Animal baiting was again suppressed in 1835 (albeit in such a way as to exclude aristocratic bloodsports) and though this still failed to effect significant change, its demise was hastened by a new found fervour for watching humans fight.

166–168 ESSEX ROAD N1

RESTORATION COMEDY

When the proprietor of the pharmacy at Nos 166–68 arrived at work one morning, he was delighted to discover that his shop had suffered criminal damage; the premises had been used as a canvas for some aerosol-based art, which was promptly attributed to the hand of the infamous Banksy. The elusive artist's satirical and subversive stencils have increased the value of walls by tens of thousands of pounds – something not lost on the pharmacist, who was quick to call in a firm of emergency glaziers to furnish his new asset with a protective perspex cover. He also astutely interpreted how Banksy's work showed clear support for small independent shops such as his own in their struggle against all-powerful supermarkets.

But in 2010, the mural's message was amended when the Tesco 'flag' to which the junior comrades are seen pledging allegiance was daubed with the tag HRH King Robbo. Robbo was London's foremost old-school graffiti artist, whose freehand works of the 1980s had been gradually obliterated by other vandals, councils and London Transport. Banksy had recently incorporated Robbo's last remaining creation (which had the distinction of being the oldest graffiti mural in London, sited somewhat ironically beneath British Transport Police Headquarters on the Regent's Canal) into one of his own – an act of 'buffing' that was viewed among the graff community as calculated disrespect, and sparked a feud between the two camps.

But the war was also waged on another front. Keenly aware of the knock-on benefits that derive from Banksy's works, Islington Council had taken the surprising step of repainting and restoring his 'street art' when it became defaced with 'graffiti', double standards that were not lost on Team Robbo. Artistic merit in acts of vandalism was appraised by the directorate of Environmental Services, a department more commonly concerned with emptying bins and filling cemeteries, and on five occasions a council rapid response team was dispatched to restore a Banksy

stencil in Martineau Road near the Emirates Stadium (now long painted over). Meanwhile, the council actively pursued the prosecution of graffiti artists for criminal damage, some of whom later gazed at prison walls, yet showed no inclination to restore Banksy's stencil of murderer Charles Manson thumbing a lift from Archway Tube station – in fact, it eventually scrubbed the hitchhiking cult leader from the neighbourhood.

Putting the sardonic boot into a successful supermarket was more socially acceptable subject matter, and to restore the artwork, persons unknown (and prime suspect must be Banksy) improvised their own conservation technique by simply covering the mess with a genuine Tesco carrier bag.

The work has since attracted significant further alteration.

SCHOMBERG HOUSE,
80–82 PALL MALL SW1

BREEDING GROUND

Doctor James Graham believed that his fellow Britons' physical and mental faculties were in grave decline so in 1781, Schomberg House (whose 1698 facade survives on Nos 80–81) became pivotal to his mission of reversing this trend; the 'Temple of Prolific Hymen' was where couples would conceive perfect offspring.

To this end, the medic-cum-impresario fitted out his house of impregnation like no other building in London. Rooms were sumptuously furnished, brightly illuminated and literally sparkled with gleaming cut glass chandeliers casting rainbows of light, gilt and silver ornaments and mirrors, and curious-looking electrical paraphernalia that emitted streams of sparks. Even the drinks were sparkling thanks to a machine that bubbled away to produce carbonated water, while the air was filled with exotic scents and ethereal music.

Through a series of public lectures, Graham regaled audiences with his peculiar ideas about reproduction such as the benefits of personal hygiene; however, the Temple's main attraction was undoubtedly his 'celestial, or medico, magnetico, musico, electrical bed which I have with so much study and at so vast an expense constructed'. His invention harnessed the powers of science 'not alone to insure the removal of barrenness when conception is at all in the nature of things possible, but likewise to improve, exalt, and invigorate the bodily, and through them, the mental faculties of the human species'. The very fate of the nation lay in this bed.

Around 12ft long and 9ft wide, the conjugal apparatus was richly carved and gilded, and its mattress, stuffed with fresh wheat and horse hair from English stallions, could be adjusted to whatever angle most conducive to its occupants. Sheets were of the finest silk with a shade 'suited to the colour of the lady who is to repose on them' and beneath the canopy were 'brilliant plates of looking-glass, so disposed as to reflect the various attractive charms of the happy recumbent couple in the most flattering, most agreeable and most enchanting style'. And the copulating couple were not alone because sat on a bed of fresh roses above them were two turtledoves. But the primary agency of this reproductive aid was electricity.

Quite how the bed was wired up is impossible to decipher from Graham's self-promotional grandiloquence but 'in a neighbouring closet is placed a cylinder [battery] by which I communicate the celestial fire to the bedchamber' causing it to conspicuously crackle. A figure of Greek god Hymen surmounted the canopy, holding in one hand a flaming torch and in the other a crown 'sparkling likewise with the effulgent fire' and across the headboard the commandment, 'Be fruitful, multiply and replenish the earth!' flickered with sparks. The doctor believed that careful calibration of the electrical current stimulated not only hair to stand on end, and ventured so far as to guarantee conception for customers – an enticing proposition for aristocrats desperate to beget an heir.

For those troubled by the prospect of exposing naked flesh near such a volatile-looking behemoth of a bedstead, Graham took pains to highlight how it was insulated by forty cut glass pillars 'invisibly incrusted with a certain transparent varnish in order to render the insulation still more complete' and further encouragement to climb into it came from his diaphanously clad female attendants who included Emma Lyon, later Lady Hamilton.

The bed also aroused other senses. Pumped through glass tubes in the canopy came 'odiferous, balmy and ethereal spices, odours and essences' to foster 'vivifying and invigorating influences', while another form of pumping generated further sensations – orchestral accompaniment. This aspect of the bed only became apparent when a couple began going through the motions, because as the mattress pulsated it acted as bellows for an assortment of organ pipes: 'the melodious tones of the harmonica, the soft sounds of the flute, the harmonious notes of the organ', accompanied by 'guitars, violins, clarionets, trumpets, horns, oboes, kettle-drums, etc.' – an ensemble that presumably puffed its way to a climactic crescendo in perfect tempo with the lovers' exertions.

Even when duties to Venus and St George were concluded and the orchestra fell silent, further forces of attraction were delivered by enormous magnets 'so disposed and arranged as to be continually pouring forth in an ever-flowing circle [of] irresistibly powerful magnetic effluxion' which thereby lent ejaculate an extra helping hand on its mysterious maiden voyage.

Bettering humankind did not come cheap and those who desired congress in this extraordinary contraption were expected to part with £50 – a fee not too exorbitant for (on separate occasions) the Duchess of Devonshire, Admiral Keppel, the Bishop of London, and politicians Charles James Fox and John Wilkes.

But for all the exterior sparkle, Graham's monetary situation was gloomy and his valiant scheme for patriotic procreation could not keep critics or creditors at bay. After a financially fraught couple of years, he fled to Scotland, where his Great Celestial State Bed was substituted with the more economical mud bath in which clients were buried up to their heads in worm-laden soil. The fate of his fornicatory furniture is unknown and Graham began his own eternal mud bath in 1794.

ADMIRALTY ARCH SW1

NOBODY NOSE

Poking from the stonework in the northern archway of Admiralty Arch, about 7ft above the ground, is a human nose. As umpteen guidebooks cheerfully explain, the addition of such an unusual architectural adornment resulted from a little-known military tradition: when the arch was built in 1912, Britain was still revelling in the defeat of its nemesis Napoleon Bonaparte so by sticking up his nose, cavalrymen could flick their old bogey as they passed by.

Other sources (which at the time of publication notably include the Royal Parks) agree that the protuberance is for the benefit of cavalry, but insist that it is not Boney's beak but the Duke of Wellington's – a facial feature for which he was singularly renowned, and the custom involves rubbing it for good luck. However, even a cursory glance reveals that the hooter's profile is not sufficiently Roman to be the Iron Duke's, and because the arch was built for the Admiralty not Army, others sniffily point out that it can only belong to Vice Admiral Horatio Nelson because it is significantly easier to rub than the one on the nearby column.

The wrangling over which military leader's nose to pick is ongoing; however, all agree that the practice is highly secretive – which explains why no one has ever witnessed any military personnel fingering it.

But more phlegmatic investigations soon blow the nose's identity – it was glued on the arch in 1997 by guerrilla artist Rick Buckley as a creative response to the proliferation of CCTV cameras across London. The impact of his artistic statement, which involved the bestowal of about thirty-five

olfactory organs on buildings across Central London (including the Southbank Centre, St Pancras Station, The National
Gallery and Tate Britain) was somewhat ineffectual because,
perhaps in a desire to keep his nose clean, he kept his involvement in the stunt entirely secret. However, he did manage to
pull off this remarkable feat right under the nose of the nas-
cent surveillance state he was critiquing.

The majority of these mystifying noses were wiped
away soon after their appearance, but the appendage on
Admiralty Arch somehow escaped architectural rhinoplasty
and the well-loved embellishment is now greatly deserving
of protected status.

By the time Buckley eventually owned up to his handiwork
in 2011, his nose (and it is indeed a cast of his nose) may
have done nothing to thwart the proliferation of video surveillance, but did elegantly illustrate how a dribble of quaint
claptrap can congest into sticky tissue of mythological drivel.

BANQUETING HOUSE SW1

LIMB OF GOD

Between 1622 and 1714, the magnificent hall of
Banqueting House regularly teemed with a throng
of wretched humanity – each disfigured by purple
excrescences on their neck, some of which had burst open
to discharge yellow-brown pus and a fetid stink. They were
victims of the King's Evil, what is now termed scrofula
and a form of tuberculosis that infects and inflames the
lymph nodes, especially in children. But thanks to magical
powers, English monarchs were able to cure the condition

(and not to be outdone, French sovereigns also possessed this epidemiological gift, no doubt on account of God's particular regard for the two kingdoms).

The mysterious royal remedy emerged following canonisation of the long-dead King Edward the Confessor in 1161 when sufferers who prayed at his tomb in Westminster Abbey reported deliverance from the disease – and though a saint might be expected to work miracles, Edward's living successors chose to confer similar virtues on themselves. Treatment entailed nothing more than the monarch's touch, thereby emulating Christ's healing of a leper and fostering an aura of mystique and godliness around the King. If physicians harboured doubts about the efficacy of the royal caress, they were wise to keep them private.

Although the Church of England dispensed with much of the supernatural ritual of former days, the cure was no less effective after the Reformation and was enormously popular during Stuart times when Banqueting House served as a suitably awe-inspiring clinic. The King sat at the far end of the room in his chair of state and the afflicted were led to him in procession; as the chaplain recited a prayer, each in turn kneeled while the King placed his hands on their weeping sores. When all had been touched they were again brought before him and after making the sign of the cross over their head, he placed a gold token hanging on a ribbon around their neck. This was their 'touch-piece', which bore the figure of an angel and was worn as a talisman to effect their cure. The gesture had originally been a gift of money, but because the King had held the coin, it became integral to the cure. When Treasury officials recognised this, the hard currency was swiftly substituted with a token of no face value. After readings from the Gospels and further prayers, the ceremony was complete.

Touching for the King's Evil was conducted during cooler months, typically at Easter, Michaelmas or Christmas, to

The Royal Gift of Healing

R. White sculp.

alleviate the nausea associated with a stiflingly hot room
teeming with sour-smelling commoners, and a schedule
of healing sessions was published to dissuade the sick from
stalking the monarch. Despite this, James I found it necessary
to prohibit sufferers from approaching him during summer,
and those seeking his touch were required to prove that they
had not already received it.

It is doubtful whether the scrofulous paid much attention to
the precise mechanism by which the King's hand operated, but
there was tacit acceptance that relief was not instantaneous and
they were obliged to go away and wait patiently for it to take
effect. Physicians were then unaware how the disease can go
into remission or heal completely – particularly with improved
sanitation or diet, but recognised that if the King was catching
a bout of something from his unfortunate subjects, scrofula it
was not. Such benign circumstances thus favoured its identification as a condition that monarchs could cure, as opposed to
say, leprosy or blindness, and rare fatal cases were put down to
a flaw in the victim's spiritual condition.

However, this left the King in competition with equally
effective folk remedies such as swigging from a human skull,
the caress of either the seventh son of a seventh son or a dead
man (the palm of someone who had committed suicide was
particularly potent), or simply submitting to the fickle inter-
ventions of a quack doctor. One of the founders of modern
chemistry (and recently purported Grand Master of the
Priory of Sion), Robert Boyle, wrote of a boy whose seeping
boils were healed after a lengthy spell of being licked by his
dog. Effort was therefore necessary to preserve the sanctity
of the Royal touch, and the nation's pulpits were employed
to convey this message. Stern proclamations belched forth
with particular vitriol aimed at those who sold or gave away
their touch-piece; the King's hand was not to be debased by
operating second-hand and grievous relapses had befallen
those who had done so.

The King's Evil was also cured by queens and Mary I, Elizabeth I and Anne all performed the ceremony – providing that they were not menstruating at the time, though the greatest rehabilitation came courtesy of Charles II – a King keen to demonstrate the special qualities of monarchs (Oliver Cromwell had known better than to attempt miracles). On one day in 1660, Charles touched 600 of his grubby subjects, and though he was less eager to stroke running sores when the plague struck London, he healed more than 92,000 during his reign.

The ceremony was last performed in 1714 when among those touched was a young Samuel Johnson; George I was so horrified by the superstitious and unhygienic ritual that he flatly refused to do it and subsequent monarchs have demurred from reviving the practice.

BARTHOLOMEW CLOSE EC1

DREAD ZEPPELIN

As darkness fell on 8 September 1915, Zeppelin L13 launched from the German North Sea coast, bound for England. Under the command of Kapitänleutnant Heinrich Mathy, the airship made landfall near King's Lynn at about 8:45 p.m. and set a course for the capital; a terrifying new form of warfare had just begun.

The Kaiser had reluctantly sanctioned the bombing of London on condition that commanders steered clear of residential districts, historic buildings, and his cousin's house, Buckingham Palace, a patently hollow plea because even with the benefit of state of the art Zeiss bombsights,

pinpointing targets from an airship gondola at 8,000ft on a
moonless night was far from an exact science. Slung beneath
L13 were both high-explosive and incendiary bombs, and
on approaching London's heart, Mathy began to drop them,
causing fatalities and destruction in areas of no strategic significance across Golders Green, Bloomsbury and Gray's Inn
as the Zeppelin glided south-eastwards across the city.

But also among the deadly payload was one colossal bomb – 660lb (300kg) of high explosive that had been bestowed with the ghoulish nickname Liebesgabe (Love Gift), and at the halfway point of Mathy's sortie he love-bombed London. This first weapon capable of causing catastrophic damage landed, perhaps fortunately, in the open area of Bartholomew Close (today, trees stand in a traffic circle on the built-up site). The explosion blasted a crater 8ft deep in the road, damaged buildings around the square and caused every window to shatter into deadly flying shards. Two men who emerged from a pub to hear the whirr of propellers scrambled for cover but were 'blown to pieces', while from aloft, Mathy noted with satisfaction how every light in the vicinity was suddenly extinguished. Yet amid the destruction was a notable act of bravery; despite head injuries, 13-year-old Violet Buckthorpe scrambled up the stairs of her devastated home to rescue her baby sister and rush her to hospital.

Mathy's path of 'air murder' did not pass unchallenged. When searchlights picked out L13 it became the target of concentrated fire from one-pounder pom-pom guns stationed across the city, but every barrage fell short and as shrapnel rained down it caused only further damage; London was conspicuously vulnerable.

The likely target of the mission was the Bank of England – and Mathy perhaps believed he had struck it because the Zeppelin changed course to drop further bombs around the Guildhall and Liverpool Street, then headed northeast where a final missile was jettisoned over Barnet – a ham bone carved with an impolite caricature of Britain's foreign secretary; by 2 a.m. the airship had passed Great Yarmouth out to safety. The raid left twenty-two civilians dead, eighty-seven injured and caused approximately one third of all damage from Zeppelin raids during the First World War.

STIR CRAZIES

The concourse of Liverpool Street Station and the hotel adjoining it stand on the site of the Bethlem lunatic asylum, whose atmosphere of frenzied mayhem gave rise to the term 'bedlam'. And although accounts of raving pandemonium have long been overplayed to satisfy a deep-rooted popular image, it is true to say that conditions for guests were not five star.

In 1247, Alderman and twice Sheriff of London Simon fitzMary founded the Priory of St Mary of Bethlehem on land he owned just outside London – an act of Christian piety concerned not with the insane but prayers for his soul. Like any religious house, the priory opened its doors to travellers, the poor and infirm, and though records from the time are scant, an inquiry into its deplorable conditions in 1403 (the first of many) states that residents included six men who were *mente capti* – mentally deranged. The monks evidently regarded this condition as curable because documents from later in the century indicate that of the many such inhabitants, some were fully restored to health. Before long it was only 'lunatikes' lodging at Bethlem – in all likelihood because everyone else simply opted to stay elsewhere.

Transformed from hostel to hospital, Bethlem's approach to accommodating the sick generally consisted of restraint; residents were routinely referred to as prisoners and an inventory of 1398 listed the essential apparatus for managing mental illness: four pairs of manacles, eleven chains of iron, six locks and keys, and two pairs of stocks – an armoury of hardware that remained indispensable until Victorian times. Furthermore, prevailing wisdom held that the insane were immune to the effects of darkness, cold and isolation, so there was no concern that these were the precise conditions in which they were kept.

Lunacy was known to be God's punishment for sin, and because Bethlem was a religious institution, treatment was directed at purifying afflicted souls by removing impediments and imbalances, both physical and spiritual. Medical techniques including bleeding – typically from the head – gargles to shift phlegm, herbal poultices, vomiting and laxatives were complemented by beatings, shock treatment such as sudden immersion in holy (but cold) water, confession, Mass and other ministrations. Physical violence became so commonplace, governors felt compelled to rule that 'no keeper or servant should beat or ill-treat a lunatic', although to allow flexibility in interpretation, brutality was permitted when 'he considered it absolutely necessary'. Other contemporary treatments included meals of roasted mouse, a remedy devised by thirteenth-century Pope John XXI, and trepanation, drilling holes into the skull to release evil spirits. What with a therapeutic regime based on purging and battering, even the most generous interpretation of the evidence indicates that treatment offered no appreciable benefit and Bethlem was not to employ a professionally trained physician until 1619.

The absence of qualified medical staff was not the only deficiency in the workforce; Bethlem suffered an unfortunate history of leadership and a succession of keepers and governors purloined property, siphoned off endowments or simply kept residents short of food with a view to pocketing the proceeds. Modest progress came in 1662 with the appointment of a female warden responsible for the women's welfare, a role primarily concerned with protecting them from men, but after both she and her replacement proved thoroughly unscrupulous, the idea was abandoned.

It was the Christian duty of visitors to offer alms to the priory and this custom was soon interpreted as an opportunity to eyeball 'Anticks' in return for an entry fee – and it is conceivable that a portion of these monies went towards patient welfare. A visitor writing in 1632 acknowledged that conditions were not conducive: 'It seems strange that any should recover here: the cryings, screechings, roarings, brawlings, shaking of chains, swearings, frettings, chafings are so many, so hideous, so great, that they are more able to drive a man that hath his wits rather out of them, than to help one that never had them, or hath lost them, to find them again.'

But although diagnosis of psychiatric illness was centuries away, it was no secret that some residents were fully *compos mentis* because the State deemed Bethlem a convenient address for a particular species of troublemaker. Anyone who voiced seditious words, railed against the established order, uttered something imprudent about the Monarch or even trespassed on royal property, ran the risk of being labelled 'crack-brained' and afforded indefinite accommodation at Bethlem. Political firebrands or mere nuisances such as these were kept in close confinement with no audience for their disagreeable opinions until they were able to demonstrate complete moral reformation.

At its cramped site, subject to inundations from the sewer it stood over, Bethlem was nevertheless the country's only repository for the insane, and acknowledgement of its woeful inadequacy was a rare positive outcome from the fire of 1666. Governors were compelled to convene at Bethlem because their usual meeting place had been burned, and such close proximity with the decrepit hovel impressed upon them what a national disgrace it was; in 1676 the hospital moved to brand new premises at Moorfields.

STEW LANE EC4

VOYAGE OF DEBAUCHERY

The street has gloried in the name Stew Lane since at least the sixteenth century and it pays homage not to piping hot casseroles but brothels. It also led to London's foremost place of fornication.

'Stew' originated from estuves, the old term for a bathhouse that itself derived from the French word for the stove used to heat one. The close association of that steamy, sweaty, bare-bodied pursuit with establishments dedicated to public bathing led to the term stew becoming synonymous with the ancient trade – even when the water-based facilities were long dispensed with.

Stews were outlawed in the City, at least in principle, so thrived along the southern riverbank where a more amenably disposed Lord of the Manor was the Bishop of Winchester.

But debauchery was not deregulated because as early as 1161
Henry II introduced licensing laws for the industry. This
was primarily to protect levies payable to the landlord and
Crown, but also to curb the spread of syphilis and establish
terms of trade. One edict prohibited whoring on Holy days,
and another denied workers the right to enjoy sex outside
their employment (the penalty for which involved the ducking
stool). There was little other commercial activity in the neighbourhood so Bankside became known as simply 'The Stews'
and in 1546 there were at least twenty resorts along the river-
side including The Cross Keys, The Unicorn, The Cardinal's
Hat and (inevitably) The Cock. According to savvy sea captain
Antonio in Shakespeare's *Twelfth Night*, The Elephant made
an agreeable place to stop by.

A convenient way to reach the amenities from the City
was via a set of river stairs at the end of Stew Lane known as
Broken Wharf (referring to their condition, not the morals of
its users), from where watermen operated a frequent shuttle
service. Stews were required to be painted white with the
establishment's name or sign across the front (to distinguish
them from alehouses whose signs jutted from the wall), so
were clearly visible to those restlessly waiting to embark.
By coincidence, watermen barked 'Oars!' when they were
available for hire – a cry that could perhaps mislead strangers
into believing that all boats headed off to the prostitutes.

But we know that one stew simmered on Stew Lane
because in 1428 its proprietor, John Baker, was hauled before
the City fathers to swear that his hot-house was run in a
respectable manner and he permitted only good and honest
men to be stewed during the times appointed. Presumably
there had been inklings that this was not the case so he was
warned that a violation attracted a £20 fine, and was barred
from allowing laundry-women to enter the premises – a penalty that reveals how magistrates made meagre distinction
between those who toiled in laundry and lechery.

67–69 CHANCERY LANE WC2

SKELETON IN THE CUPBOARD

There is a simple explanation for anything untoward occurring at 67–69 Chancery Lane: former resident Aleister Crowley.

For those not familiar with the occult, Crowley was, *inter alia*, a member of the Hermetic Order of the Golden Dawn, a tenth degree adept in occult society Ordo Templi Orientis, founder of spiritual organisation Argentium Astrum A∴A∴, creator of Thelema religion (although he credited Aiwass, an emissary of Egyptian deity Horus, with dictating its texts to him) and went by the names Frater Perdurabo, Lord of the New Aeon, Prince Chioa Khan, Mahatma Guru Sri Paramahansa Shivaji, The Great Beast whose Number is 666 and Mrs Bloomer Greymare. He also made liberal use of cocaine, cannabis, ether, mescaline, opium, heroin, alcohol and magic mushrooms. A self-appointed master of magick (he added the 'k' lest his craft be confused with pulling rabbits out of hats), Crowley revelled in the fact that others dubbed him the wickedest man in the world.

Posing as Russian aristocrat Count Vladimir Svareff, Crowley took a lease on a luxury apartment in the building in 1898. Why he adopted this particular pseudonym is not clear and although vanity undoubtedly played a part (as is the case with the more sensational rumours of his work for British Intelligence), it may have simply been a ruse to escape his devout Plymouth Brethren mother. It goes without saying that the fanatical religious zeal of Crowley's parents did not pass undefiled to their son, although the

enfant terrible did have them to thank for a most favourable inheritance, allowing him to circumvent the mundane
necessity of gainful employment.

The new tenant built himself two temples at the property
– one for white magic, the other for black. While the former
comprised six 6ft by 8ft mirrors covering the walls, pentagrams
and a magic circle on the floor and everything else painted
white, the black temple was significantly darker because it was,
in fact, a cupboard. Inside it, Crowley kept both an ebony
wood carving of a black man standing on his hands with his
feet supporting an altar, and a human skeleton that he fed
blood and small birds with the intention of restoring it to life.
Crowley later admitted (with uncharacteristic candour) that he
succeeded in nothing more than covering it in 'viscous slime'.

Somewhat more spirited company was provided by Allan
Bennett, an impoverished occultist friend who Crowley invited
to move in and become his personal tutor. The pair wasted
no time in experimenting with magick and drugs, and the student later wrote how he was left awestruck when his mentor
wielded his 'blasting rod' (a glass chandelier lustre mounted
on a wooden handle) to render a sceptic incapacitated for
fourteen hours. But summoning dark forces had its downsides;
Crowley recalled how on one occasion they returned home
to discover that malevolent spirits had laid waste to the white
temple and a procession of no fewer than 316 semi-material-
ised beings were tramping around his living room.

Such shenanigans could not have escaped the notice of
neighbours, and police began to take an interest in activities at Chancery Lane – though less for the convocation of
demons than Crowley's suspected homosexual relationships.
Oscar Wilde's trial was still fresh in the collective memory
and had whipped Victorian society into a feverish horror of
that abominable crime not to be named.

As Crowley dabbled with more extreme forms of magick, the unsuitability of his lodgings became evident. He wished to perform a spell known as the Abramelin Operation – an elaborate and lengthy ritual that demanded a room with windows on all sides leading to an outside terrace covered with fine river sand to the depth of two fingers. Clearly, an upstairs London flat would not be sufficient to satisfy the spirits and what with police sniffing around, Svareff swanned off to Scotland in late 1899 to establish 'The House of the Beast' beside Loch Ness.

Although Crowley inhabited the building for just one year, its malignant atmosphere intensified in 1906 with the publication of a horror story by Algernon Blackwood entitled 'Smith: An Episode in a Lodging House'. Blackwood was on nodding terms with Crowley and his story of an unsettling neighbour performing dangerous experiments in magic was inspired by The Great Beast's exploits at Chancery Lane – its fictional details now bearing uncanny resemblance to fact. Crowley gladly fuelled the speculation by writing how the flat was unsafe to visit, such was its aura of evil – not only from his own magick, but also the confluence of nefarious forces out to destroy him. One such detractor was poet W.B. Yeats, who he believed was waging supernatural warfare on him, driven by bitter jealousy. With much satisfaction, Crowley let it be known that workmen were struck dumb in the building, visitors were seized with anything from cramp to apoplexy, and it was a long time before the rooms were re-let.

With the sinister influence of the address firmly established, every unexplained phenomenon, from headaches to blocked drains could be linked back to the world's wickedest man, who might smile to learn of his apartment's exorcism, because in 2006 the building's owner saw fit to demolish all but its facade.

ST MARK'S CHURCH,
KENNINGTON SE11

BLOCK BOOKING

St Mark's occupies a site formerly known as Gallows Common where felons were hanged and their corpses displayed to full effect inside a metal gibbet. In 1738, a man named Gill Smith underwent this treatment for murdering his wife and, for reasons unknown, thieves shinned up the post and made off one of his legs – perhaps to pocket a few pence from anatomists because 'they endeavoured to cut off one of his arms on Tuesday last but was prevented by the irons in which he was inclosed'. This was no mean feat considering that the body hung 20ft aloft, nails around the base of the gallows made climbing it awkward, and the penalty for doing so was transportation. Notwithstanding human and avian robbers, corpses were thus left to decompose *in situ*, making a powerful sensory impact on passing traffic until disarticulated chunks eventually fell to earth through the gaps.

Not every victim enjoyed such exposure; in 1746, the gallows were busy with a higher class of wrong-doer when nine Jacobite rebels were dragged through the streets from Southwark to be hanged, drawn and quartered. Although their sentence stipulated that they should be alive during dis-embowelling, in practice, the point at which to commence the butchery was left to the discretion of the hangman. After the men recited some final devotions, they cast their hats and prayer books into the crowd, and were turned off.

About five minutes later, the executioner cut down Colonel Towneley and stripped him naked (a perk of his profession was his victim's clothing so he was sensible to appropriate

Towneley's black velvet suit before it became unfavourably soiled). As the body was dumped on the block, it became apparent that he was not entirely dead so in a surprising act of mercy, the executioner struck Towneley violently on the chest, but it 'not having the effect designed, he immediately cut his throat, after which he took his head off'.

Next came the gruesome ritual of pulling out Towneley's bowels and heart, throwing them into a fire, then quartering the headless body, and after the hangman had diligently

worked through his other eight candidates he cried 'God save King George!' to which spectators responded with a muted cheer.

A fortnight later, three more rebels were served in the same manner; however, 'a chair-man who plies in Great Ormond Street having got from the fire the liver of one of the unhappy sufferers, broiled and ate it, whether out of derision, or to imitate a cannibal is not known'. The unnamed omnivore was spotted about an hour and a half later 'surrounded by a mob and complaining of a great sickness in his stomach'.

4 GRAY'S INN SQUARE WC1

VICTORIAN'S SECRET

To outward appearances, Henry Spencer Ashbee was the very model of a respectable Victorian gentleman: he was senior partner in a prosperous export company, owned a handsome house near the British Museum, and was happily married with three children. But he pursued a hobby so dangerously unwholesome, it necessitated private rooms at No. 4 Gray's Inn Square.

Ashbee collected erotic literature and did so obsessively – something he understandably kept from all but a few close associates. The family home was not appropriate for piling up porn, whereas discreet lodgings at Gray's Inn were conveniently nearby (though not too convenient) among lawyers' chambers, an exclusively male and ostensibly law-abiding environment. Here, carefully selected gentleman connoisseurs could join him in perusing the publications and perhaps find themselves a little hot under their immaculately starched collars. For almost thirty years Ashbee amassed erotica old and new to form probably the finest (if that is the correct word) hoard of pornography ever accumulated by an individual.

Possessing indecent literature was technically lawful (though clearly not something to shout about) but the Obscene Publications Act 1857 made it illegal to sell such material, creating somewhat of an obstacle to the collector. Fortunately for Ashbee, he travelled widely courtesy of his employment and this took him to countries with far less repressive attitudes, principally France and Belgium where he was well known to specialist suppliers, so much of his lewd library materialised from his luggage on such forays.

Safely ensconced at Gray's Inn, Ashbee began to compile a meticulous catalogue of his burgeoning collection and published it (anonymously of course) in 1877 under the pseudonym Pisanus Fraxi – a scatological anagram of *fraxinus* and *apis*: Latin for ash and bee. The work's title, *Index Librorum Prohibitorum*, was a cheeky appropriation of the Roman Catholic church's list of heretical and immoral books, and Ashbee used its introduction to lament: 'That English erotic literature should never have had its bibliographer is not difficult to understand. First and foremost the English nation possesses an ultra-squeamishness and hyperprudery peculiar to itself, sufficient alone to deter any author of position and talent from taking in hand so tabooed a subject.' However, he also mourned the mediocre artistic merit in home-grown erotica, 'written with so little talent, delicacy, or art' – although Spanish porn was dealt equally short shrift.

It took Ashbee two further decades and two weighty volumes to complete the catalogue, owing not only to the size of his stash, but also because the work was no mere inventory; along with bibliographic information on each title, Ashbee penned synopses and critical remarks (especially withering on matters of punctuation), offered lengthy quotations and

translations, as well as copious footnotes deciphering authors'
pseudonyms or intentionally misleading publication notices.
One title on his bookshelf was:

> The Romance of Chastisement; or, The Revelations of Miss
> Darcey. 8vo; pp. 112; 8 coloured lithographs, badly executed;
> published by W Dugdale in 1866. Belinda Darcey visits her
> friend Dora Forester who initiates her into the pleasing myster-
> ies of flagellation and reveals to her experiences at Belvidere
> House, an academy where the birch is much used. Other scenes
> are introduced, such as a penitence in a convent, a domestic
> whipping, &c ... The literary worth of this book is rather above
> the average and in its way it is readable, and even entertaining.

The catalogue's exhaustive index alone would have taken
Ashbee months to compile: 'Abbysinia; Arab women able
to constrict the muscles of the vagina, ... *Boarding School
Bumbrusher, The*, ... clitoris, excessive size of, ... dress, men's
effeminate described, ...'

With such expertise and erudition in his specialist subject,
Ashbee dispensed unique insight through his masterwork,
such as the fetish or 'lech' peculiar to each nation. While
the English cherished flagellation, 'sodomy, so prevalent
among the ancient Greeks and brought into modern Europe
by the Bulgarians, has found a permanent home in Turkey
and Italy ... tribadism is chiefly indulged in by Turkish and
French women ... corpse profanation, a crime so strange
and so utterly contrary to nature that its very existence will
possibly be unknown to many of my readers, is practiced in
Italy and even in France ... bestiality, so dear to ...' etc.

While discretion was paramount during his lifetime,
Ashbee was happy for his name to be known to posterity
because he bequeathed all 2,379 volumes of his libidinous
library to the British Museum – and he gazes impassively
from a bookplate mounted in each. Anticipating that

trustees would baulk at this tsunami of smut, he included with it his priceless collection of Cervantes' *Don Quixote*, literature he obviously enjoyed when spent with chronicles of the flesh. However, the bequest authorised the destruction of any book should the museum already own a copy and it was not 'expedient' to send elsewhere; correspondence from the time suggests that this clause was interpreted as carte blanche to destroy at least six boxes of 'offensive matter', predominantly illustrated editions that Ashbee's scrupulous catalogue indicates were among his collection but are now nowhere to be found. Those that survived were safely placed under lock and key where, in what is now the British Library, they still reside.

CABLE STREET/
CANNON STREET ROAD E1

SUICIDE MISSION

Suicide was once shrouded in superstition; life was a gift from God, so those deprived themselves of it committed an abominable offence against Him. And the crime was codified through a posthumous trial to determine whether the perpetrator acted though insanity – a marginally lesser wrongdoing, or *felo de se*, a 'felon of himself' or self-murderer. Satan, as the guiding hand behind suicide, was very real to Londoners and all manner of mischief was attributed to his skullduggery, so precautions were necessary to protect the population. Seen as an ungodly threat, the malignant corpse was removed from the murder scene not through a door but a window or specially made opening to hamper the ghost's endeavours at finding its way back in. Then its legs might be broken or tied to frustrate any attempt at walking, before it was buried by means of a brutal ritual enshrined in law.

In 1811, while John Williams languished in prison awaiting trial for seven grisly murders in Shadwell, he hanged himself. Although Williams's involvement in the crimes was not clear cut, in his absence magistrates resolved that he was solely responsible and his suicide was a self-evident admission of guilt. Williams's meagre possessions were forfeited to the Crown and, although in all likelihood he had saved the authorities the trouble and expense of a hanging, it was now incumbent on the State to stage manage the manner of his burial.

Suicides were buried at night in the middle of crossroads, traditionally at remote rural sites, though as London expanded this became increasingly inconvenient, so instead the junction nearest the self-annihilation was settled upon. However, the peculiar circumstances of Williams as both mass murderer and self-murderer meant the need for a daytime spectacle took precedence; it was important for the neighbourhood to witness that he posed no further danger, and evil spirits were purged.

On 31 December 1811, Williams's four-day-old corpse was strapped to a cart and slowly paraded through Shadwell past upwards of 10,000 people lining its streets in complete silence. To ensure a satisfactory view for all, the body was arranged on an elevated and angled platform, and onlookers thought it looked surprisingly fresh, with the exception of the hands and lower arms, which had turned a deep purple. Accompanying Williams were the grisly implements of his presumed crimes – a large chisel and a shipwright's mallet, still caked in blood.

Amid concern that locals might wreak revenge on the corpse, the loathsome cortège was escorted by more than 300 constables with cutlasses drawn, and the only disturbance came from a coachman who took the opportunity to whip Williams's head three times with his crop. At the site of each murder, the procession paused for a quarter of an hour as an act of redress, and a dramatic moment occurred at one when Williams's head suddenly flopped to the side, as if to look away. A volunteer obligingly ascended the platform to ensure that his face ghoulishly stared at the crime scene.

At the centre of the crossroads between Cable Street and Cannon Street Road, a shallow pit had been dug, deliberately too small to take the body comfortably and likely orientated north–south. Despite the obvious religious symbolism of a cross, crossroads burials were the antithesis of Christian burial and scuppered any hope the victim's soul might have for salvation. The corpse was roughly manhandled face down into the distinctly unconsecrated ground, and an official took the blood-stained mallet and drove a wooden stake through Williams's heart. At this, the spectators finally broke their silence: 'The populace gave three groans, accompanied by deep and unfeigned execrations.' Impaling a suicide in this way served to anchor its wandering spirit – though in the event it did escape, the crossroads offered a second line of defence by leaving it flummoxed as to which road to follow.

Quicklime was thrown over William's body to hasten decomposition, the hole filled in and cobblestones rammed back into place – though not before someone had carefully collected splinters from the stake to sell as souvenirs. As a final precaution, the procession headed home by a different route and with Shadwell's denizens feeling somewhat safer, traffic on Cable Street returned to normal.

But it was not the last sighting of Williams. When a gas main was installed in 1886, unsuspecting workmen were surprised to discover his grave beneath the road – the stake still stuck between two ribs and a prison shackle around a leg bone. The relics were divvied up as mementos and the local publican honoured with the skull.

Impetus to abolish crossroads burial was hastened by the
suicide of Foreign Secretary and Leader of the House of
Commons, Viscount Castlereagh, in 1822. Because of his
drastic actions with a penknife, his Lordship escaped the
need to explain an incident in a brothel with a transvestite
but left the coroner facing an uncomfortable choice between
felony and insanity. In opting for the latter he invited unwelcome comments about the state of Government, but cleared
the way for Castlereagh to be buried not at a crossroads but
in Westminster Abbey.

Suicide and attempted suicide remained illegal until 1961.

NATURAL HISTORY MUSEUM SW7

FRIGHT AT THE MUSEUM

Where herds of stuffed mammals now lounge, there was
once formerly a display of rats bloated with explosive.

Between 1942 and 1945, a museum gallery was quietly appropriated by the Special Operations Executive, the
organisation tasked with espionage and sabotage in occupied
territory, or in Churchill's words, to 'go and set Europe ablaze'.
With the greatest secrecy, six rooms were sealed off and their
natural history rehomed to make way for a smorgasbord of
spy paraphernalia such that the site's official name, Station
XVB, was inevitably usurped by its nickname: the Toy Shop.

But this was no plaything. Before agents entered the field
they could peruse an array of ingenious and deadly gadgetry
that they might find use for, including a one-person submarine,
a crossbow powered by elastic bands, a folding motorbike,
food that looked like driftwood, or tools that appeared to

be turnips. They might wish to observe the enemy through a telescope concealed in a cigarette holder, or throw them off the scent by slipping on a pair of over-shoes 'bearing the imprint of the native foot'. There were radio sets hidden inside clocks, Bibles, petrol cans, blocks of wood, record players and vacuum cleaners, while explosives were to be found inside soap, briefcases, logs, clogs, chocolate, Chianti bottles, cigarettes, hammers, bicycle pumps, lumps of coal and (imitation) cowpats. The excrement theme continued in a range of tyre bursters masquerading as dog, horse or mule droppings, and devices were tailored for specific war zones, so bombs were concealed inside exotic fruits, tins of Japanese sauce or Balinese wood carvings, while detonating dung came in both elephant and camel manure variants.

Many of the camouflage and decoy components were manufactured at the Victoria and Albert Museum, where secret workshops employed technicians and prop-makers from the film industry, while others originated from Station XV – a factory based conveniently near to Elstree Film Studios.

The rodents on display were not plaster props but the genuine article, harvested from the streets of Tottenham by a professional rat-catcher labouring under the impression that London University required them for protracted experimentation. They were expertly skinned, stuffed with plastic explosive and primed with a timer fuse poking from their anus. Exploding vermin did not alter the course of the war but after the Nazis discovered the first colony dispatched to France, unnecessary caution was exercised around the creatures, and fear of self-immolation from exploding coal or cigarettes caused a similarly powerful psychological effect.

This Aladdin's cave of spyware had unexpected impact in another quarter: novelist Ian Fleming served with Naval Intelligence during the war and it is no coincidence that the Toy Shop bears an uncanny resemblance to James Bond's gadget gurus 'Q Branch'.

COCK LANE EC1

KNOCK KNOCK JOKE

Cock Lane was the chosen haunt of one of London's most famed ghosts.

In October 1759, William Kent and his pregnant wife, Fanny, took lodgings with Richard Parsons and his family at their drab house on the lane (now the site of 1 Giltspur Street). Fanny came from a wealthy family, so the couple were not typical tenants for such dingy surroundings, but Kent explained that they had bought a house in need of renovation before they could move in.

However, this was not the entire truth. Kent had been married to Fanny's sister and had a son, but both died; the law prohibited him from marrying Fanny so they were living in sin and fear of her family, but to ensure her security should he die, he wrote a will in her favour and Fanny reciprocated with Kent as beneficiary. Parsons was a liquor-soaked good-for-nothing but he was canny and not slow to tease this useful information out of Kent, along with the loan of twelve guineas.

The ghost first manifested itself not long after the couple's arrival; while Kent was away on business, Fanny asked Parsons' 10-year-old daughter, Betty, if she would share her bedroom and for several nights she was kept awake by peculiar knocking and scratching. But when Kent returned, they faced a problem more troubling than a ghost; Kent had asked that Parsons repay some of the loan and a bitter quarrel ensued, culminating with their eviction onto the street. They moved to their unfinished house, only to discover that Fanny had smallpox; within days she was dead.

This tragic turn of events left the ghost distinctly subdued until shortly after Kent had successfully sued Parsons for the debt. Suddenly its nightly noisemaking could even be heard by passers-by in the street and word rapidly spread that Fanny's troubled spirit was being channelled through Parsons' sleeping daughter.

Supernatural communication seemed a perfectly logical explanation to local clergyman John Moore and when invited into Betty's bedroom for an audience with the unhappy phantom, he guilefully inquired whether it might answer questions using one knock to signify 'yes' and two for 'no'. After a short pause, a single knock rang out. By this means, and with the supposition that scratching noises signalled disquiet, Moore confirmed that the ghost was indeed the spirit of Fanny – and Kent had poisoned her.

Parsons was itching for 'Scratching Fanny' to enjoy a wider audience, so every night twenty a time crammed into his daughter's bedroom, following commensurate remuneration. Accusations of deceit were forestalled by allowing spectators to study Betty as she undressed and climbed into bed, and a neighbour acted as intermediary between Fanny's spirit and the rapt assembly; local alehouses were pleased to exploit the upturn in passing trade, the ever-alert newspapers had a field day and all of London was agog.

Kent could not fail to hear of the ghost's allegation and in an effort to halt the frenzy, arranged to meet with Moore. The clergyman left the encounter convinced of Kent's guilt; Kent went away resigned to the fact that his fate lay in the hands of a percussive phantom, who, during a question and answer session in his presence, informed him that he would hang for his crime. More alarmingly, it repeated the assertion when Betty slept at other houses in the neighbourhood.

Gleaning information solely through knocks had its challenges, but one night the ghost made the surprising revelation that should Kent venture near Fanny's coffin, she would

strike on its lid. It was now high time for learned gentleman of rank to assume control of the matter so a committee was formed with Samuel Johnson among its number – though the necessity of subjecting Betty to intimate scrutiny meant an invitation was also extended to a matron from the local hospital. The distinguished company duly escorted Kent to the vaults of St John Clerkenwell and must have felt an inkling that their reputations were in jeopardy when Fanny's corpse remained obstinately mute.

Listening to coffins finally instigated some long overdue scepticism and following close examination of Betty's sleeping arrangements, many including Reverend Moore and Dr Johnson were disappointed to learn that the girl was creating the din through the mundane agency of a wooden board. Whenever she was put to bed with arms and legs spreadeagled and secured, there was no Scratching Fanny; with this news, Kent had Parsons arrested for conspiracy.

The ensuing trial was notable for Rev. Moore's sudden reinterpretation of events to declare Kent innocent, and the unexpected appearance of Fanny's ghost, although it turned out to be a gentleman who had somehow become trapped on the roof. Parsons had no change of heart so the court was left to ponder the existence or otherwise of spirits. To his dismay, witnesses testified to Parsons' penchant for another species of spirits and the character assessment sealed his fate. He was handed a two-year prison term and a spell in the pillory, appropriately at the end of Cock Lane, where locals showed their appreciation for the months of entertainment by passing a hat around to buy him some drink.

RIVER THAMES, GALLION'S REACH E6/SE28

CRASH COURSE

On the evening of 3 September 1878, paddle steamer *Princess Alice* was navigating up the Thames following a day's pleasure cruise to Gravesend. It was a popular excursion and enjoying the happy atmosphere of singing and dancing were about 800 passengers (the exact number is unknown because children did not warrant tickets). At about 7.45 p.m. the 220ft vessel took a starboard helm to wend its way around the bend in the river at Tripcock Point, and as it did so a lookout informed Captain Grinstead of the 890-tonne, 250ft iron-built coal ship *Bywell Castle* heading downstream. The collier's pilot had already spotted the pleasure steamer and judged that they would approach head-on, so ported the helm as standard procedure for ships to pass on the port side. Alas, this was a rule more honoured in the breach than the observance; neither vessel slowed sufficiently to assess the other's course and with only a few seconds warning the collier struck *Princess Alice* amidships, just forward of the paddle box where an ensemble of elderly ladies stood singing hymns. A huge burst of steam erupted as it carved deep into her side and water engulfed its furnaces.

The paddle steamer immediately began to sink and panicked screams were almost overpowered by the doleful moans of the ships' whistles, blowing in desperate hope of assistance. Three passengers managed to climb the funnel stays then clamber onto the collier's anchor chains; others clung to ropes cast from its bow – some of whom were hauled up while others fell back into the writhing mass of bodies beneath. Within four minutes, *Princess Alice* had broken in two and vanished, dragging down anyone who had not jumped clear. Hundreds below deck in the lower saloons met a terrifying end, along with the one man who could have shed most light on the disaster, Captain Grinstead.

A handful of survivors were pulled into the collier's lifeboats and others clung to buoys, ladders or planks cast from the ship, but those in the water faced another peril. At high tide, London's main sewer outfall discharged into the Thames immediately opposite Tripcock Point and its sluice gates had not long since belched 'two continuous columns of decomposed fermenting sewage, hissing like soda water with baneful gases, so black the water stained for miles, and discharging a corrupt charnel house odour'. The impracticality of Victorian fashion left women in particular with little hope of reaching the riverbank and as darkness fell nothing further could be done.

Next morning, the grisly scene of swollen bodies floating in sewage did not deter enterprising watermen from taking to their boats in the knowledge that retrieving a corpse merited a 5s reward, even if it entailed fisticuffs over their valuable catch. Such labours were necessary because the authorities faced an acutely challenging task; the dead, who it was known numbered at least 500, had to be buried as speedily as possible because they posed a noxious health hazard. But to retrieve so many of bodies, many of which washed up far from the scene, identify them and release them to relatives posed all manner of difficulties. There was also the dilemma of the living such as a little boy taken to Plumstead Infirmary, where he gave his name as Edward Newman and told staff that his mother sold sweets, but was never claimed.

Two days after the disaster, a diver was sent down to examine the wreck in preparation for raising it, and due to the filthy state of the water, he was compelled to perform the task

solely by touch, by which means he identified how the cabins were crammed with a serried mass of bodies that were particularly tightly congested around doorways. When the wreck was raised a few days later, several of the dead became dislodged and among the first recovered was a woman dressed in black silk with a small boy clinging to her neck and his toy trumpet entangled in her hair – a horrifying scene to which an estimated 100,000 sightseers had flocked. Pandemonium broke out when souvenir hunters took to rowing boats to hack a memento from the wreck while criminals appreciated the opportunity to pickpocket both the living and the dead.

Recovered bodies were laid out in a shed at Woolwich dockyard where a pitiful procession of grieving relatives traipsed past the slimy, rank-smelling exhibits in the hope of recognising loved ones from their blackened, swollen features; remarkably, one woman was identified when her blind husband felt her jewellery. However, more than a week after the accident, four naked, bloated and badly decomposed corpses were discovered in a shed in Silvertown and it was never ascertained who they were, how they ended up there, or even whether they had been involved in the tragedy at all; they were among the thirty-one unidentified bodies buried in Woolwich Cemetery alongside 120 others who were never claimed.

While the exact death toll will never be known, the consensus is that about 650 people perished in the disaster.

STATUE OF ACHILLES, HYDE PARK W2

BARE NECESSITIES

The 18ft bronze statue of Achilles, unveiled in 1822, honours the Duke of Wellington and is unusual for being funded entirely by women. Their generosity may have been somehow connected with the eye-catching manner in which the sculpture stuck out; it was Britain's first nude created for public display since Roman times – a circumstance that revealed the figure's anatomical weakness not to be its heel.

Although the subject was named Achilles, it was modelled on an ancient marble statue of a muscular horse tamer that stands in Rome's Piazza del Quirinale. Divesting the nameless horseman of his stallion and furnishing him with shield and sword were thought sufficient to transform him into the mythological warrior, although *The Times* struck a dissenting note by sneeringly summing up the work as 'nonsense'. (The success of the makeover was not fostered by the fact that for reasons never fully explained, the battlefield hero remained bereft of a weapon for more than forty years, prompting pranksters to regularly arm him with a broom.)

Female sculpture lovers raised in excess of £10,000 for their idol – munificence egged on in some quarters by the misconception that the undraped statue was modelled on the Duke himself. In fact, convention prohibited the erection of his likeness because Wellington was still very much alive, although this circumstance did enable His Lordship to graciously supply much of its metal in the form of twelve, 24-pounder cannon acquired at his victories across Europe. But while the more discerning benefactors may have wished to preserve Classical ideals and accuracy, it was men who

oversaw important decision-making, and gentlemen of the statue committee were obliged to tackle the matter of gentlemen's tackle. It came as no surprise that in the interests of public decency and decorum, the sculptor was instructed to beautify the inappropriate part with a fig leaf, in spite of which, the popular press delighted in naming the figure 'The Ladies' Trophy'.

In 1961, the temptation to reveal what lay beneath proved too much for one young lawyer and, emboldened by preparatory refreshment in a nearby hostelry, he saw fit to hacksaw through the three substantial bolts employed to secure the foliage. However, it was nuts that made his task especially arduous because he happened to be simultaneously castrating the Greek hero. Liberal 1960s attitudes did not extend to the presentment of larger-than-life mutilated manhood in a Royal Park, so substitute foliation was affixed post-haste, but his enterprise triggered a spate of copycat prunings and the Ministry of Works found itself compelled to stockpile spare vegetation.

In the early 1990s the now remorseful Queen's Counsel meekly returned his plunder to the park authorities and paid for it to be reinstated.

COVENT GARDEN WC2

STIMULATION MANUAL

For much of the eighteenth century, Covent Garden was synonymous with sex – its exalted status due in no small measure to activities at the Shakespear's Head tavern in the north-east corner of the piazza. A popular haunt for the lubri-

cious (now an entrance to the Royal Opera House) it was here
that head waiter John Harrison – or Jack Harris to regulars
– liberally greased the workings of the flesh industry by means
of a well-thumbed ledger, bulging with notes on the salient features of the local daughters of pleasure. Its itemised particulars
ranged from age, address and admission fee to specialisms and
salubrity, thereby helping the self-declared 'Pimp-General of
All England' match whoredom's purchasers with its purvey-
ors, while the magnum opus lined his pockets in more ways
than one through mutually favourable arrangements with the
workforce. Such was the demand for its precious contents that
in 1757 publication became imperative.

But Harris was a pimp not poet, so it is suspected that he
struck a deal whereby penniless hack Samuel Derrick would
ghostwrite the guide. Derrick was suited to the task through
extensive first-hand experience of its subjects, though whoever
its author, it was their way with words that turned Harris's List
of Covent Garden Ladies into a best-seller. A few extracts from
its most lyrical waxing demonstrate how the book appealed to
both savvy shopper and armchair aficionado.

'Tall and genteel, of a mild temper, and not more than
twenty-one,' was how it introduced the enticing delights of
Miss Maria C–ck–tt (names might be feebly obscured) before
elaborating on her 'fine regular set of white teeth, light
blue eyes, carrots above and below, tempting lips below and
above' etc. available for a guinea. As to a visit's climax, 'this
damsel is peculiarly skilful in extracting all its sweets; for …
just as the liquid minute is pouring down, her wanton lecherous hand with eager but gentle compressure, squeezes the
circular balls in nature's treasure bag'. For those of more limited means, Mrs Howard possessed 'such a habit of intimacy
with the gin bottle that unless a person is particularly partial
to it, it is almost intolerable to approach her', although 'the
grove below is well thatched, and ample enough in size to
take in any guest; but still she has learnt the knack of con-

tracting it and a small made gentleman may feel the tender
friction' for which she 'does not turn away any money offered
her'. In no time, London's voluptuaries were beating a path
to the tavern to secure a copy of this scholarly tome.

Gentlemen 'who prefer the pleasure without the expensive consequences' were directed towards Miss Lucas who 'is
said, like the river Nile, frequently to overflow, but somehow
or another her inundations differ from those of that river,

HARRIS'S LIST; or CUPID'S LONDON DIRECTORY.

as they do not produce fecundity; some skilful gardeners are of opinion that she drowns the seed, which is the reason that it does not take root'. Alternatively, Betsy Miles offered 'entrance at the front door tolerably reasonable but nothing less than two pounds for the back way'.

'We may conclude from Mrs Dod,' the writer mused, 'that a woman in years may be perfectly alluring; she is indeed turned of forty, rather fat and short, yet ... will give you a comfortable cup of tea in the morning for one pound one,' whereas an engagement with Miss Clicamp accorded, 'one of the finest, fattest figures as fully finished for fun and frolick as fertile fancy ever formed'.

Topographical euphemisms were the author's stock in trade; Miss Devonshire's 'port is said to be well guarded by a light brown chevaux-de-frieze and parted from Bum-bay by a very small pleasant isthmus' while Madam D–sl–z 'has one qualification which many English girls want, which is a certain cleanliness in the Netherlands.' Miss Wood mean-while 'is really a delicious piece and her terra incognita is so very agreeable to every traveller therein, that it hath ceased to deserve that name and is become a well-known and much frequented country'.

The indulgence of specialised fetishes was diligently documented, such as services offered by Miss Grant, who charged two guineas for a client to wash her soiled under-garments: 'These being produced with the maid's dirty bed gown which he puts on ... he sets to work and in a few sec-onds gets up to the elbows in suds.' For the more submissive, Mrs D–l–v–t 'is celebrated for bush-fighting with a birchen rod, which she wields with dexterity to the uncommon grati-fication of many gentlemen'.

Punches were not pulled when it came to shortcomings; Miss Hamilton 'looks much best when in a serious humour for when a smile forces itself she is under the disagreeable necessity of exposing a set of teeth not at all to her advantage', and as for Miss Jenkinson: 'for the time you are with her, divest yourself of hearing, or your nose from smelling the salubrity of her breath'. But even when less than complementary, inclusion in Harris's List was considered beneficial for business.

The guide made such compulsive reading, and presumably, trustworthy insight, it was kept updated for close to forty years and sold in excess of 250,000 copies, the majority of which were later consumed not by pleasure-seekers but in the fireplaces of Victorian moralisers.

NOTRE DAME DE FRANCE CHURCH WC2

NEW TESTAMENT

Aficionados of Dan Brown's novel *The Da Vinci Code* flock to Notre Dame because the church is circular, a form favoured by the enigmatic Knights Templar, and home to an image that, according to the book, conceals a portentous message. Jean Cocteau's 1959 mural in the north chapel includes a haunting image of Mary beside Christ's feet at the Crucifixion. Or does it?

Although Brown's novel is a fantastical concoction of mysticism, symbolism and historical alternativism, it opens by asserting as fact the existence of a mysterious secret society named The Priory of Sion – and a disparate bundle of modern documents alluding to its history were indeed stumbled upon in 1967 after the organisation had successfully remained unheard of for almost 900 years. The dossier revealed that Cocteau, as well as being master of more creative pursuits than are easily listed here, was its Grand

Master. Brown then takes up a hypothesis already proven to shift books: that the Frenchman, like earlier holders of the office such as Leonardo da Vinci and Sir Isaac Newton, safeguarded heretical knowledge of a bloodline descended from Jesus and Mary Magdalene. With this privileged information in mind, the mysteries of Cocteau's art may be unravelled.

While the central mural might at first glance appear to depict a traditional Crucifixion scene, unexpected features fuel alternative interpretation: black rays glower from a black sun (or *sol niger* – an alchemical and occult symbol), a rose at the base of the cross alludes to the Rosicrucians, an order claiming to guard ancient wisdom, and an appearance is made by the falcon-headed Egyptian god Horus, who, it is perhaps irrelevant to add, was born of Isis courtesy of a magic phallus after Osiris's penis was gobbled by a fish. Also present at the Crucifixion is Cocteau himself in self-portrait, but with his back to the scene and an eyebrow quizzically raised – as if to question the orthodox version of events. But most significantly, the crucified figure is visible only from the knees down and a curiously green-tinged onlooker has what might be interpreted as the ichthys symbol of Christ for an eye, which to the suggestible signals that Jesus is witnessing the death of someone else. Had Cocteau's secret knowledge remained so we might innocently assume that the mural was merely the work of an eccentric and enigmatic artist cramming a vertically orientated subject into a panoramic space.

Which brings us to the mundane reason for the church's unusual shape. Although the building dates from 1955, it replaced a church that was heavily damaged during the Blitz. This earlier building had been circular because it was constructed inside 'The Panorama' of 1793 – a popular visitor attraction exhibiting 360-degree paintings (with no hidden messages) in a 90ft circle.

CUCKOLD'S POINT, ROTHERHITHE SE16

HORNY MEN

Until prudish twenty-first-century cartographers rubbed it from the map, the north-east tip of the Rotherhithe peninsula rejoiced in the name Cuckold's Point or Cuckold's Haven. But quite how the riverbank of this nondescript neighbourhood came to be known by the term for a man whose wife takes delight in sexual relations with others, is agonisingly vague.

Although it was the conspiratorial cuckoo that lent its name to cuckoldry, its defining symbol was a set of horns or antlers – something long associated with male potency because in the field of sexual prowess, stags, bulls, rams and billygoats were considered the animal kingdom's greatest players. But how horns became a humiliating reference to a wife's infidelity is also frustratingly enigmatic and although prime suspects include scapegoats, castrated oxen and the devil, another pleasing explanation relates how during the Crusades, soldiers wore crests on their helmets, many of which featured horns. After years away fighting, it was a fair supposition that the horned men returned home to their wives as cuckolds.

An early reference to the name comes from 1562 when there was 'set up at the cuckold haven a great Maypole by butchers and fishermen, full of horns; and they made great cheer for there was two firkins of fresh sturgeons … and great plenty of wine'. In 1598, a visitor remarked upon 'a long pole with ram's horns on it, the intention of which was vulgarly said to be a reflection upon wilful and contented cuckolds', but groping for an innocent explanation, a Victorian writer optimistically suggested that the marker denoted an ancient toll for cattle, though he confessed reluctance to mention the indecorous topic of cuckoldry or 'that word of fear, unpleasing to a married ear'.

In the absence of a plausible explanation for the two-timing toponym, an implausible one has stepped into the void and goes thus: during the thirteenth century a miller and his wife lived in the locality and one day while the husband was out, King John made an unexpected appearance at their door and indulged in pleasures of the flesh with the man's comely wife. When the miller returned home to a surprise guest and uneasy atmosphere, the King, by way of reparation, offered him a stretch of land as far as he was able to see, provided that on each anniversary of the incident, he walked there with a pair of stag's horns on his head. As the miller sharpened his vision and eyed up London, the King hastily added that he was offering only land downriver, at which the cuckold managed to make out Charlton on the slopes of Shooter's Hill.

Later versions of the romance maintain that the miller lived in Charlton and spotted Rotherhithe, but either way no record exists of a humble labourer owning vast swathes of land across Greenwich. Yet veracity was of scant importance to those seeking an excuse for Bacchanalian revelry and on 18 October each year, the miller's supposed stroll was re-enacted by men proudly sporting horns on their heads. The two-hour ramble, invariably prolonged by interludes for participants to slake their thirst, culminated in a riotous Horn Fair at Charlton, where an eighteenth-century writer noted: 'So many indecencies were committed … such as the whipping of females with furze, that it gave rise to the proverb of All is fair at Horn Fair.' For one day, all notions of sexual propriety were cast-off and the hoi polloi considered itself free to make advances on all and sundry: 'The mob at that time take all kinds of liberties and the women are especially impudent that day, as if it was a day that justified the giving themselves loose to all manner of indecency without any reproach.'

Cross-dressing played no part in the legend but the fair was also thought a seemly occasion for men to drag up: 'I was dressed in my landlady's best gown and other women's attire and to Horn Fair we went, and as we were coming back by water all the clothes were spoiled by dirty water that was flung on us in an inundation for which I was obliged to present her with two guineas to make atonement for the damages.'

Perhaps surprisingly, the revelry centred on Charlton church: 'Though it's the rudest fair in England, it begins with a sermon which makes another old saying good, viz. in the name of the Lord begins all mischief. They say the parson usually takes his text upon this occasion out of Solomon's proverbs; and I asking why he did so was told, because Solomon was a great cuckold-maker.' Those hoping to find a more prosaic origin for the festivities point out that 18 October is the feast day of St Luke – one of whose symbols is an ox, and to whom the church at Charlton is dedicated.

Needless to say, the Victorians eyed such debauchery with great alarm and the jamboree was outlawed; however, it has since been revived in more sober, family-friendly form.

Oddly, another entirely unremarkable patch of ground 6 miles north-east on the Barking Creek is also known as Cuckold's Haven; the site currently awaits a comparably colourful legend.

DOMINION THEATRE W1

PORTERY GRAVE

For the impoverished residents of the parish of St Giles, alcohol posed a daily peril but on 17 October 1814 it proved uncommonly deadly.

The day began as any other at Meux's Horse Shoe brewery (on the site of today's theatre) where atop the storehouse, an enormous vat of porter was quietly maturing. At about 5 p.m. a clerk spotted that one of its iron hoops had slipped off, but was unconcerned because it had occurred before and there were twenty others still securing it. He penned a note

to say that a repair was necessary and was about to deliver it when the vat exploded. Such was the force of flying debris, it caused several nearby hogsheads to rupture and knocked out the cock from another mammoth vat.

A tsunami of strong black beer, between 8,000 and 9,000 barrels (more than 2 million pints) smashed its way through the brewery walls and engulfed the surrounding neighbourhood, inundating cellars where 'the inhabitants had to save themselves from drowning by mounting their highest pieces of furniture'. Two houses immediately behind the brewery were completely demolished by the deluge and in the cellar of one, a grieving family was holding a wake for a dead child; five drowned (and sometime later their corpses could be inspected at a local public house in exchange for a donation). On the first floor 'a mother and daughter were at tea; the mother was washed out of the window, and the daughter was swept away by the current through a partition and dashed to pieces'. Inside the brewery, employees waded waist-deep through beer to rescue colleagues and save as much of the brew as possible – while also recovering the corpse of a 60-year-old woman who had floated onto the premises, along with the constituent parts of an illegal still.

Newspapers generally spoke of the bravery shown by survivors and rescuers; however, *The Bury and Norwich Post* welcomed the opportunity to sneer how 'when the beer began to flow, the neighbourhood, consisting of the lower classes of Irish, were busily employed in putting in their claim to a share, and every vessel, from a kettle to a cask, were put into requisition, and many of them were seen enjoying themselves at the expense of the proprietors'. While the editor may have presumed this to be the case, there is no evidence to show that locals hastened the flood-water's retreat by gulping it down.

Four women and four children lost their lives in the London Beer Flood but happily for the brewery, the coroner returned verdicts of death 'accidentally and by misfortune', so it dodged any demands for damages, and the Government waived thousands of pounds of duty on its next brew.

FULHAM PALACE SW6

WHIPPING BOYS

Henry VIII executed tens of thousands of his subjects (including two he had married) yet it is his daughter Queen Mary who bears the sobriquet 'Bloody', despite condemning fewer than 300 to death; such is the power of propaganda. The Bishop of London during Mary's reign is similarly immortalised as Edmund 'Bloody' Bonner because punishing those in his diocese who resisted the shift back to

Roman Catholic worship came under his purview, and his palace at Fulham became an important venue for this work.

Nineteen-year-old Thomas Hinshaw spent three months of 1558 imprisoned at Newgate for his insistence that Christ's body and blood were not truly present in consecrated bread and wine – a matter of particular concern to Bonner. Prison stimulated no shift in his views so the Bishop ferried him aboard his barge to Fulham for a more personal approach; Hinshaw was locked in the set of stocks that Bonner kept for such occasions and after an uncomfortable night to rethink his ideas, was interrogated by his host. But the captive held to his convictions and the bishop became increasing irate with the 'peevish boy', so decided to change tactics from cerebral to corporal: he would escort Hinshaw to his orchard and thrash his buttocks. Bonner 'sent for a couple of rods and caused him to kneel against a long bench in an arbor in his garden where the said Thomas, without any enforcement on his part, offered himself to the beating and did abide the fury of the said Bonner'. In truth, it was unlikely that the prisoner submitted quite so meekly because Bonner found it neces-sary to have a flunkey hold Hinshaw's head firmly between his legs, but the stubborn teenager was in luck because the comfortable life of a prelate had left Bonner decidedly out of shape. The beating continued 'so long as the fat-paunched Bishop could endure with breath and till for weariness he was fain to cease; he had two willow rods but he wasted but one and so left off'.

Bonner was unapologetic about his hands-on approach to religious conversion and when shown a picture of himself excitedly flailing at Hinshaw's backside it was reported that he roared with laughter saying: 'A vengeance on the fool! How could he get my picture drawn so right?'

The bishop also confined religious wrongdoers in the coal-cellar of his house beside St Paul's Cathedral and one of them, John Milles, whose brother had experienced live

cremation on Bonner's instructions, was brought to Fulham
for a change of scenery. Milles spent more than a week in the
stocks while the bishop employed a stick as a supplementary
means of persuasion, 'oft-times rapping him on the head
and striking him under the chin and on the ears'. Again,
the prisoner was not tempted to reconsider his opinions, so
he too was led to the orchard, his breeches slackened, and
Bonner 'with his own hands beat him, first with a willow rod
and that being worn well nigh to the stump he called for a
birch rod which a lad brought out of his chamber'.

An invitation to the palace orchard was also extended to
James Harris, 'a stripling of the age of seventeen years' who
came to Bonner's attention for failing to attend church for
more than a year. The bishop may have found himself short
of weaponry because he 'took the poor lad into his garden
and there with a rod gathered out of the cherry tree did most
cruelly whip him'.

On another occasion, perhaps because blushing the glu-
teal flesh of heretics was not satisfying his urges, Bonner
took exception to some young boys who were washing and
swimming in the river. His henchmen were dispatched to
apprehend the youths and those unfortunate enough not to
escape were brought before him; Bonner proceeded to whip
some of them with stinging nettles, had the others dragged
naked through nettle bushes, then after watching his men
beat up another bunch of boys, headed off to evensong.

Not all those summoned to Fulham felt the sharp sting of
religious persecution on their backside; Thomas Tomkins
was forced to spend a summer labouring in the fields of
the estate while he pondered his principles, although the
bishop took a particular dislike to his captive's hirsute chin
so 'bruised him in the face and plucked off the greatest part
of the hair of his beard'. Once more, Bonner's techniques
failed to trigger a change of heart, so this time he turned
to his other area of expertise: burning. In the Great Hall
at Fulham and in front of spectators including Archdeacon
of London John Harpsfield, he held Tomkins' hand over
a large candle with several wicks; the skin blistered until
'the veins shrank and the sinews burst and the water did
spurt in Mr Harpsfield's face'. Watching his hand burn in
front of him, Tomkins feared his end was nigh; however, it
was only after a spell in Newgate that he was delivered to
Smithfield, where Bonner had arranged for the rest of his
body to be burned.

THE ELIZABETH TOWER (BIG BEN) SW1

TOWER OF STENCH

Summer 1858 was decidedly unpleasant at Westminster. For the best part of 2,000 years, London's waste removal system, the River Thames, had served the city admirably. But matters had now reached boiling point. Not only did sewers empty into the river but it acted as a dump for the more abominable by-products of slaughterhouses, skin and bone boilers, wool scouring works, soap makers, tanners' yards, dyers and glue factories; the necessity of breaking and churning up its foamy crust made travelling by boat particularly perilous. May and June were among the hottest on record and as the river dropped to a shallow channel, a deep blanket of scum and sewage was exposed, densely pocked with rotting fish. Baked by the sun, the putrefying slime then began to fizz and London was hit by a stench so fetid it defied description. Its effects were thoroughly observed, however: 'nausea and pain, beginning most commonly in the temples and spreading over the head,' recorded a doctor when examining river workers. This was complemented with 'giddiness and in many of them temporary loss or impairment of sight, the presence of black spots before their eyes and often utter mental confusion', while a slew of sewer workers suffocated in the course of their employment.

Science was called upon to analyse the city's plight: 'Two highly scientific gentlemen found that taking the population of London at 2,600,000, the solid matter contained in excreta amounts daily to 266 tons. The calculation was carefully made from an average of several experiments of not a very pleasant nature.' Equally unpleasant investigations

determined that the specific gravity of human stools lay somewhere between that of fresh water and sea water and as a result, faecal matter was carried down the Thames in suspension, gently sinking until it hit incoming salt water, which floated it back up into town.

Science was less helpful in its conviction that putrid smells spread disease, but the misconception hastened efforts to mitigate the situation as those worst hit by 'The Great Stink' were politicians at the Palace of Westminster. The building enjoyed more than 800ft of riverfront beside a main sewage outflow granting unfettered views of parliamentary motions fermenting on its banks; 'The intense heat had driven our legislators from those portions of their building which overlooked the river. A few members, indeed bent upon investigating the subject to its very depth, ventured into the library, but they were instantaneously driven to retreat, each man with a handkerchief to his nose.' Honourable members gladly united behind a policy of dumping hundreds of tons of chloride of lime in the river to disinfect and deodorise it, then as a secondary precaution, hang canvas sheets soaked in the chemical from the windows. But the respite was short-lived.

Into this mess leapt gentleman scientist Goldsworthy Gurney, a man with first-hand experience of the dangers of sewage vapours. A few years earlier when providing evidence at the inquest into five deaths in a nearby sewer, he described how when a cover was lifted to retrieve the bodies, someone ill-advisedly lit a match and the flame burst 20ft in the air. It was perhaps an omen. With a varied list of achievements and disappointments to his name (his patented musical instrument that stroked silk ribbons across different-sized wine goblets failed to set the artistic world alight), Gurney had recently become responsible for heating, lighting and ventilation at the palace and therefore tasked with remedying the nuisance. However, his brief was not to cleanse the river for the benefit of all Londoners, but simply purge the pong from the corridors of power.

In a rank-smelling committee room, a council of war was convened at which Gurney proposed tightly sealing all sewers in the vicinity to trap the noxious gases, then draw them up a chimney to be harmlessly burned off. In the absence of alternatives, despairing MPs gave Gurney the go-ahead and his stink pipe soon adorned a conveniently sited tall structure – the Big Ben clock tower. Then, also up in the tower, he installed his patented steam-jet furnace – and lit it.

The first noticeable effect of Gurney's endeavours was a huge explosion; fortunately, it was only down in the sewer, from where an assistant emerged dazed but otherwise unscathed. The blast was felt up in the tower, where the furnace had begun to melt and there must have been a palpable sense that the building had been lucky to escape detonation. But though Gurney joined Guy Fawkes in failing to blow up Parliament, he was less pleased that acclaimed engineer Joseph Bazalgette happened to be on hand to highlight the scheme's folly and point out that coal gas was leaking into the sewer. Parliamentarians were now prepared to pay for the stink to go away; Gurney was knighted in expectation of his imminent retirement, Bazalgette spent the next fifteen years constructing a new sewer network and replacing the feculent riverbank with the Embankment, and Big Ben thus escaped the ignominy of blowing-off fart gas.

HARLEYFORD STREET, OVAL SE11

FARTHER LAND

Air raid sirens sounded across Kennington shortly after midday on 15 September 1940 as twenty-five Dornier Do 17 bombers with an escort of some thirty Messerschmitt Me 109 fighters approached from the south-east. The Luftwaffe had recently begun large-scale attacks on London as a prelude to invasion and daring daylight raids were its latest tactic to beat Britain into submission. While the date would be passed down to history as Battle of Britain Day, Oval was to witness a little-known skirmish amid the day's combat.

Engine problems in a Dornier piloted by 27-year-old Oberleutnant Robert Zehbe left it trailing half a mile behind the formation and it quickly attracted the determined attentions of RAF fighters. Sustained attacks tore into the bomber and killed two of its crew, while in the burning cockpit Zehbe ordered the remaining two to bail out, before setting the doomed aircraft to autopilot and bailing out himself.

The first two airmen were taken into captivity no sooner had they landed in the suburbs but the welcome awaiting Zehbe was markedly different. People had gathered in the street to watch the dogfight and tracked the injured pilot as he floated down towards Oval – faster than he would have hoped because his parachute was damaged, and between the cricket ground and Underground the chute snagged on telegraph cables, leaving him unceremoniously dangling just above ground.

Exactly what happened next is a matter of dispute. Locals had suffered a week of relentless bombing so the niceties of the Geneva Convention may not have been uppermost in their minds, and an eyewitness remarked how Zehbe was unlucky to land near a rest centre filled with the homeless survivors of East End bombing the previous weekend. Amid cries of 'Kill him!', a mob of mostly women, some armed with kitchen knives and pokers, pulled on the airman's legs – an image that does not sit well with indomitable 'Blitz spirit'. The account of another bystander – and one that newspapers chose to print, asserted that the women were simply fighting for the silk of his parachute.

While it was not unusual for enemy airmen to be roughed up somewhat, whether Zehbe suffered calculated cruelty is a question many would rather not investigate. He was rescued from the mob's clutches by the police, and a van whisked him away to the military hospital at Millbank.

Meanwhile, his Dornier flew on and a Hurricane pilot who found himself spent of ammunition sliced his wing tip through the bomber's tail fin, causing its fuselage to catastrophically break in two, its bombs to catapult into Buckingham Palace, and the aircraft to land on the forecourt of Victoria Station.

Robert Zehbe died of his injuries the following day.

GREAT TOWER STREET/
BYWARD STREET EC3

DOCTOR'S DISORDERS

John Wilmot, Earl of Rochester, was a man highly disposed to offences against sobriety, propriety and chastity – qualities that made him particularly popular among the court of Charles II; he even enjoyed a generous allowance for somewhat ill-defined 'services to the King'.

With limited capacity for knowing when to temper his drinking, whoring and mischief, Wilmot habitually found himself in a spot of bother and an early mishap arose when he forcibly abducted a 15-year-old courtier with the intention of marrying her, for which he instead endured trouble and strife at the Tower. He also courted controversy through satirical and scurrilous verse, although when Charles learned that Wilmot had penned a poem entitled Signior Dildo in which he mocked the ladies at court – many of whom had graced Charles' bedsheets – the King was cheerfully game for reading it. However, by accident, or reckless design, he instead handed Charles a ditty that viciously lampooned him; Wilmot was banished from court and his grants revoked.

Peace was restored, though only momentarily because a hopelessly inebriated Wilmot then chose to pick a fight with Charles' new sundial at Whitehall. No ordinary timepiece, it was an elaborate astronomical instrument replete with delicate glass spheres and etched panels bearing portraits of the Royal family – perhaps the most valuable object of its kind in Europe. By the time Wilmot had finished slashing at it with his sword, it was a sorry pile of shattered fragments;

Charles was livid and Wilmot wisely chose to spend some time in the countryside.

In 1676, Wilmot found himself in the last chance saloon following another long day of exuberance with the bottle; accompanied by his merry companions he had staggered off in search of a strumpet but instead managed to cause a misunderstanding at the house of a constable, and in the ensuing scuffle a friend was killed. But while Wilmot was again holed up somewhere, rumour had it, in France, word spread of an intriguing doctor recently arrived from Italy who had set up beside the Black Swan tavern on Tower Street (now Great Tower Street, at the junction with Byward Street).

Dr Alexander Bendo was a sight to behold; clad in the rich attire of his homeland, he flaunted an oversized green gown lined with exotic furs of many colours, an antique cap, and a showy jewel-encrusted medallion dangling from a gold chain around his neck – an ensemble set off by an implausibly thick beard. With limited command of English, the noble doctor expressed himself through an outlandish shtick of gesticulations and gibberish, though fortunately for someone so unfamiliar with the native tongue, his handbills were remarkably fluent, berating impostors who pretended to his trade and listing the multitude of maladies he could cure, from broken hearts to bad breath.

The Italian quack was, of course, none other than Wilmot and this was his inimitable way of laying low for a while; 'being under an unlucky accident which obliged him to keep out of the way, he disguised himself so that his nearest friends could not have known him.' But acquaintances may have recognised Wilmot trademarks because Bendo's particular field of interest was the female form: 'I assure you of great secrecy as well as care in diseases ... whether venereal or others as some peculiar to women, the green sickness, weaknesses, inflammations or obstructions ... I cure all suffocations in these parts producing fits of the mother,

convulsions, nocturnal inquietudes and other strange accidents not fit to be set down here.' Those not in on the joke could even view the laboratory in which his accomplices brewed up balms, tinctures, tablets and philtres; unbeknown to credulous spectators, their ingredients included soot, soap, brick dust and urine.

However, the therapy that especially favoured the gratification of Bendo's ambitions was administering to infertile women: 'I have the knowledge of a great secret to cure barrenness with great success – I have cured one woman that had been married twenty-one years, and two women that had been three times married.' It takes little imagination to surmise what the wily Wilmot was getting up to: 'The medicines I use cleanse and strengthen the womb and because I do not intend to deceive any person, upon discourse with them I will tell them whether I am likely to do them any good.' Those selected for treatment paid 'one-half of what is agreed when the party shall be with child, the other half when she is brought to bed [gives birth]'.

For those of the fairer sex with qualms about exposing themselves to the flamboyant doctor, Bendo had another trick up his fur-lined sleeve – he graciously offered the services of his wife, the dour and matronly Mrs Bendo. Following the reconfiguring of his disguise, Wilmot was invited into private bedchambers where he was at liberty to apply unctions and scrutinise women's bodies for prophetic birthmarks, moles or whatever else his wandering eye fancied.

But no sooner had his latest transgression been forgiven, Bendo bid *buongiorno* to Tower Street and Wilmot effected an impossibly swift passage from France to reappear at court and resume seizing the moral low ground. Such a libertine lifestyle could not continue indefinitely and the consequences of syphilis and alcoholism meant Wilmot failed to reach his thirty-fourth birthday.

SAVOY CHAPEL WC2

AT LIBERTY

The Liberty of the Savoy, a half mile strip of land between the Thames and Strand, was for many years a law unto itself. Granted manorial independence from the Crown in the fourteenth century, the area held great appeal to those wishing to evade prosecution, so became 'the chief nursery of evil people, rogues and masterless men' and 'a lodging for loiterers, vagabonds and strumpets'.

Even during the eighteenth century the chapel's minister considered himself immune from outside interference and Dr Wilkinson conducted a lively trade in no-questions-asked marriages, reaping 'a profusion of cash ... all was rat tat tat at the street-door'. It was a wonder he found time to answer it – within two years he had helped about 1,400 couples tie the knot; 'many came distressed out of the country, big with child ... some who could not be married anywhere else'. Many were underage.

But rapping on his door in 1755 were constables brandishing an arrest warrant and the portly, gout-ridden minister was compelled to effect a rapid escape over the rooftop, then hoof it along the muddy riverbank. From exile in Kent, he continued to feather his nest by engaging the services of another clergyman but the honeymoon was over; both were sentenced to fourteen years' transportation and died en route to America. However, feathers were truly ruffled in an earlier incident.

In 1696 when tailor Roger Roberts wished to recover an outstanding £4 5s from William Hughes, who resided near Savoy Chapel, he plucked up courage to venture into the liberty and ask the proprietor of a tavern on Somerset House Yard, Sarah Morgan, to send for him. 'Hughes came in a

riotous manner with a mob, which Roberts perceiving would
have made his escape from them; but the said Sarah Morgan
stopped him and he was knocked down and much wounded,
and a cane, tobacco-box and a pair of buckskin gloves taken.'

Roberts now had second thoughts and desperately offered
a full discharge of the debt, along with 5s for the mob in
return for his freedom, but the gesture was thought insufficient. Following some consultation amongst the Savoyards,
they 'stripped him stark naked and besmeared him all over
with tar, and strewed feathers upon him' (with one newspaper here adding the telling comment: 'according to usual
custom) then 'tied a rope about his middle and led him about
the Savoy where they pleased'. Next, the feathered creditor
was unceremoniously dumped in a wheelbarrow and 'they
led him all along the Strand crying out A Bailiff! A Bailiff!
and in that condition tied him to the maypole where they
made him kneel down upon his knees and curse his father
and mother'. Roberts was saved further abuse by the timely
arrival of some constables, on sight of which the fugitives
promptly scarpered back to safety.

HIGHGATE CEMETERY (WEST) N6

POETIC LICENSE

'The book in question is bound in rough grey calf and has I am almost sure red edges to the leaves,' was how Dante Gabriel Rossetti described the volume of poetry that he urged a friend to obtain for him – not from a bookshop or library, but the coffin of his long-dead wife.

Elizabeth Siddal was both muse and model for Rossetti, and her pale, angular face framed by luxuriant copper hair gazes pensively from many of his drawings and paintings. Following a turbulent relationship, the couple married in 1860, but the stillborn birth of their daughter drove Siddal into depression and Rossetti returned home one evening to find her dying from a laudanum overdose; pinned to her nightgown was a suicide note, which he promptly burned because suicide was illegal and would deny a Christian burial – as well as heap shame on the family name.

Rossetti refused to acknowledge that Siddal was dead so kept her corpse at their house until, six days later, indications convinced him otherwise; then in a tender gesture before her coffin was sealed, he placed a notebook of his poems next to her cheek and covered by her hair, deeming that they were for her and her alone. She was then consigned to his family plot at Highgate, and Rossetti renounced poetry.

But seven years later, he thought otherwise. Ruing the fact that he had neglected to make a copy of his compositions, Rossetti discussed the idea of recovering the notebook with his flamboyant and somewhat unscrupulous agent, Charles Augustus Howell. Regrettably, however, exhumation required consent from the grave owner, Rossetti's

mother, whose husband and other family members lay in
the plot, and she would scarcely sanction such a sacrilegious
act. Rossetti also required authorisation from the Home
Secretary but on this count he had some luck. He happened
to be acquainted with Henry Austin Bruce through the commission of a painting for Llandaff Cathedral in the MP's
constituency; Bruce saw no need to trouble Mrs Rossetti
and, following payment of the fee, permission was granted.

Needless to say, Rossetti was anxious that the utmost
secrecy surrounded his grave-robbing, so it was the dead of
night on 5 October 1869 when its undertakers mustered at
Siddal's graveside. Alongside Howell there was a solicitor
to foil any foul play, a doctor to prevent infection, and two
gravediggers drafted in for the spadework. To add to the
ghoulishness of the scene, the exhumation took place by the
light of a bonfire – though this did offer the benefit of purging the gases of putrefaction and keeping observers warm.
As for Rossetti, he had no intention of dirtying his hands so
waited at Howell's house, reassuring himself that his wife
would have wished him to retrieve the poetry, but also fret-
ting that they might unearth the wrong body; his aunt had
been interred at Highgate sometime after Siddal, and he was
unsure exactly where.

Once the heavy headstone and slab were removed and
the earth dug away to reveal the coffin, its lid was prised
open. Howell reported (at least, to Rossetti), that its contents
were 'quite perfect' and he was undoubtedly the source of
rumours that Siddal's hair had grown to fill the space – a
suitably Pre-Raphaelite image. His depiction was what
might be politely called romanticised, but it was a consid-
erate one to plant in Rossetti's increasingly perturbed mind
because, in truth, the decayed coffin was waterlogged with
the fetid liquid of decomposition and when Howell retrieved
the book, taking care to extract the poems but not the Bible
that Siddal also enjoyed as post-mortem reading matter, it

emerged soaked-through and bearing the heavy scent of rotting. The poetry was promptly confiscated by the doctor, who dunked it in disinfectant before the long process of drying it leaf by leaf could begin.

A week later, in a letter to his brother Rossetti owned up to his subterranean adventures and expressed concern that Howell might not hold his tongue, though in a poor choice of words for a poet, he conceded that the truth would likely 'ooze out'. (In contrast, his other correspondence of the time describe the comic antics of his latest companion – a pet wombat.) The following week he took possession of the dried notebook and although much of the text was still legible after seven years in a saturated coffin, it quickly dawned on Rossetti that he could not simply hand it to someone to transcribe – he would have to handle it himself and was disappointed to discover that it smelt 'dreadful'. Furthermore, the poem he was most keen to recover, Jenny, the lengthy musings of a young man over a prostitute, had also been of interest to an earthworm, which had munched a hole through each page of it. Reconciling his wife's perfectly preserved remains with the presence of a hungry worm in a sodden coffin cannot have been trouble-free.

Rossetti's mother went to her grave in the plot oblivious to the desecration, while her son made it abundantly clear that he was not to be buried at Highgate.

LINCOLN'S INN FIELDS WC2

KETCH UP

Any open space in London lent itself to hosting public executions so on 21 July 1683, a scaffold was erected in the centre of Lincoln's Inn Fields to allow crowds an unobstructed view of Lord Russell's beheading. On scant evidence, the politician had been found guilty of conspiring to assassinate Charles II and his brother James.

Russell approached his death stoically, remarking that he 'did not consider it with so much apprehension as the drawing of a tooth', but even accounting for the standards of seventeenth-century dentistry his optimism was misplaced, because the man tasked with his execution was Jack Ketch – the notoriously inept hangman who had never yet undertaken a live beheading.

Russell divested himself of his waistcoat, cravat and periwig, then pulled on his nightcap – an essential garment for 'the big sleep' – and handed Ketch a bag of coins in the hope he might perform his task efficiently. He need not have bothered; an eyewitness reported 'three blows, besides sawing with ye ax', and even seasoned onlookers were appalled by the spectacle.

In fact, such was the outrage, Ketch felt compelled to pen a public apology, and if he did indeed write it himself, it discloses that the reviled butcher might have enjoyed an alternative career as a thoughtful man of letters. 'It is an old saying and a true one,' he began, 'that one story's good till another's heard, but it is one of the most difficult things imaginable to dispossess the world of any censure or prejudice that is once fixed or hath taken root in the hearts of the people.' But though he wielded the pen better than the axe,

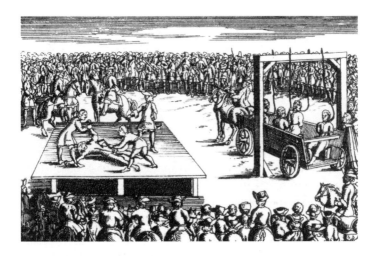

Ketch was obliged to address the less poetic matter of his 'bungling and supine negligence', so swiftly refuted allegations that after drinking all night he had been sotted on the scaffold: 'neighbours can testify I went orderly to bed and wholly undisguised in drink'. He then chose to disabuse his critics of a suspiciously vivid detail, stating that when his first blow came to rest in Russell's shoulder, His Lordship did not turn and snarl: 'You dog! Did I give you ten guineas to use me so inhumanly?'

Ketch placed blame for his wholly unsatisfactory decapitative work squarely with someone who was now unable to dispossess the world of censure; it was Russell who would not be persuaded to pull the nightcap over his eyes, give a signal, or 'dispose him[self] for receiving of the fatal stroke in such a posture as was most suitable'. Nevertheless, some obesrvers credited Ketch with nuanced dexterity to exact such brutal butchery under the guise of hapless incompetence.

When Ketch was poised to behead the Duke of Monmouth on Tower Hill two years later, his victim begged: 'Do not hack me as you did Lord Russell,' though such pleas proved entirely in vain.

HOLLAND STREET/HOPTON STREET SE1

MATE IN CAPTIVITY

As with many of London's street names, Holland Street recalls a renowned figure from the city's past, but instead of a monarch, aristocrat or politician, the public servant it celebrates is the madam of a whorehouse established on the site sometime around 1600 – Mrs Elizabeth Holland.

A respectable background and astute marriage did not discourage Elizabeth from taking up professional life as a high-class lady of negotiable affections, and a yearning for greater job satisfaction and remuneration soon led her to establish her own brothel. In accordance with the customary pretence that foreign bawds were more accomplished than their native counterparts, she adopted the *nom de guerre* Donna Britannica Hollandia but suffered an immediate skirmish with the forces of law and order because she set up shop in the City of London. Prostitution was overlooked in the City if it operated out of the public eye and appropriate bribes were doled out, but should it became an embarrassment through popular or religious outrage, the authorities were compelled to submit to the burdensome obligation of prosecutions; Holland found herself in Newgate and was only released through the good offices of her rich and influential clients. She thus began to contemplate a more amenable situation in which to continue her vocation and it came to her notice that the old manor of Paris Garden was available – and could not have been more suited to her purposes.

Paris (a leisurely spelling of Parish) Garden was an ancient liberty over which the City fathers held no sway and law enforcement was instead somewhat ill-defined by a local marshall – someone who might thoroughly abuse their power, moralise fanatically, be wholeheartedly corruptible, or a combination of all three. The seedy purlieus of Bankside already bustled with licentious entertainments such as alehouses, gaming dens and stews (which Holland noted with satisfaction posed no threat to her section of the market), while theatres and animal baiting attracted the wealthy elite. As for the manor house, it was a veritable fortress: the building benefitted from its own moat so that the front door, complete with portcullis, was reached across a drawbridge.

Holland fitted up her whorehouse in a manner that equalled if not exceeded the Royal palace immediately upstream; rooms were sumptuously appointed, and both beds and personnel were clad with fresh linen courtesy of an

on-site laundry – unusual for an age when washing was not commonplace. She also catered to more than mere sexual cravings; the bill of fare included fine food (and stewed prunes were though a suitably fortifying dish), choice wines from the cellar, a gambling salon and plumbed privies which kept rooms sweet smelling by emptying directly into the moat – an appropriate destination for cantankerous customers. To uphold her house's reputation a doctor regularly cast a forensic eye over the workforce and unceremoniously ejected those indisposed by infections, while its safety was preserved by a burly doorman who raised the portcullis only on presentation of suitable demeanour and sufficient wherewithal. Troublemakers became acquainted with the in-house prison cell and whipping post (as could clients, if so disposed), and the brothel even contained a chapel should fornicators wish to repent.

As to the carnal main course, immigrant labour ensured that Holland's hand-picked whores were proficient in a wide repertoire of customs, languages and skills, and should trading became uncommonly brisk, domestic staff were pressed into alternative service. Each and every working girl was well versed in the art of convincing the most unappealing specimen that he was the most charming and well-endowed she had the good fortune to come across, and masterful at encouraging him to enjoy the full menu of services until nothing more could be squeezed. A cash-only establishment, this was a brothel for those with the deepest pockets – perhaps including King James I himself.

But James's death in 1625 spelled the end for Holland's reign; Charles I set about mopping up the widespread vice left by his father, not least the bawdy houses. The court and aristocracy were compelled to temper their whoring and without the King's endorsement, the calibre of Holland's clientele nose-dived. The end seemed nigh in 1631 when soldiers were dispatched to storm the house and arrest its occupants, although the platoon was pleasantly surprised to see the drawbridge lowered for their benefit – though less so when thanks to a special mechanism it collapsed, consigning them to the stinking moat. Undeterred, the men brushed themselves down and launched another offensive, this time assisted by crack reinforcements, but the besieged sisters-in-arms gave battle with missiles originating from used chamber pots – much to the delight of spectators. Not wishing further embarrassment, the troops limped home.

But Holland knew her time was up. Her beleaguered brothel became known to posterity as 'Holland's Leaguer' and she managed to vanish without trace, and presumably without punishment, until the 1790s when her name was unwittingly immortalised in the street name. Ironically, twentieth-century municipal meddling left Mrs Holland's street rudely deprived of half of its domain, so her brothel stood just beyond Holland Street on today's Hopton Street.

EARL HAIG MEMORIAL, WHITEHALL SW1

LEAKING INFORMATION

The manner in which to commemorate the Commander in Chief of British forces in France during the First World War, Field Marshall Earl Haig (and by extension, the war itself with its unprecedented human slaughter), proved perilous.

Although Haig found limited opportunity for gallant cavalry charges during the conflict, a knightly figure on horseback was thought appropriate and Parliament passed responsibility for its details to a civil servant, Sir Lionel Earle. He in turn opted for a competition adjudicated by a trio of specialists from eminent artistic institutions – though when he discovered their identity he hastily added two more of his own choosing. Unfortunately, this left judges outnumbering entrants because leading sculptors refused to either lower themselves to a contest or compete against anyone who was not a member of the Royal Academy. The predicament intensified when George V expressed misgivings over a monument to Haig so close to the Cenotaph, and Westminster Council voiced concerns about obstructing vehicles (though on this point Earle deftly highlighted the benefits of traffic calming and a mounted policeman was posted in the middle of the road for a dummy run).

Three little-known sculptors submitted entries and Alfred Hardiman was declared winner; however, his design did not please the *Daily Mail*, which immediately started a campaign against it, supported by Lady Haig. While one bone of contention was the absence of headwear (to observe military etiquette rather than afford the Field Marshall's face protection from the unwelcome attentions of pigeons), most objectionable was his steed, whose stylised form was thought to jar with its realistic rider. Hardiman was instructed to try again and his second offering, in its effort to appease his many critics, united them in reluctant preference for the first.

Hardiman waged one last battle with Haig in a third attempt, though his confidence cannot have been boosted when renowned equestrian sculptor Georges Malissard delicately offered his assistance on the quiet. After seven years' toil, his necessarily final rendition was unveiled on 10 November 1937 – just in time for the build-up to another world war. Lady Haig was said to be too ill to attend the ceremony, but she had already notified the press that nothing would drag her to Whitehall to dignify the 'monstrous' memorial with her presence, and articulated her sincerest wishes that the work was irreplaceably damaged in transit.

She was not alone in her sentiments: amid a chorus of derision there were headlines about a circus horse, comments from cavalrymen that Haig would not twist a German's neck in such a way let alone his charger's, and the knife was cruelly twisted by the suggestion that Jacob Epstein could have done better. And anyone with close experience of horses will recognise that its posture signals the passage of urine.

BARKING UP THE
WRONG TREE

The illness that was to blight King George III for more than thirty years made its first appearance at Kew in 1788: the Royal family was spending summer at the White House (whose outline is marked by a sundial opposite Kew Palace) when George suffered violent stomach spasms. Their cause was put down to the unusually dry weather so the King's physician prescribed castor oil and senna to bring about robust evacuation of the Royal bowels – a course of treatment that failed to avert another attack, this time because George wore wet stockings and consumed four large pears for supper.

The family headed to Windsor for the winter but the King's symptoms worsened, accompanied by quickness of speech, darkened urine and, most worrisomely, bouts of mental disturbance. With a rumour circulating that the King discussed matters of continental politics with a tree in the belief it was the King of Prussia, anxious physicians, Parliament and the Prince of Wales concluded that he would benefit from quiet seclusion at the White House – while his profligate heir also voiced how privacy would facilitate more forceful treatment.

But a change of scenery was not to everyone's taste and when advised he was moving to Kew, a home not suited to winter, George obstinately refused to leave his bed. Trickery failed to entice him out and nothing but the threat of force persuaded him to make the journey, only to find himself separated from his family and imprisoned in a ground-floor room.

The King now refused to go to bed, calculating that if left alone he might have an opportunity for escape, a strategy that was thwarted by a vicious fight with his pages at 4 o'clock in the morning. Cutlery and razors were confiscated and the patient tightly strapped to his bed at night.

The greatest medical minds were applied to the King's condition and a treatment plan formulated. To draw morbid humours from his head, George's legs were blistered – the skin burned with powerful irritant then pierced to drain off serum (and, after they became infected, prolific quantities of pus); he was doused in cold baths, cupped with burning hot glass bowls on his back, his temples catered to hungry leeches and he was dosed with opium to calm him, antimony to provoke vomiting, as well as calomel, camphor, digitalis, musk, quinine and unremitting purgatives. Bewildered doctors noted how George's incessant chatter was now liberally peppered with choice obscenities, which only abated when foam spewed from his mouth.

His language did not improve with the arrival of Rev. Francis Willis – a 70-year-old clergyman who had enjoyed modest success with patients at his mad-house in Lincolnshire and now presumed sole charge of the King's therapy. Willis found his patient enjoying a moment of lucidity because George sternly rebuked him for abandoning his sacred calling, a profession he loved, for medicine, one he utterly detested. 'Jesus cured the sick,' retorted Willis; 'Yes', snapped the King, 'but He did not get seven hundred a-year for it.' From that inauspicious introduction, George quickly formed a violent loathing for his new keeper and instead directed his affections (and, to the great discomfort of all, wanton sexual urges) towards several ladies of the court.

Aided by his sons and 'physical assistants' from his asylum, Willis treated the King as if he were a disobedient child and the slightest infraction called for the straight-jacket. If this proved insufficient, a handkerchief was stuffed in George's mouth and he was strapped into a specially adapted chair, which had been fixed to the floor so he was unable to tip it over; with dark humour George dubbed it his 'Coronation chair'. However, despite the bullying and intimidation, the King showed signs of recovery; his legs healed sufficiently for him to chase one of the Queen's ladies-in-waiting around the gardens and kiss her, and in February 1789, the Prince of Wales was dismayed to learn that his father had been declared fully recovered.

However, in 1801 he suffered a relapse. Rev. Willis had retired but his sons gladly stepped into his shoes and ambushed the King in his library at Kew; when George tried to escape they took him hostage in the now empty and derelict White House. Fortunately, within a few months the symptoms eased and generous remuneration stimulated the brothers' departure.

But following another recurrence in 1804 they effected a hasty return, only to find their access blocked by two of the King's sons; George had evidently planned ahead and even demolished the despised White House, choosing instead to build himself a forbidding Bastille-like castle overlooking Brentford. Nevertheless, the King's new physician still saw fit to restrain him in a straight-jacket day and night at Kew Palace. George now enjoyed no respite from his condition and a particular low point was noted when he suggested creating honours for women; the King departed Kew for the last time in 1806 to spend his final years at Windsor.

89 PALL MALL SW1

BONE IDOL

Another location in which those with an appetite for the weird and wonderful could sate their hunger pangs was Pall Mall. In 1824, crowds flocked to the Grand Saloon at No. 94 (now site of the Royal Automobile Club) to gawp at Napoleon's horse Marengo, captured alive at Waterloo and bearing the Imperial crown and letter N branded on its hind quarters, and scars of battle including (according to its hand-bill) a bullet lodged in its tail. Boney's steed – if indeed it ever was – is still on display (albeit in bony form) at the National Army Museum in Chelsea.

Having cleared up behind Marengo, the curious could then inspect Gallic bones in the form of an emaci-ated Frenchman. Bearing the attractive title 'The Living Skeleton', Claude Ambroise Seurat offered a spectacle that one visitor considered 'one of the most impudent and dis-gusting attempts to make a profit of the public appetite for novelty', which doubtless inspired countless others to turn up and decide for themselves. But although business in a shrivelled foreigner was brisk, nagging discomfort about cap-italising on human suffering was perhaps why the exhibition also went under the billing L'Anatomie Vivante, thus lending it an air of scientific respectability and warranting the exor-bitant half a crown admission.

According to carefully phrased letters published under Seurat's name, he was no hapless dupe but leading a blissful existence and he gushed how 'my present situation is more happy than I ever yet enjoyed during my whole life, and is entirely conformable to my desires'. That being so, his wishes encompassed standing naked but for a skimpy purple apron with openings to admit his hip bones, while submitting to clammy hands grabbing and poking at his pinched, parchment-like skin. For the better scrutiny of his leathery skull, his hair was shaved off, allowing viewers to inspect the cranial flatness that betrayed his intellectual shortcomings – though when he became especially cold he was permitted to don a wig.

Seurat was not predisposed to lively performance; there was no dancing, and his condition, the result of a skeletal abnormality, restricted his breathing, leaving him able to sing only 'in a faint tone of voice'. However, to his credit, he took only one day off sick after 'an odd fancy he took to breakfast on stewed eels' left him much indisposed (and further underweight).

With regard to Seurat's transition from a living skeleton to a dead one, the body of information is thin. One source asserts that he sold his late self to the Royal College of Surgeons and was deposited in its museum; another equally dubious account claims that he died in France, where a post-mortem opened his wasted frame to discover a 5m tapeworm.

STRAND/ALDWYCH TUBE
STATION (DISUSED) WC2

SKIRT THE ISSUE

On 28 April 1870, crowds thronged the Strand Theatre (which stood on the site until 1905) for its latest burlesque 'St George and the Dragon'. The venue was renowned for its raucous and risqué productions which, thought one critic 'would fall dead at the first night but for the services of a horde of jigging hussies … liberal in the display of their pectoral and femoral muscles and in the suggestion of their glutei maximi.'

Theatregoers that night included Messrs Mundell and Thomas who were sharing a private box with the glamorous acquaintances they had the pleasure of chaperoning, Misses Stella Boulton and Fanny Graham. The ladies, both in their early twenties, were dressed to the nines and revelling in the flat-tering attentions of ogling men, many of whose gaze carefully followed Fanny as she promenaded to the ladies' retiring room and had an attendant fasten some loose stitching in her skirt.

However, three in particular were intently absorbed in mentally undressing them, and at the end of the evening as the party was about to leave, one of them pounced. Bursting into their carriage he announced that he was a police con-stable and would be escorting them to Bow Street station. In a flash, Thomas leaped for the door and made good his escape down the Strand, but the others were discouraged from doing the same by the appearance of more police, and in the case of the womenfolk, the unsuitability of their attire.

A bewildered Fanny and Stella were taken into custody and although Mundell was free to leave, his gentlemanly instincts compelled him to stay with his distressed lady-friends. The prisoners were then ordered to disencumber themselves of clothing and to Mundell's dismay it became perfectly apparent that both were men.

But the spectacle of male genitalia came as no surprise to police, who for some time had been casting a suspicious eye over Ernest Boulton and Frederick Park.

Their appearance in a teeming courtroom the following morning did not radiate the dignified, ladylike demeanour both would have wished – what with a night in the cells and thoroughly inadequate toilette, and a gasp arose when the dishevelled duo were charged with 'that horrible crime not to be named among Christians', inducing others to do the same, and outraging public decency by disguising themselves as women. While evidence for the last offence was plain to see, securing proof of sodomy would prove more troublesome.

Focus turned to Bloomsbury, and specifically, No. 13 Wakefield Street (now long demolished) where the pair kept lodgings courtesy of a landlady who specialised in letting rooms to respectable men with a penchant for cross-dressing and its associated pursuits. What confronted constables there was all the trappings of a lady's boudoir, and officers set about drawing up a meticulous inventory of the paraphernalia they came upon: 'Dresses – mauve satin trimmed with blond lace, white corded rep silk trimmed with white lace, pink satin and tulle, white glacé trimmed with blue satin … also a number of skirts and petticoats in tulle, tarlatan, white frilled cambric …' and so it went on. There were bonnets, boots, bodices, stockings, stays, garters and drawers, along with cosmetics, jewellery, wigs, curling tongs, a bottle of chloroform, artificial flowers and 'a great quantity of wadding, apparently used for padding'. Incriminating evidence would have to be sought in other locations.

To that end, Fanny and Stella became the subject of a more rigorous medical examination. Police surgeon Dr Paul considered himself an authority on anuses and after poking his nose into the subject, solemnly declared that what the suspects presented were two strikingly loose examples of that orifice. Further proctological points of view were sought and three other doctors found nothing untoward between the pair's buttocks, so in an effort to reach a consensus, six eminent physicians were appointed to get to the bottom of the matter. But even before they met, The Lancet expressed reservations about English doctors and whether they had enough experience of this 'very repulsive subject', suggesting men from Paris, Spain or Constantinople considerably more qualified. However, in a poky consulting room at Newgate with barely enough room to bend over, the specialists unpacked their instruments and set about investigations, though after much probing and jabbing of the tenderest recesses, theirs was the only proven instance of anal penetration.

On 9 May 1871, one year after that fateful night at the theatre, Fanny and Stella stood before the highest court in the land, where to the dismay of those in the public gallery, both sported sober suits, Stella had grown a thin moustache, and Fanny flaunted whiskers. Cross-examination steered clear of the pair's posteriors because the sodomy charge had been prudently withdrawn – a decision perhaps motivated by evidence that intimately connected the defendants with an aristocrat and former MP. However the indictment of conspiring to incite others remained, so for six days the public lapped up the particulars of Fanny and Stella's colourful lifestyle with equal measures of delight and disgust. Much of the second day comprised an exhibition of their couture so that a dressmaker summoned as expert witness could cast a critical eye over it. In their defence, the pair declared that they simply shared a singular passion for amateur dramatics, and both were acquitted, at which Stella, with impeccable timing, fainted.

THE HIGHWAY/ARTICHOKE HILL E1

PILLORY TO POST

Of the myriad royal memorials, plaques and statues that litter London, one monarch is notably under-represented. This particular king has not been afforded the honour of presiding over Trafalgar Square or standing guard at Westminster, neither is he immortalised in a street name – or even a pub, park or playing field. Edward VIII is commemorated solely by no more than twenty pillar boxes across the capital, and they are almost universally overlooked. But such a situation is not without reason.

To the establishment, King Edward VIII was not sufficiently 'Kingly'; the Government was horrified by his interference in its domain, and the Church and Windsor dynasty were appalled by his playboy lifestyle and insistence on marrying the thoroughly unsuitable Mrs Simpson. Not only was she American, she was already twice married and seemed to hold some kind of dominating – to some, even sadomasochistic – power over the King. What with suspicions that Edward harboured Nazi sympathies and was vulnerable to blackmail, the Prime Minister took the unprecedented step of asking security services to tap the King's telephone and intercept his telegrams – an extraordinary and supremely secretive surveillance operation, ably facilitated by the General Post Office.

Although the constitutional crisis went to the brink with plans put in place for the King to marry Simpson in a secular wedding at Banqueting House, Edward abdicated, ostensibly of his own accord, after $325\frac{1}{2}$ days on the throne and his brother, Bertie, became George VI.

During Edward's brief reign, 271 post boxes bearing his royal cypher were erected across the country (though for reasons never fully explained, prior to the approval of its design, a number were also installed with the initials of Edward VII). It was not standard protocol to purge former monarchs'

monograms, but following Edward's abdication the nation found itself in far from ordinary circumstances and the Post Office set about unobtrusively replacing them with that of the new King. Justification may have been found from the fact that Edward's cypher bears the crown and he never quite made it as far as his Coronation – though other reasons probably held greater sway. Edward was excised from almost every rectangular post box and costs were obtained for replacing the rounded doors of all 161 pillar boxes, but in the end, it is likely that penny-pinching saved Edward from complete national obliteration.

The playboy prince may have wished for a statue of himself, particularly if it showed his fashionable parting, but a handful of disregarded pillar boxes look likely to remain his only public monument. The example on the busy dual-carriageway in Wapping is the closest that Edward comes to central London – a situation elegantly summed up by a comment attributed to Simpson: 'You can't abdicate and eat it.'

TRAFALGAR SQUARE WC2

MISERY, GUTS

When the outcome of the Battle of Trafalgar inspired a triumphalist makeover of the road junction, it erased not only its former name, Charing Cross, but also its long association with public executions. One such occasion was the demise of Thomas Harrison on 13 October 1660.

Harrison had signed the death warrant of Charles I and this earned him no favours with his victim's heir. Newly restored King Charles II sought both retribution and a vivid tableau for any potential republicans to behold. A platform and gibbet were erected where the equestrian statue of Charles I stands – originally the site of the ancient stone cross that gave the area its name, and whose railings now provided a convenient means of crowd control.

Harrison put on a brave face but when he was seen trembling at the foot of the ladder the mob cruelly taunted him and continued to do so after he attempted to explain away his shaking as the result of war wounds. After the noose had been placed around his neck and his face positioned towards the site of Charles I's beheading on Whitehall, Harrison forgave his executioner and spoke of his deep faith that God would make his end an easy one.

In this he was entirely mistaken – his sentence specified a cruel, lingering death and the hangman was obliged to accomplish it. Harrison was hanged with a short drop to deny him the benefit of a fractured neck and resultant unconsciousness, and when his frantic thrashing about subsided, he was cut down and revived. He was then stripped naked so that the hangman could slice off his genitalia – a customary element of traitors' executions, though one not always mentioned – and the articles were dangled in front of their former owner's eyes before being tossed in a bucket; they later provided nourishment for stray dogs. The executioner then carved open his victim's chest and began pulling out organs and yards of intestines to throw on a burning brazier but, as he did so, eyewitnesses reported how Harrison rose up and punched him in the face. Further resistance was impeded by the swift removal of his head, which along with his heart was held aloft, prompting 'great shouts of joy'. The head was then carefully set aside, the heart cast into the flames, and the rest of the body quartered to provide ornamentation for the City gates.

A few days later, two more traitors, John Cook and Hugh Peters, were dragged on sledges to their execution at Charing

Cross and, in an extra touch of detail, Harrison's head accompanied Cook on his journey 'with the face uncovered and directed towards him'. Neither was Peters denied special treatment and he was invited to stand beside Cook's corpse while it was emasculated and disembowelled: 'The hangman came to him all besmeared in blood and rubbing his bloody hands together, tauntingly asked him, "Come, how do you like this – how do you like this work?"'

The lingering stench of burned bowels was not something welcomed by residents of Charing Cross and they successfully petitioned the King to relocate traitor's executions to Tyburn; however, this did not signal the end of entertainments on their doorstep because also erected at Charing Cross was a pillory, one of whose victims was Japhet Crook.

Crook was a master forger who, perhaps aware that his infelicitous surname might expose his line of business, adopted the pseudonym Sir Peter Stranger, his baronetcy as fictitious as the documents he created. Following a lengthy criminal career, Crook was caught attempting to mortgage a valuable estate in Essex for which he had fashioned his own title deeds, but was doubtless aware that the punish-

ment for forgery was comparatively lenient. While theft of a handkerchief might warrant hanging, on 10 June 1731 the 69-year-old was brought to Charing Cross and clamped in the pillory for an hour in front of an unusually good-humoured crowd.

However, that was not the sum total of his sentence because Crook was then chained into a chair and 'the hangman, dressed like a butcher came to him and with a knife made like a gardener's pruning knife, cut off his ears'. He held the lobes aloft for the benefit of eager spectators then 'with a pair of scissors slit both his nostrils; all which Crook bore with great patience, but at the searing (with a hot iron) of his right nostril the pain was so violent that he got up from his chair; his left nostril was not seared so he went from the pillory bleeding'. A surgeon was on hand to clap bandages around his wounds and Crook's defiant show of courage – even making light of the protracted ordeal – earned him a trip to the nearby Ship Tavern, where he languished for the rest of the afternoon before he was carted off to begin what turned out to be a relatively short life sentence. Crook's performance stimulated Parliament to resolve that forgery was a capital crime and six days later another forger was hanged at Tyburn.

THE SAVOY HOTEL WC2

WILDE OATS

The Savoy proudly lists Oscar Wilde among its many distinguished guests, but is less voluble about the Irishman's exploits in rooms on the third floor.

Wilde's appreciation for aesthetic beauty extended to the

person of Lord Alfred Douglas (better known as 'Bosie') and in March 1893 the pair took a suite of rooms at the hotel for a hedonistic month of gourmet food, fine wine and unrefined young men. Bosie's father, the Marquess of Queensbury, was distinctly nonplussed by his son's choice of company and hotel staff were among those from whom he gathered evidence to bring a charge of gross indecency against Wilde. He even claimed that the lovers were kicked out for their conduct, although the management, who were doubtless fond of the hotel's reputation, remained tight lipped on the subject. However, the three subsequent trials allowed Queensbury a line of questioning that graphically hung out the playwright's dirty laundry. 'I do not examine bed-linen,' Wilde declared imperiously on the topic; 'I am not a housemaid.'

Wilde's supposition regarding the observational habits of housekeeping staff was entirely correct because a chambermaid testified that after clapping eyes on his sheets she promptly resigned her employment in disgust – despite a half sovereign tip from the room's occupant. (The hotel's prepubescent pageboys kissed by Wilde were given 2s 6d for their trouble, although Herbert, his favourite, pocketed half a crown.) Pressed for particulars she hesitated, but when prevailed upon, described stains of a brown colour. Wilde's counsel proffered an entirely innocent explanation and gently familiarised the jury with his client's bouts of diarrhoea, but it failed to avert further filth from dribbling out. The Savoy's masseur had spotted a young man, about 16 to 18 years old, recumbent in Wilde's bed, as did another maid who spied 'a common boy, rough looking' among the bedclothes; she also objected to changing the linen because of 'indications on the sheets that conduct of the grossest kind had been indulged in'. (A contemporary account of the trials helpfully explained to the less au fait how 'the sodomistic act has much the same effect as an enema inserted up the rectum. There is an almost immediate discharge, though not, of course, to the [same] extent'). However, the maid was sufficiently attentive to distinguish faeces, Vaseline and semen, and note how Wilde's nightshirt exhibited similarly unsavoury soiling.

Sex between men, let alone of different ages and classes was, as the judge thundered, something 'one shudders to contemplate in a first-class hotel' and what with testimonies from a succession of rent boys, no heights of wit or eloquence could save Wilde from conviction and two years' hard labour.

Wilde later acknowledged that he was not an innocent man but also divulged that Savoy staff had been describing not his room but that of Bosie, who, just like his legal adversaries, he did everything to protect.

CIRCUS PLACE, LONDON WALL EC2

UNSTATELY HOME

In 1676, Bethlem Hospital went from the ridiculous to the sublime.

The asylum's dilapidated site at Bishopsgate was condemned as both inadequate and insanitary, while new premises on London Wall appeared to take inspiration from the Louvre or Tuileries palaces in Paris. Flaunting more than 500ft of elegant facade, Bethlem was now perhaps the most grand edifice in London, an inconsistency that prompted one writer to voice a not uncommon sentiment: 'It was a pity so fine a building should not be possessed by such who had a sense of their happiness,' adding: 'They were mad that built so costly a college for such a crack-brained society.'

But for all its palatial exterior, what took place inside was considerably less dignified. The purpose-built hospital quickly proved wholly unsuited to its purpose; its 140 lunatic tenants were banished from the front lest they spoil its orderly appearance, and in keeping with medical advice that mental disturbance was exacerbated by heat, cells were unglazed and unheated, with occupants typically naked but for a chain connecting them to the floor. Little attempt was made at segregation beyond separating the sexes and congregating violent cases on the upper floors, and whatever the diagnosis (were indeed one made), standard treatment for all comprised routine bleeding, emetics to induce vomiting and purgatives to void the bowels. Those who were unable or unwilling to shit in a pot languished in a 'dirty room', though when this facility proved inadequate, the basement was fitted out with cells to accommodate the soiled and uncooperative. The idea of patient consent was unheard of and those who refused medication had it concealed in their food.

Visitors were warmly welcomed and the hospital governors highlighted how the instructive and moralistic display of lunatics stimulated donations and endowments, along with hundreds of pounds reaped from the admission fee.

It also generated eyewitness accounts and many mention the expectation of entertainment, and how if necessary, audiences were at liberty to use provocation to elicit some. As one observer lugubriously recorded:

> The distempered fancies of the miserable patients most unaccountably provoked mirth and loud laughter in the unthinking auditors; and the many hideous roarings and wild motions of others seemed equally entertaining to them. Nay, so shamefully inhuman were some, among whom (I am sorry to say it!) were several of my own sex, as to endeavour to provoke the patients into rage, to make them sport.

Prisoners' wild and unruly behaviour – and in particular their uninhibited wantonness – was regarded as licence for visitors to behave in precisely the same manner and Bethlem rapidly gained a reputation as a Mecca for lecherous voyeurism and sexual encounters: ''Tis an alms-house for madmen, a showing room for whores, a sure market for lechers, a dry walk for loiterers.' While there is no record of visitors extracting the full value of admission through sexual relations with inmates, during the 1680s, two staff were discharged for freely creating pregnancies among patients. Carnal liaisons were otherwise solely between sightseers: 'We observed an abundance of intriguing; mistresses we found were to be had of all ranks, qualities, colours, prices and sizes ... for there wanted not a suitable Jack to every Jill.'

The calamitous consequences of embracing spectators was plain to see and after 1770 public access to Bethlem was curtailed – but concealing madness behind locked doors also had its disadvantages.

American seaman James Norris (pictured on page 22) was admitted to Bethlem with violent tendencies in 1800 and because he suspected that his food was being doctored with poison, he made his dissatisfaction known by extracting himself from his shackles and forcefully employing them against his keepers. Doctors had limited techniques at their disposal for dealing with such behaviour, so a piece of apparatus was constructed exclusively for Norris's therapy. It consisted of a stout iron hoop riveted around his neck and attached by a 12in chain to an iron bar mounted horizontally on the wall, allowing him the freedom to stand up and sit down, while another hoop was riveted around his waist to pinion his arms tightly to his sides. Supplementary treatment came in the form of a chain connecting one leg to the floor.

Norris was confined in this ironmongery day and night for a decade until Quaker philanthropist Edward Wakefield 'discovered' him in 1814. Wakefield noted that Norris 'read a great deal of books of all kinds, history, lives, or anything that the keepers could get him; the newspapers every day and conversed perfectly coherently on the passing topics and the events of the war, in which he felt a particular interest'. Wakefield's revelations caused a scandal and when a doctor was asked whether such treatment could in itself cause derangement, he ruefully admitted: 'No man could be sane under so much restraint.' Norris was cut free from his irons and keepers were pleased to note how placid he appeared, doubtless because he was emaciated and weak; he died of tuberculosis a few months later.

Bethlem was soon on the move again; the grand building was perilously sinking into the rubbish-filled ditch it had been built on, so the hospital relocated to Lambeth in 1815.

KING WILLIAM STREET EC4/
MONUMENT STREET EC3

OFF THE RAILS

An unfortunate consequence of pioneering enterprises
is the high risk of failure and though King William
Street Underground Station was in one respect a landmark
achievement, it was also an unmitigated disaster.

In 1886, work began on a railway tunnel running north–
south under the Thames between King William Street
and Borough (inexplicably, a station at London Bridge was
thought unnecessary) with the line continuing to Stockwell.
Underground trains were pulled by steam locomotives but
because passengers would choke to death in such a long
stretch of unventilated tunnel, carriages on its single track
would instead be hauled by cables attached to a steam
engine at each end. Engineers were nervous, however; the
system had proven unreliable in the Tower Subway and
King William Street Station had been awkwardly orientated
east–west, partly for fear of toppling the Monument, and
this created both a steep incline and tight curve on the way
into it. At the last minute, the courageous decision was taken
to use a newfangled system styled 'electrization'.

While the gradient helped propel trains out of the station,
it was a hit-or-miss affair for those coming in. The electrical generator had been sited at Stockwell, which could not
have been further away, and locomotives struggled to muster
enough power to reach the platform, so drivers had no
option but to roll the train back to the bottom of the tunnel
and try again. And the roller coaster ride was not always so
premeditated – locomotives were under such strain, their

motors had an unfortunate propensity to short circuit amidst a shower of sparks.

Not surprisingly, the public also found the journey difficult. It was assumed no one would wish to gaze at a tunnel wall, so carriage windows were narrow slits above head height, thus making it also impossible to see the train's whereabouts and obliging the guard to bellow each destination at the top of his voice. Generous upholstery alleviated the bumpy ride but what with only one class of travel, being hurled against other passengers caused social as well as physical discomfort. The stifling, claustrophobic carriages swiftly earned the nickname 'padded cells'.

On accomplishing a successful ascent there was one further obstacle for passengers; the station was 75ft below ground and escalators had not yet been invented. The lifts proved barely more reliable than trains and in 1893 a full car of fifty people discovered what it was like when the rope snapped: 'The lift rushed down with terrific force, but beyond a severe shaking, no one appeared injured.'

The world's first deep level underground station was, as the company chairman admitted, 'an engineering blunder', so it closed in 1900 and the proposition was made that the tunnels were instead devoted to cultivating mushrooms.

6 BEDFORD STREET WC2

GUT FEELING

Sometime around the turn of the eighteenth century, a new kind of emporium opened on Half Moon Street (now Bedford Street) 'seven doors from the Strand on the left-hand side'. It could be identified by its sign above the doorway, a green canister, and while this symbol indicated that the premises was either currently, formerly, or merely pretending to be a tea merchant, its particular field of commerce was condoms. However, the intimate particulars of London's first sex shop are impenetrably sheathed in mystery.

Of one detail there is reasonable certainty: the proprietor of The Green Canister was a Mrs Phillips (or Philips), whose name was sufficiently renowned to merit mention in a play performed in London in 1701. During a dialogue between the fittingly named Lady Lovetoy and elderly magistrate Sir Testy Dolt, Her Ladyship explains how country girls should adopt fashionable habits such as: 'buy all their silks at an India house, their looking-glass at Gumly's, and all their tea at Phillips's'. Bald mention of this last name leaves Dolt aghast, while Lovetoy playfully muses how ladies are no longer secretive about their love lives. Condoms first appeared in London only a few decades earlier, yet audiences were evidently aware that the implied merchandise was not for the purpose of brewing a hot beverage.

'Phillips' may have been synonymous with condoms but precious little else is known about the shopkeeper (as may also be said for the slippery etymology of the condom). Some historians link the premises with infamous courtesan Theresa Constantia Phillips, whose expertise in matters sexual was extensive and widely known courtesy of her deliciously indiscreet memoirs. However, she was born in 1709 so her notoriety and serendipitous surname were perhaps shrewdly appropriated to lend the shop further repute.

Presiding over The Green Canister from 1765 was a Mary Perkins, whose advertisements proclaimed it 'the old original shop, still continued by the successor of the late Mrs Philips, where gentlemen's orders shall be punctually observed in the best manner as usual'. This provoked an indignant response from the aforementioned Mrs Philips, disputing her death and stating that she could be found behind the counter of her new condom warehouse at Orange Court, Leicester Fields (now the National Portrait Gallery – which sadly lacks her portrait); she had been coaxed out of retirement after customers pleaded that 'they cannot procure any goods comparable to those she used to vend'. A war of words then broke out between the two over use of the surname, further confusing the Phillips/Philips genealogy, and clarity is not forthcoming from the delicate tiptoeing around the subject by contemporary writers. In fact, one description of the shop's wares was so linguistically indeterminate, it led an early twentieth-century sexologist to believe that The Green Canister supplied a more established item, the dildo, despite the unlikelihood that widow's comforters featured among its product range. (Dildos also enjoy a somewhat shaky etymology.) The Phillips name was still held in high esteem in the late 1780s but after that time the chronicles of condom ancestry go limp and lose interest.

Although Mrs Phillips and her heirs remain elusive, plenty is known about her esteemed goods (or as they were variously termed at the time: machines, engines, purses, armour, bladders, balloons, preservatives, insurance caps, gloves and riding coats – as well as condons, condums or cundums). They were manufactured on the premises from sheep intestine – something available in abundance from London's slaughterhouses – and preferably using the caecum, which has the convenience of a closed end. This did not make their manufacture straightforward, however, because the section of gut had to be 'soaked for some hours in water, turned inside out, macerated again in weak alkaline – changed every twelve hours – and scraped carefully to abstract the mucous membrane, leaving the peritoneal and muscular coats exposed to the vapour of burning brimstone, and afterwards washed with soap and water'. Following that, they were

'blown up, dried, cut to the length of seven or eight inches and bordered at the open end with a riband'; the pretty silk ribbon served to bridle the ovine bowel to its wearer and prevent them from parting company during an engagement.

Also available was a superfine condom that demanded further soaking in soapy water, infusing with essences of flowers and spices, stretching over a specially blown glass mould then vigorous rubbing to a polished finish; little wonder that condoms were costly and owners rinsed them after use in readiness for their next deployment. (The superfine justified its additional expense because the wearer was afforded reduced likelihood of brimstone burns on sensitive parts and in operation they exuded a less meaty smell.) And not only were prices stiff; prior to emplacement, a rigid condom required moistening to render it flaccid, and James Boswell's diary describes how he limbered one up in readiness by dunking it in the Serpentine in Hyde Park.

Another distinguishing feature by which passers-by might recognise the shop was a picture of the Archbishop of Canterbury gazing from the shop window; condoms came in a range of sizes and the most capacious – and doubtless most frequently requested – was known as 'The Bishop'.

OLD BAILEY EC4

HELPING HAND

In 1783, the chaotic and troublesome ritual of parading condemned prisoners from Newgate Gaol to the gallows at Tyburn came to an end and hanging instead took place on Old Bailey, immediately outside the prison (and did so until 1868). In truth, the relocation was less for reasons of expedience than deference to West End property developers who felt that dangling corpses were not conducive to gentrification. However, thousands still eagerly thronged to the new venue to scrutinise the slaughter – and what occurred immediately afterwards.

Perhaps counter-intuitively, the dead were thought to possess health-giving properties and most potent were those whose life had been taken prematurely. Following an unnatural death, 'the vital spirit being greatly afraid of the dead carcass, doth depart or retire', and this unused life force could be readily harvested by the living. Such beliefs comfortably co-existed with the notion that through sympathetic magic, the body of an evil criminal could dispel evil disorders – the worse the felon, the better the remedy. Naturally, people knew full well that the cure was not instantaneous but took effect as the corpse slowly rotted in its grave, and

both mechanisms operated through the medium of touch. So no sooner had a hanging concluded, there began a frantic scramble to grab the body.

Ailments most commonly cured by corpses were swellings or 'wens' – anything from moles to tumours – and the excrescence simply required stroking by what was thought the most effective agent, the deceased's hand. Needless to say, the hangman was happy to encourage the practice and following appropriate recompense acted as puppeteer with his dead charge, though should the disfigured be unable to muster the 2s 6d (at 1818 prices) he could later be found in a local watering hole peddling sections of the fateful rope, which he vouched were imbued with this same magic.

In 1814, a spectator on Old Bailey remarked how 'three females were introduced for the application of the dead man's hand, supposed to remove marks, wens etc. The first was a young woman of interesting appearance who was so much affected by the ceremony that she was obliged to be supported'. Also taking particular interest in ladies' swellings was an onlooker in 1799: 'I observed a number of men and women carried to the scaffold to be stroked by the hands, still quivering in the agony of death … amongst the rest I remarked a young woman with an appearance of beauty, all pale and trembling in the arms of the executioner, who submitted to have her bosom uncovered in the presence of thousands of spectators and the dead man's hand placed upon it.' She could at least take comfort that the hand was still warm.

17 IRVING STREET WC2

NAKED AMBITION

For generations, lawmakers diligently safeguarded Britons from theatrical performances that were 'indecent' – a somewhat loosely defined characteristic adjudicated by the incumbent Lord Chamberlain. So, many were surprised when, during the 1930s, nudity was first glimpsed on a British stage at the Windmill Theatre in nearby Great Windmill Street. A shrewd line of argument had questioned how it could be that naked statues, which were freely available for intimate examination in museums, were not considered indecent, yet similarly posed living persons were. Guileful logic won the day but obliged girls (and it was only females, because male nudity remained indecent for another three decades) to be presented 'artistically' under subdued lighting and completely motionless, as if 'living statues' or *tableaux vivants*. Needless to say, connoisseurs found much merit in this distant relation of the plastic arts and ploys were soon contrived to test the limits of the legislation, such as rotating platforms that enabled movement to be performed on a girl's behalf.

But two decades later, licensing laws remained as rigid as the nudes so it was perhaps inevitable that a lawyer would find another wheeze to circumvent them. Yet although Dhurjati Chaudhuri was a former barrister, he was otherwise a most unlikely figure to establish London's first strip club.

In 1950, Chaudhuri founded the Asian Institute, an organisation dedicated to better understanding between East and West through art, literature and performance, and opened a gallery and theatre at No. 17 to serve this purpose.

But his lofty aims sustained deep losses, so Chaudhuri looked elsewhere to recoup his outlay. After dabbling with graphic horror shows for audiences aware that they might faint or vomit at gouged eyeballs and seared flesh – and a uniformed nurse was on hand to render assistance – he concluded that naked girls held greater appeal. And because licensing laws governed only public venues, not private clubs, by the simple expedient of charging not for entry but membership he neatly sidestepped the Lord Chamberlain's roving eye.

In 1957, the Irving Theatre proudly made its attractions known with a sign proclaiming: 'The Only Theatre in London Where the Nudes Can Move' picked out in lights – a proposition that immediately attracted the gaze of a particular group of art aficionados. Associate membership was conferred by the not insignificant £1 6s 6d, which granted one complimentary admission, although owing to further licensing regulations purchasers were obliged to endure a frustrating forty-eight-hour cooling off period before reaping the fruits of their outlay, with subsequent renewals costing 16s 6d. However, for gentlemen who sought fuller membership through unfettered scrutiny of the female form, Chaudhuri charged an annual fee of £26 5s. Such sums amply overcame the irritation that because the council declined to issue the necessary Public Music and Dancing Licence, the management was also in receipt of a monthly £100 fine.

Between 2.30 p.m. and 11 p.m. Monday to Saturday, the show ran five times with only a fleeting comfort break between each (just three performances on Sundays) – a gruelling schedule of disrobing that necessitated two companies performing alternate days. There was no jukebox or piped music, so The Irving Girls set pulses racing in revue-style turns bearing such enchanting titles as 'Jungle Tit Bits', 'Let's Bathe', 'Three Mormon Maids' and 'Watery Passage' accompanied by the meagre combo of piano and drums.

Within a year of opening, Chaudhuri claimed to have 50,000 members – an extraordinary achievement considering that the theatre seated barely 100, although this butt-cheek by jowl intimacy was undoubtedly the secret of its appeal, and teetering on the smallest stage in the West End, girls soon learned to ignore a hat or newspaper quivering in a gentleman's lap beneath. Between numbers, a compère did his utmost to keep members entertained, aided by a quartet of sprightly soubrettes to impart visual interest; however, ending routines naked fortunately favoured prompt turnarounds to comply with the club's 'non-stop' billing. Even by the standards of the day, productions were cringingly amateur but with acres of exposed flesh in such close proximity, no one was complaining.

Not one to miss an opportunity, Chaudhuri published a quarterly magazine featuring partially adorned Irving Girls interspersed with contributions by 'literary giants needing no introduction' which most purchasers doubtless skipped over. He also proved himself porn pioneer by selling sets of stereo photographs of his girls in various alluring poses, complete with a plastic 3D viewer. There was no skirting the law on pubic hair in publications, however, so tresses had to be excised either physically or photographically.

The Irving's success did not pass unnoticed because by 1960 there were an estimated 200 strip joints across London and punters quickly recognised that Chaudhuri's creativity with the law did not extend to the stage. His dogged insistence that Irving girls were proficient at singing, acting and dancing made productions appear dowdy and wholesome compared to his sexier and riskier competitors, whose girls simply peeled off to pop music; the club closed in 1964.

THE TOWER OF LONDON EC3

DEFENDERS OF THE FAITH

A brief footnote in an official guide to the Tower states that during a violent siege in 1267 (one of few instances of conflict in the Tower's annals), the iconic castle was successfully defended by Jews and the Papal legate – a statement that positively begs for further explanation.

Jews of thirteenth-century London enjoyed intimate knowledge of the Tower thanks to their unusual relationship with English society; there was no place for them in a Christian feudal system so they belonged directly to the King, who entrusted their governance to the Constable of the Tower. Consequently, the fortress became the administrative centre for Jewish affairs; it was where they paid taxes (which funded the castle's building programme during the 1270s), were summoned to court, or were imprisoned.

But the Tower was also at their service. Christians were prohibited from lending money at interest (although a blind eye was turned towards Knights Templar) and while Jews were bound by a similar regulation, it did not preclude making profit from Gentiles. Loans of capital were vital for trade or war-making, so the King had a vested interest in the physical and economic well-being of Jews – and ecclesiastical laws created no impediment to his occasional extortion of their assets. In looking to the King for protection, Jews benefited from criminal and civil courts at the Tower, their strongbox containing financial transactions could be safeguarded within its walls (where Treasury officials might conveniently scrutinise it), and whenever under threat, they took refuge in it – a not uncommon occurrence when their peculiar status and occupation led to persecution.

Thus, when the Papal legate was in London to mediate in a war between Henry III and a group of rebellious barons then occupying the city (a conflict, like countless others in which the curious customs of the Jews were interpreted as sorcery against Christians), he found himself holed up in the fortress in the company of sheltering Jews. The rebels cut off supplies to the garrison, denounced the legate for presuming to control it, alleging 'it was a post not to be trusted in the hands of a foreigner, much less of an ecclesiastic' and were doubtless even less impressed when the unlikely coalition came off triumphant.

But Jews were also subject to the King's whims and in 1278 when 600 were accused of clipping coins, they were manacled together and imprisoned in the Tower for five months wherever space could be found – including the animal enclosures; close to 300 were later executed. In 1290, Jews' insatiable thirst for Christian blood could be tolerated no longer, so they were expelled from England – minus their money and property – and the Constable oversaw the exodus of nearly 1,500 from the Tower's wharf. His powers extended to the levy of tolls, so as they embarked, he extracted 4*d* from each – though banishment for 126 paupers cost them just 2*d*.

IN BAD FAITH

In July 1901, 99 Gower Street became home to the Theocratic Unity Temple and Purity League – a house of worship quite unlike what its virtuous name implied.

Authors of its unorthodox doctrine were an American couple: Ann O'Delia Diss Debar, a veteran spirit medium who went by countless aliases but whose latest moniker was Swami Horos, and her young husband du jour, Frank Dutton Jackson, alias Theodore Horos, a conman and sexual predator. Altercations with law enforcement in America regarding certain swindling operations had made their presence there unwelcome, so the pair washed up in London hoping that the reception would be more benign.

It certainly appeared that way; to drum up disciples for their creed, the couple placed advertisements in rural newspapers announcing that a handsome, highly educated gentleman of exemplary habits was desirous of marriage. Young ladies replied in droves and the pair singled out those most suited to their schemes; each was invited to meet the eligible bachelor (Jackson, of course) who, after gaining their confidence, introduced them to 'his mother' (the Swami). Should they exhibit sufficient naivety, they were then invited to move in. But nuptials were not forthcoming; on arrival at Gower Street, girls were swept into a phantasmagoria of cabbalistic hocus-pocus as they were inducted into the Temple – or as others chose to describe it: brainwashed into a harem.

Rather than take pains to devise rituals specific to Theocratic Unity, the Horoses instead appropriated those they had pillaged from occult organisation The Hermetic

Order of the Golden Dawn; blindfolded novices had a rope
tied around their waist, were ushered into a room heavy
with incense and led around it three times. They were consecrated in front of an altar bearing sundry sacred objects,
then kneeled as the blindfold was lifted – whereupon they
peered up to find a sword poised above their head. However,
the couple refashioned liturgies to their own end by pep-
pering them with passages culled from Kabbalah, Indian
tantras, the Marquis de Sade, Egyptian mythology, the Black
Mass and any other beguiling incantations that emphasised
both the obscene and the obedience of womankind. And in
another modification, Jackson performed the rituals naked
but for a formidable wax phallus, which he brandished over
prostrated neophytes in lieu of the sword; it was a taste of
what was to come.

Four girls swallowed the bait including Vera Croysdale from Yorkshire, who was promptly divested of her money and jewellery in order to further the Temple's mission, and 16-year-old Daisy Adams of Birkenhead, who was also pleased to hand over her possessions. The disciples did not see fit to question their strict diet of fruit, nuts and water, or Jackson's fumbled explanations for the throng of prospective brides residing at the house.

Needless to say, their induction also placed heavy emphasis on a solemn oath of secrecy because the first step to enlightenment in the Theocratic Mysteries was achieved through Jackson's tutoring in mutual masturbation. Should the pupil take her schooling well, he then progressed to the next level and had intercourse with her while the Swami watched – even holding the novice down should it become necessary. And yet the girls stayed.

However, it was perhaps the sight of their elders tucking in to steak and wine that persuaded Vera to inform police that her money had been stolen, and when two constables arrived at Gower Street, the girls innocently acquainted them with the more intimate ways of Theocratic Unity while the Horoses made themselves scarce. Given that the sect's devotional rites involved obtaining money by false pretences, procuring women for immoral purposes and criminal assault, the guru and her confederate were tracked down and arrested.

The British public was always ready to take interest in a lurid amalgam of sex and the occult, so the couple's trial attracted generous newspaper coverage, with especial delight taken when Daisy explained how she was under threat of instantaneous incineration by lightning bolt should she reveal the Temple's secrets. Then, to a spellbound courtroom, she proceeded to divulge precisely what went on at Gower Street, including graphic accounts of sharing a bed with both defendants – something that

obliged the judge to excuse women from the room, and
frustrated reporters who feared it too explicit to publish.
Her testimony was particularly uncomfortable for members of the Golden Dawn, whose arcane rituals became the
object of public merriment.

But despite Daisy's testimony that the 'act of submission' was administered on several occasions, Jackson took
everyone by surprise when he suddenly blurted out that his
alleged crime was a physical impossibility because he had
made himself a eunuch for God. It was a bold claim, and
one that failed to outlive the subsequent medical examination. Similarly dismissed were the couple's assertions that
as a holy mission based on the principles of Christ's life,
their order espoused celibacy. It took the jury five minutes
to return guilty verdicts; Jackson was handed a fifteen-year
prison sentence, the Swami seven. She earned the ultimate
compliment when Harry Houdini characterised her as one
of the most extraordinary fake mediums and mystery swin-
dlers the world has ever known.

RIVER THAMES, WOOLWICH SE18

THE INESCAPABLE HULK

The 1776 United States Declaration of Independence
had a dramatic effect on the river at Woolwich; overnight, Britain was dispossessed not only of sovereignty over
its American colonies, but also its dumping ground for criminals. This created an uncomfortable dilemma because the
stability of British society relied on the expulsion of unde-
sirables to far-flung places, and what with a harsh penal code

that criminalised minor offences, a remedy for overcrowded prisons suddenly became imperative.

The Government's solution was to deploy broken-down ships as floating prisons and – in a surprisingly modern approach – transfer their management to a private contractor. Within weeks, rotting former transportation ship *Justitia* and frigate *Censor* were crudely converted into jails moored in the river at Woolwich, where each housed fifty men permanently shackled in heavy irons – a persuasive deterrent to prospective swimmers. The strategy was envisaged as a short-term expedient but within three years, prisoner numbers escalated to more than 250 in each, and other decrepit ships were pressed into service; the era of the hulk had begun.

We owe a debt of gratitude to the contemptible swindler and thief James Hardy Vaux because he left a first-hand account of life aboard the hulks in his memoirs, published in 1819:

> At four o'clock in the morning myself and eleven others were conveyed by water on board the Retribution hulk at Woolwich. I had now a new scene of misery to contemplate; and, of all the shocking scenes I have ever beheld, this was the most distressing. There were confined in this floating dungeon nearly six hundred men, most of them double ironed and the reader may conceive the horrible effects arising from the continual rattling of chains, the filth and vermin naturally produced by such a crowd of miserable inhabitants, the oaths and execrations constantly heard among them, and above all, from the shocking necessity of associating and communicating more or less with so depraved a set of beings.

At night, prisoners were locked down below with free run of the lower decks and at no time were guards foolish enough to venture into this abyss. 'On descending the hatch-way, no conception can be formed of the scene which presented

itself. I shall not attempt to describe it, but nothing short of
a descent to the infernal regions can be at all worthy of a
comparison with it.' Conditions were particularly favourable
for fleas, rats and lice, while gaol fever (typhus) and violent
dysentery from drinking Thames water caused the hulk's
human population to drop like flies; during their first twenty
years, one in four died.

During the day inmates offered a spectacle for sightseers
by performing hard labour at Woolwich dockyard:

> Every morning at seven o'clock all the convicts capable
> of work, or in fact all who are capable of getting into the
> boats, are taken ashore to the Warren in which the Royal
> Arsenal and other public buildings are situated and are
> there employed at various kinds of labour, some of them
> very fatiguing; and while so employed, each gang of six-
> teen or twenty men is watched and directed by a guard.
> These guards are most commonly of the lowest class of
> human beings; wretches devoid of all feeling; ignorant in
> the extreme, brutal by nature and rendered tyrannical and
> cruel by the consciousness of the power they possess. They

invariably carry a large and ponderous stick with which, without the smallest provocation, they will fell an unfortunate convict to the ground, and frequently repeat their blows long after the poor sufferer is insensible.

As for the food, the stipulated ration is very scanty, but even part of that they are defrauded. Their provisions being supplied by contractors and not by government are of the worst kind, such as would not be considered eatable or wholesome elsewhere and both the weight and measure are always deficient.

But with regard to another appetite, some convicts were pleasantly sated. Vaux coyly mentions how 'unnatural crimes' were openly committed and while sodomy was endemic, rape was a matter of course for new arrivals, as noted by prison reformer Jeremy Bentham: 'At Woolwich, an initiation of this sort stands in the place of garnish [extortion] and is exacted with equal rigour,' adding mournfully: 'such things ever must be'. Boys as young as 12 were not exempt and these passive recipients of old lags' attentions were known as punks – though if taken under the protective wing of a controlling guardian, they were christened with girls names such as Polly, Bet or Nancy.

Those who departed the hulks hammered inside a coffin were buried in unmarked graves, originally among the marshes and later in Woolwich dockyard, though following one exceptionally virulent cholera outbreak, the officiating chaplain refused to perform the ceremony until a significant pile had accumulated. He then delivered the funeral service from the safety of a boat, where on reaching the words 'dust to dust', he dropped a handkerchief to signal that the bodies be committed to their grave.

Transportation to Australia commenced just a decade after prison hulks first appeared, yet they continued in service for eighty years; those at Woolwich were finally towed to the breakers' yard in 1857.

CHARLES I STATUE,
TRAFALGAR SQUARE WC2

TAKEN FOR A RIDE

The equestrian statue of Charles I is the work of French sculptor Hubert Le Sueur and was cast during Charles's reign in 1633. But it was never intended for Charing Cross (as Trafalgar Square formerly was) and certainly not to gaze down Whitehall to the site of the King's execution. It was commissioned by Sir Richard Weston, first Earl of Portland and Lord High Treasurer, for the garden of his estate at Roehampton in Surrey, but following the King's demise in 1649 Parliament was evidently aware of its existence because it ordered that the relic was auctioned for scrap and destroyed.

Brazier John Rivet bagged the statue for the knock down price of £215 and shrewdly chose not to melt it down, but instead secretly bury it – and such was his secrecy it is not certain whether this was in his Holborn garden or elsewhere. However, to demonstrate that he had fulfilled his obligations, he presented lumps of brass that, he explained, originated from the condemned statue. Touches of romance may have found their way into the story because Rivet's opportunistic ingenuity supposedly went further. Recognising the symbolic (and by extension, monetary) value in any old brass he might have laying around his workshop, he offered for sale various paraphernalia ostensibly fashioned from Charles and his steed: 'Accordingly, he furnished his shop with a prodigious number of knives and forks with a bronze mounting. In a short time his warehouse was full of customers.' Such knick-knacks could be either kingly relics or republican trophies, so

netted him a small fortune: 'To the royalists it afforded a melancholy but precious remembrance of their dear master; and
as to their antagonists, this extraordinary circumstance was
not a little flattering to their republican pride.' However, the
cutlery chronicle has a strangely familiar forerunner because
prophet and piss artiste William Lilly noted that when the
earlier royal monument on the site – Charing Cross was
torn down in 1647, he saw 'knife-hafts made of some of the
stones, which being well polished, look like marble'.

Following the restoration of King Charles II in 1660, the statue promptly re-materialised from its grave, stimulating the second Earl of Portland to request that it be returned to his family (and there are no records of how any recent purchasers of tableware reacted to this news). But Rivet – no doubt eager to once again flog an inanimate horse – dissented, and was only convinced of the error of his ways after the Earl issued a lawsuit. He duly relinquished the statue, but only after publishing a print of it, which sold handsomely.

Some years later, the Earl's widow sold the statue to the King for £1,600 and it was erected on the site in 1675.

INNER TEMPLE HALL EC4

DEVIL'S ADVOCATE

L ondon escaped the worst excesses of seventeenth-century witch hunting but the population knew full well from both their religious and medical superiors that misfortunes too complex to be explained through conventional means were likely the malevolent scheming of ostensibly frail old ladies – and Inner Temple found itself on the frontline of this confrontation with Beelzebub.

In 1602, petty bickering between Mary Glover, the 14-year-old daughter of a Thames Street shopkeeper, and Elizabeth Jackson, an elderly woman who lived nearby, turned sour. During a heated confrontation, Jackson wished the girl an evil death and sometime after this Glover suffered a sudden tightening of the throat and convulsive fits. Over the next few weeks her choking and seizures intensified and were accompanied by violent contortions – symptoms that were exacerbated whenever Jackson was near. Glover's pious Puritan parents feared the worst and had the church bell tolled in expectation of her death; on hearing it, Jackson crowed how she had silenced her foe.

But Glover clung to life despite losing her speech, sight and having great difficulty breathing and swallowing. For months, some of the country's most qualified physicians attempted to diagnose her illness, and while some thought it the result of natural causes such as 'maid's melancholy' (hysteria),

others concluded it was supernatural – Jackson had indeed cursed the girl and she was now diabolically possessed. Such a prospect made it a matter for the church, so the Bishop of London urged the city's most senior legal official, Sir John Crooke, to investigate; Glover was brought to his chambers at Inner Temple (in buildings now long demolished), where he performed a dramatic series of experiments.

In front of an audience including Glover's mother, several neighbours and clergymen, he first had a woman disguised as Jackson enter the room and touch the sickly girl – to which she showed no reaction. When the real Jackson was ushered in dressed 'like a country-market woman with a mufflet hiding her face, and an old hat and a short cloak spattered with mire' Glover immediately fell to the floor – 'her eyes drawn into her head, her tongue toward her throat, her mouth drawn up to her ear, her body became stiff and sense-less. Her lips being shut close, a plain and audible voice came out of her nostrils saying: Hang her, Hang her.'

Following that spectacle, Crooke wished to determine whether Glover felt pain – a well-established test for bewitchment. He held a flame to her palm until it blis-tered, then 'the blister did break and water came out which dropped down upon the floor, the maid lying still senseless as a dead body with the voice coming out of her nose'. For the avoidance of doubt, he then heated a long pin in a flame until it was red hot and 'thrust the head of it into her nostrils to see if that would make her sneeze, wink or bend her brows or stir her head'. The girl did not so much as wince, and when Crooke repeated the test on Jackson, the woman instantly recoiled in agony.

Next, he told Jackson to recite the Lord's Prayer and when she stumbled over the words 'deliver us from evil' Crooke compelled her to articulate the line, at which Glover sud-denly began convulsing violently and whining 'Hang her!' through her nose.

Lastly, Glover was laid on a bed with cloths over her eyes and as her mother and neighbours gently placed their hands on her she remained still and calm 'till the witch laid her hand upon her then all the cloths were thrown off and the maid tossed towards her'. Crooke had his proof of witchcraft and Jackson was despatched to Newgate.

The trial of Elizabeth Jackson was made all the more dramatic for Glover's presence in the courtroom, writhing and intoning 'Hang her!' throughout. Two physicians asserted that the teenager was suffering from a natural disease but struggled to offer a specific diagnosis, so Glover was again burned on the hand to demonstrate her insensitivity to pain, and Jackson instructed to recite the Lord's Prayer – her fumbling interpreted not as simple ignorance but the work of demons. And lest the jury harbour misgivings about Jackson's allegiance to Satan, the judge thoughtfully reminded them that no one knew more about witches than him, and Jackson was the archetype – a cursing, scheming old woman with marks on her body where the Devil sucked blood. Following that guidance, the verdict was fait accompli; Jackson was handed the maximum sentence for a first offence under the 1563 Witchcraft Act – twelve months in prison and four sessions in the pillory. She was fortunate, as only two years later her 'crime' was punishable by death.

But Crooke was disappointed that the passage of justice was not sufficient for Satan to take leave of Glover, so he urged Puritan clergymen to perform an exorcism. Their account attests that He put up a determined fight until she 'did throw white froth out of her throat and mouth round about the chamber ... then suddenly life came in to her whole body. She looked up with a cheerful countenance ... saying: "The comforter is come, I am delivered."'

ROYAL OBSERVATORY SE10

UNLUCKY STARS

G reenwich is famous for its position on an imaginary line from pole to pole, but its journey there was not altogether stellar.

Charles II established the Royal Observatory in 1675 but proved reluctant to fund it. A meagre £500 raised from the sale of decayed gunpowder forced its builder, one Christopher Wren, to salvage materials from a decrepit gatehouse at the Tower of London and reuse existing foundations on the hilltop – with the result that the building was not even aligned north–south.

Princely miserliness also obliged Astronomer Royal John Flamsteed to purchase his own instruments, but fortunately for the nation's subsequent maritime and global supremacy, his father died, leaving enough funds for an accurate telescope. But peering through it, Flamsteed noticed how fixed stars were imperceptibly rising, and it was several years before he realised that his shoddily built observatory was subsiding.

He also experienced a sinking feeling because his profession became the target of scorn, as epitomised by the tale of a nameless astronomer among the newly founded Royal Society. On surveying the moon through his telescope, the scientist was surprised to spot an elephant bounding across its surface, so began writing up his sensational discovery only for a footboy to take a peek and see that a mouse had crawled inside the instrument. The Elephant in the Moon may have been satire but it summed up the popular view of star-gazers with astronomical pretensions.

Flamsteed was loath to publish his observations until he
was confident of their accuracy (he even diligently calculated
the rate of subsidence – which he noted, was increasing) and
this reluctance greatly annoyed Isaac Newton, who hankered
after the data for his labours on gravitation. The animosity
did not diminish when Flamsteed highlighted a number of
blunders in one of Newton's books, remarking: 'I always
found him insidious, ambitious and excessively covetous of
praise and impatient of contradiction.'

Their quarrelling simmered for several years, the elephant
in the room being exactly who owned Flamsteed's readings,
and in 1711 Newton upped the ante by publishing them,
claiming they were public property. Flamsteed, who had spent
close to forty years stargazing, was livid: 'They cost him not an
hour's labour or watching, nor was he at one penny expense
for making them; but besides my daily labour and watchings
when he was asleep in his warm bed, it had cost me above
£2,000.' The embattled astronomer successfully petitioned
that copies of Newton's book were surrendered to him (or at
least those its author had not already despatched elsewhere)
and in April 1716, after setting aside a few as evidence of 'the
malice of godless persons', he piled 300 in the courtyard and
made 'a sacrifice of them to Heavenly truth' by burning them.

SADLER'S WELLS THEATRE EC1

THIRST ACT

During the 1680s, Edward Sadler was digging gravel
from his garden when, to his delight, he discovered
a natural spring. To the enterprising Mr Sadler (who for

reasons unknown, history has generally chosen to call Richard) this was a gold mine; Sadler was proprietor of a public house and by all accounts the water gave rise to exceptional beer.

But it was soon decided that brewing was unnecessary. Sadler let it be known that the spring was an ancient holy well famed for miraculous healing – though he had a physician examine the water for a more precise list of its qualities, including cure of 'dropsy, black and yellow jaundice, swelling of the spleen, scurvy, green sickness and other distempers incident to the female sex … those that make bloody urine … all inveterate dysenteries, or bloody fluxes' as well as a host of other ghastly ailments. London's hypochondriacs, who included among their number the Royal family, flocked to what became known as Sadler's Wells.

Clientele were encouraged to take the water for at least two weeks with nothing but caraway seeds, tobacco and a glass of wine, which, as luck would have it, Sadler could also provide by virtue of being a confectioner, tobacconist and vintner. And to create a pleasant ambiance for weakly imbibers he laid on ornamental gardens, musicians, acrobats and boghouses – a prerequisite because the steely water stimulated drinkers 'to stool at the first taking … and where it meets with a very foul stomach, provokes to vomit'.

Entertainments quickly proved more appetising than the water, then took a noticeable turn down-market – a slide hastened by the stipulation that in order to sidestep theatre licensing laws, admission required the purchase of a beverage, which by choice was now alcoholic. Under new proprietorship in 1700, regulars were, according to one visitor: 'Butchers, bailiffs, prize-fighters, deer-stealers, buttocks [prostitutes], files [pickpockets] and vermin [self-explanatory]' and such was the level of obscene phraseology directed towards female performers it became necessary for police to mingle among the insalubrious throng.

One spectacle feasted upon by patrons was the Hibernian Cannibal: 'A table was spread with a dirty cloth in the middle of the room, furnished with bread, pepper, oil and vinegar but neither knife, plate, fork or napkin and when the beholders had conveniently mounted themselves upon one another's shoulders to take a fair view of his Beastylness's banquet, in comes the lord of the feast, disguised in an Antick's cap and with a smutty face like a country hangman.' In true showman tradition, 'cannibal' turned out to be a mild overstatement: 'A live cock was given into the ravenous paws of this ingurgitating monster which after trifling with for some time he ate up, feathers and all.' Half a pint of brandy washed down any remaining morsels from the Irishman's throat, sufficient for him to announce that five guineas said he could shortly devour another fowl feast.

A much-loved staple of the Sadler's Wells roster was
Isabella Wilkinson, who danced and played the violin, pipe,
drum and cymbal while balanced on a tightrope – a feat she
performed unencumbered by skirt or petticoat, which thus
greatly favoured the inspection of her legs. It was no secret
that Wilkinson supplemented her income through prostitution. However, both careers were interrupted in 1759 when
the rope snapped and she broke a leg, obliging her to instead
perform melodies on the musical glasses.

But what pulled the greatest crowds was not human but
bestial. Treading the boards at Sadler's Wells was a hare that
stood on its hind legs and beat a tambourine, two horses
that danced a minuet, bulldogs sent into the air in a balloon
primed with fireworks, a singing duck and a troupe of fourteen dancing dogs: 'The actors were so well dressed and so
much in earnest – Moustache particularly as the Deserter in
his little uniform with smart musket and helmet.' The dogs'
theatrical spirit was fostered by the fact that they had not
been fed all day: 'By the temptation of a hot supper which
was unseen by the audience they were made among other
feats to ascend scaling ladders and storm a fort.'

However, it was pigs that hogged the limelight. Despite a
popular impression that the obstinate creatures had a natural antipathy towards schooling, audiences were soon in awe
of their intelligence – in the words of one astounded spectator: 'A far greater object of admiration to the English nation
than ever was Sir Isaac Newton.' By means of cards laid in
a circle, the perceptive porkers told the time from a gentleman's watch, recognised unmarried audience members,
solved mathematical puzzles, read ladies' minds (after obtaining their permission of course), and acted as porcine prophet
in telling fortunes – even performing such feats blindfolded.
(The creatures would have been less accomplished had their
ears been covered.) Members of a French acrobatic troupe
were most indignant when it became apparent that they

were second billing to swine, so issued that time-honoured theatrical ultimatum – either the pig went, or they did. The acrobats sought immediate employment elsewhere.

SAYES COURT PARK SE8

RUSSIAN REBELLION

The neighbourhood was once perhaps the most elegant country estate in London – until it was ravaged by a visiting foreign dignitary.

During the seventeenth century a handsome house named Sayes Court stood on the site and it was leased from the Crown by diarist John Evelyn. His overriding passion was its 100-acre garden in which he spent four decades creating then lovingly tending an elaborate parterre, ornamental lake, lawns, flower beds, avenues and orchards, and although he lavished attention on scarce and unusual plants, he was especially proud of his mighty holly hedge, which stood 9ft high, 5ft thick and 400ft long.

An innocuous entry in Evelyn's diary for 30 January 1698 reads: 'The Czar of Muscovy being come to England, and having a mind to see the building of ships, hired my house at Sayes Court and made it his court and palace.' Evelyn's abode offered convenient quarters for the youthful Tsar Pyotr Alexeyevich Romanov (later Peter the Great) and his not inconsiderable entourage of 'one court marshal, one equerry, one major-domo, four chamberlains … six pages, six trumpeters, one cup-bearer, one cook, one quarter-master, twelve lacqueys, six coachmen and postillions, twenty-four serving men, thirty-two footmen', as well as four dwarves and a monkey.

But the Russian's interests did not overlap with Evelyn's;
'He is a man of a very hot temper, soon inflamed, and very
brutal in his passion,' concluded the Bishop of Salisbury, one
of Peter's chaperones. 'He raises his natural heat by drinking
much brandy, which he rectifies himself with great application: he is subject to convulsive motions all over his body and
his head seems to be affected with these.' The Tsar and his
retinue, dubbed 'right nasty' by Evelyn's manservant, worked
up a prodigious thirst during their stay and spent three
months drunkenly ransacking their accommodation.

On the despot's departure, a lengthy inventory of repairs was drawn up, including 300 panes of glass, many hundred feet of floor tiles, replacement of torn and soiled bedding, curtains, carpets and tapestries, a new floor for the bog-house, almost 100 chairs, tables, cabinets and doors for those broken or missing – presumably last seen in one of the (broken) stoves, and the restoration of twenty paintings that had evidently served as targets for pistol practice.

Yet what most dismayed Evelyn was the scene of destruction in his garden: 'great dammages are done to the trees and plants which cannot be repaired … all the grass worke is out of order and broke into holes by their leaping and shewing tricks upon it'. But worse, his beloved hedge was a trampled mess because the Tsar delighted in nothing more than being raced through it in a wheelbarrow. Repairs cost the Treasury £350, including £1 for the replacement of three wrecked wheelbarrows.

ST JAMES'S PALACE SW1

COURT CONTROVERSY

In 1724, residents of the German town of Hamelin (that of the Pied Piper legend) discovered a curious creature living in the nearby forest. It was a curly haired brute aged between 11 and 15 who walked on all fours and was naked but for the tattered remains of shirt collar. When towns-people attempted to catch the beast, it scampered up a tree 'as naturally as a squirrel'; the tree was duly felled and the quarry taken captive.

The being possessed no understanding of language, so was unable to explain its rustic circumstances, and though some suggested that it must have been suckled by a she-wolf or bear, the consensus was that the boy had been abandoned some years earlier and survived without human contact by eating leaves, acorns, berries and tree bark.

Such peculiar fauna did not escape the attention of George I when he visited nearby Hanover shortly afterwards, and it was summoned for royal inspection. The King was charmed by the encounter and the mute boy raised no objection when George declared that he would be taken to London to join his household at St James's. Meanwhile, the name Peter was conferred on the oddity because he appeared to respond to it – though it was later observed how he responded to any name.

'Peter the Wild Boy' unwittingly proved the equal of any royal jester. With his natural propensity to laughter and innocence of social graces he scandalously flouted the court's stuffy conventions, provoking horror and delight alike – though should his comic antics transgress the behaviour allowed of him, the delivery of a sharp strike on his legs from a leather strap unambiguously signalled his master's displeasure.

The house guest was not entirely appreciative of his upgrade in accommodation, however; he spurned the comfortable apartment set aside for him and instead slept on the floor, raw vegetables were favoured over the ambrosial delights on tap from the Royal kitchen, and there was limited success at tempering his inclination to bound around naked by coaxing him into suitably courtly dress. But Peter proved himself a natural pick-pocket, if only in the hope of finding nuts, and possessed fine teeth, acute hearing and a heightened sense of smell – with the exception of his own excrement, to which, it was ruefully noted, he appeared entirely insensitive.

Novelties were usually made available for public scrutiny, but with Peter kept captive at the palace, a wax effigy was instead exhibited on the Strand; column inches unreliably filled in the absent details and London buzzed with excitement about 'one of the greatest curiosities that has appeared in the world since the time of Adam'. For some, the fact that an ignoramus lived among the court was an invitation too tempting to pass up, and Peter's presence was gleefully exploited to satirise the establishment.

But serious discussions focused on exactly who or what Peter was. Devoid of language, how could Peter think? Did he possess a soul? Was such a primitive being capable of learning? Debate over the differences between man and beast led some to conclude that Peter was a missing link between the two and proof could be found in his hairline, which lay lower on his forehead than was usual. But perplexingly, he otherwise showed no excessive hairiness – in fact, 'his face was not at all ugly or disagreeable, and he had a look that might be called sensible or sagacious for a savage' – an air of wisdom that did not discourage Swedish taxonomist Carl Linnaeus from classifying Peter in the feral sub-species *Homo ferus*.

The King made an attempt to tame the brute by asking his physician, Dr Arbuthnot, to educate Peter, and the boy learned the correct way to bow, how to articulate his master's name and, as a spiritual contingency, was baptised. But his schooling advanced little further and rumours circulated that Peter had breached all principles of civilised decorum by donning his hat before the King had done so. George was not known for unlimited forbearance and what with Peter's fondness for dining on raw onions and failure to get to grips with the purpose of a chamber pot, he quickly tired of his human pet and passed him to the Princess of Wales.

As it happened, Caroline had taken a particular fancy to Peter and was pleased to keep him at Leicester House (on the site of Leicester Square), where thoughts of his uninhibited animal virility among the Maids of Honour may have created quite a frisson. But Peter had no designs on ladies' chastity and when Caroline became Queen he was moved on again. The public was now preoccupied with a woman who had given birth to rabbits, so Peter was pensioned off to a farm in Hertfordshire where he could scamper into the woodland he pined for. With the exception of a possible incident in which he disappeared and was later arrested as a Scottish spy, he lived quietly and long outlived his royal masters, dying in his late seventies in 1785.

Peter's curved Cupid's-bow upper lip, drooping eyelids and happy, excitable demeanour suggest that he may have suffered from the rare genetic disorder Pitt–Hopkins syndrome.

ROYAL MINT STREET E1

COINING IT

When the Shadwell Basin dock was excavated during the 1850s, hoards of treasure emerged from the sticky mud. Or so experts thought.

William Smith and Charles Eaton toiled as shore rakers with a sideline selling any items they scavenged from the river-bank – typically lumps of coal though occasionally an antique artefact or two. However, it did not take Billy and Charley long to recognise that their occupation would be less strenuous and more lucrative if they simply manufactured antiquities themselves. At a workshop on Rosemary Lane, ironically right beside the Royal Mint (hence now Royal Mint Street, though their exact address remains a mystery) the pair cast a miscellany of lead objects that were then carefully aged with acid, dirt and an occasional clout from a hammer, to foster an appearance that seemed to date from somewhere between the eleventh and sixteenth centuries. After nightfall, the fruits of their labour were carried down to the dock and deposited in the mud to be discovered the following day – no doubt accompanied by a certain amount of breathless theatre.

The duo's negligible grasp of history lent a colourful individuality to the medieval kings, warriors or saints they depicted – idiosyncrasies that along with their crude tech-niques, only enhanced the items' curiosity value. Up to twenty-five treasures a week were 'discovered' at Shadwell and snapped up by an acquaintance in the antique trade, who in turn sold them on to dealers and connoisseurs includ-ing the British Museum. Medallions required the least effort to turn out, and what with materials for a dozen costing $2s$

and each making between 2*s* and 5*s*, the pair were coining it; their annual income for 1858 was a tidy £400.

Though Messrs Smith and Eaton were pleased to discover that no one questioned their handiwork, specialists struggled to explain the abundance of finds pouring forth from a site of no particular historical significance. And the quest for plausible theories was greatly hindered by the fact that both men were illiterate, so dating the artefacts from their meaningless jumble of numbers and letters proved acutely challenging.

Their authenticity became a matter for the courts, however, when a magazine accused a London dealer of hawking fakes, but fortunately for the amateur artisans, an expert witness declared the curios genuine simply because he believed that no one would choose to contrive something so preposterous – and the publicity occasioned a welcome boost in sales.

But not everyone was convinced. One wag sketched a statue of a bishop with the word 'Fabricatus' on its pedestal, then put it about that he collected antiques of that nature; lo and behold, within twelve hours just such a figure emerged from the mud.

Despite being rumbled, it was not apparent what crime Billy and Charley could be accused of, so they escaped prosecution and forged on with their enterprise, though fakes were regrettably now worth only pennies.

SAFFRON HILL EC1

INTEREST PER ANUM

Not without reason was the area thoroughly remodelled during the 1860s: the southernmost stretch of
Saffron Hill (formerly styled the bucolic Field Lane) had
the unhappy distinction of providing Dickens with inspiration for Fagin's den in his 1839 novel *Oliver Twist*: 'A dirtier
or more wretched place he had never seen. The street was
very narrow and muddy and the air was impregnated with
filthy odours ... drunken men and women were positively
wallowing in the filth and from several of the doorways great
ill-looking fellows were cautiously emerging.' But a century
earlier, decidedly different fellows were cautiously emerging
from Field Lane.

During the 1720s, John and Margaret Clap were proprietors of a coffee house beside the Bunch o'Grapes tavern on
the lane. 'Coffee house' was an all-encompassing term and if
the Claps did indeed serve the beverage, it was certainly not
the establishment's primary line of business; Mother Clap's
molly-house was London's premier gay rendezvous.

Men of a homosexual bent referred to each other as 'mollies' (perhaps from *mollis*, Latin for soft) and were then busy
forming what we would now term a gay subculture, employing a recognised pattern of behaviour, dress and language, and
congregating in specific resorts such as markets, taverns, boghouses and molly-houses. The comfort, facilities and service
at Mother Clap's made it particularly popular – so much so,
some mollies were permanent lodgers: 'For the better conven-
iency of her customers she had provided beds in every room
in her house, she usually had 30 or 40 of such persons there

every night, more on a Sunday.' The patriarch of the frater-
nity appears to have kept a low profile in proceedings, whereas
Margaret – likely an ageing bawd whose true surname had
been eclipsed by a reference to the pox (and who presumably
earned the honorific 'Mother' from her convivial and caring
instincts) – may have run the house as much for pleasure as
profit: the earliest documented fag hag.

But it was a dangerous vocation. By condoning and facilitating sodomy, the Claps were applauding both a capital
offence and an affront to nature, and this attracted some
considerable opprobrium; even whores took a dim view
of molly-houses for fear that they posed a threat to their
own livelihood. So as well as mollies, this Valhalla of vice
caught the attention of The Society for the Reformation
of Manners, a coterie of religious zealots with their own
particular interest in its sexual irregularities. Fearing that
London would suffer divine fury as was wreaked on the
Biblical cities of Sodom and Gomorrah, members endeavoured to avert fire and brimstone by energetically pursuing
the prosecution of homosexuals – and such was their cru-
sade they were prepared to get stuck in under cover. One
such regular was Samuel Stephens, who made note of some
molly pageantry: 'I found between 40 and 50 men making
love to one another, as they called it. Sometimes they would
sit in one another's laps, kissing in a lewd manner and using
their hand indecently. Then they would get up, dance and
make curtsies and mimic the voices of women. O fie Sir! –
Pray, Sir, – Dear Sir, – Lord how can you serve me so? – I
swear I'll cry out. – You're a wicked Devil – and you're a
bold face. – Eh! ye little dear toad! Come buss! [kiss].'

In 1726, such queer goings on inspired an unheralded visit
from police to arrest Mother Clap along with the forty clientele on the premises, and at her trial Stephens was pleased to
recount what he clapped eyes on: 'They'd hug and play and
toy and go out by couples into another room on the same

floor to be married as they called it.' Such nuptials took place
in the 'chapel' and were evidently concerned not with com-
mitment but consummation, while 'the door of that room
was kept by Eccleston, who used to stand pimp for them to
prevent anybody from disturbing them in their diversions.
When they came out they used to brag in plain terms of
what they had been doing. I went to the same house on two
or three Sunday nights following and found much the same
practices as before. The company talked all manner of gross
and vile obscenity in the prisoner's hearing and she appeared
to be wonderfully pleased with it.'

But while the brotherhood of bedfellows may have found
the incursion of a great number of constabulary a regret-
table interruption, none were demonstrably *in flagrante
delicto* – and proof of sodomy was necessary for conviction.
Prosecutors knew the hazards of acquiring such evidence,
so called upon the services of their own, more provocative,
agents provocateurs in return for immunity – and perhaps
more besides; these informants' indelicate testimonies later
sent several of Mother Clap's regulars to the gallows.

As for the matriarch herself, when she rose to address the
jury she drew attention to her gender 'and therefore it cannot
be thought that I would ever be concerned in such practices'
(another wily molly-house proprietor had explained how
witnesses had merely seen surgeons examining patients) – a
valiant effort but inadequate to avert conviction for keeping
a disorderly house, attracting two years' imprisonment with
time in the pillory. This sealed the fate of her enterprise and
emboldened the vigilantes, who gleefully returned to work,
shutting down another sixteen 'hellish clubs of sodomites'.

DANCE WITH DEATH

Aside of heaven or hell, Londoners have long fretted where they might go when dead. Overcrowded graveyards, fear of body-snatchers and wanting the best for one's soul led most to aspire to eternal rest inside church vaults, and by offering such a domicile for the deceased, Baptist minister Mr Howse smelt opportunity. In 1822 he opened Enon Chapel for the acclamation of God upstairs and accumulation of bodies below – and passage to paradise had never been so cheap.

Interment cost 12*s* for adults, 8*s* for children, a fraction of the fee at nearby St Clement Danes (admittedly, without the classical splendour), and because Howse harboured no sectarian prejudice and the chapel stood amid a slum whose population was prone to premature death, he was soon deluged with the departed. Over the next two decades it is thought that the minister deposited 12,000 in a space appropriate for 1,200 – and locals now paid the price for this hell-hole.

All that separated the chapel from putrefying cadavers were thin floorboards, yet services doggedly continued, despite headaches, blackouts, and a sickening taste in the mouth; children must have found the six hours of Sunday school particularly challenging. And as well as the fetid exhalations of the dead – which rapidly turned any fresh meat in the neighbourhood rancid, worshippers watched swarms of peculiar black bugs emerge from cracks in the floor, and later found them crawling in their hair and clothes.

Howse likely achieved such a feat of disposal through liberal application of quicklime combined with the utility of fuelling his kitchen stove with coffin-wood – appropriated at the earliest opportunity because 'when the wood has become saturated with the death-gas, the stench which it gives out in burning is intolerable in a house'. Further space was freed up because the chapel stood over an open sewer in which bodies could slip away to a netherworld somewhere beyond the Strand – their transport perhaps aided by prior dismemberment. Some time later when the sewer was necessarily enlarged, sixty cartloads of the less destructible portions of the deceased had to be excavated, then dumped near the southern end of Waterloo Bridge as landfill for a new path.

Following Mr Howse's demise the chapel reopened as a Temperance Hall staging: 'Plain and fancy dress balls … quadrilles, waltzes, country dances, gallopades, reels etc.' The shindigs were known locally as 'Dances on the Dead' and mercifully, the floor never collapsed.

In the 1840s, local surgeon George 'Graveyard' Walker arranged for the remaining remains to be properly buried at his own expense in Norwood and 6,000 sightseers came to see them off – although not all made the journey. Bones were still being pulled from the ground in 1967 when the site was excavated for redevelopment.

GARDEN OF INIQUITY

In the 1660s, when Charles II remodelled St James's Park in the elegant French manner, it inspired politician Edmund Waller to compose 'A Poem on St James's Park as lately improved by his Majesty', in which with choking sycophancy, he eulogised the king: 'his shape so lovely, and his limbs so strong ...' and his Garden of Eden.

But that was not the situation on the ground and in 1672, John Wilmot Earl of Rochester penned 'A Ramble in St James's Park' to set the record straight. Rather than portray heavenly paradise, he brought to life the earthy pursuits it hosted, commencing:

> Much wine had passed, with grave discourse
> Of who fucks who, and who does worse,
> Such as you usually do hear
> From them that diet at the Bear,
> When I, who still take care to see
> Drunkenness relieved by lechery,
> Went out into St James's Park
> To cool my head, and fire my heart,
> But though St James has th' honour on't
> 'Tis consecrate to prick and cunt.

His poetry makes it perfectly evident that the park provided a backdrop for all levels of society to indulge in al fresco sexual adventures:

Unto this all sin sheltering grove
Whores of the bulk and the alcove,
Great ladies, chamber maids and drudges
The rag-picker and heiress trudges,
Car-men, divines, great Lords and tailors
Pimps, poets, 'prentices and jailors,
Footboys, fine fops do here arrive
And here promiscuously they swive.

By the time the reign of the 'Merry Monarch' ended,
St James's Park was well established as the favoured resort of
the licentious.

Not only heterosexuals sustained grass stains on their clothing; the adjacent barracks supplied ready trade for a cruising
ground along Birdcage Walk: 'They are easily discovered by
their signals … one of them sits on a bench, he pats the back
of his hands; if you follow them they put a white handkerchief thro' the skirts of their coat, and wave it to and fro.' But
retiring to nearby shrubbery had its risks: one sashaying soldier blackmailed at least 500 suitors by threatening to disclose
their proclivities; another boasted that he 'could show nine

inches ... and that when he wanted money, he took a walk in the park, and got four or five guineas a night of gentlemen because they would not be exposed'.

In 1710 a French visitor remarked upon another activity:

> Every day in London's St James's Park we see women carrying baskets full of dolls and young women of all conditions haggling to buy them. Under the skirt of the doll we find instead of legs a cylinder with a cloth cover, about six inches long and an inch in diameter – we say not its purpose. [For the avoidance of doubt, he is describing a delightfully embellished dildo.]
>
> A woman one day bought one of these dolls whose cylinder seemed too oversize for her; she asked the saleswoman if she had one smaller, whereupon the saleswoman answered no. She ordered a smaller one and the vendor insisted upon payment in advance because if the woman did not collect the doll she would be burdened with it because everyone wanted big ones.

Rochester personified these sex toys as 'A Noble Italian call'd Signior Dildo' thus observing the custom of attributing depraved or unnatural activities to degenerate countries such as France or Italy. However, one Italian not known for his moral rectitude was appalled by more base activities. Casanova visited London in 1763 and related 'a small anecdote that paints well the English humour':

> You know the paths of the palace gardens are separated by numerous arbours and openings. Pembroke and I were walking in the avenues one afternoon when I see six individuals squatting (we guess why) with their backs towards us. Verily, my Lord, these are very ill-mannered people.
>
> What do you mean?
>
> At least these gentlemen could face the other way.

That would be wrong because in that posture we would recognise them.

Lord Pembroke's response suggests that unashamedly emptying one's bowels in the park was also commonplace.

Such underfoot hazards did not discourage lechery because that same year when writer James Boswell felt a different urge from within his breeches, he knew exactly where to head: 'As I was coming home this night, I felt carnal inclinations raging through my frame. I determined to gratify them. I went to St James's Park and, like Sir John Brute, picked up a whore. For the first time I did engage in armour, which I found but a dull satisfaction.' Boswell had outfitted himself with a condom, which conveniently were openly sold in the park; 'She who submitted to my lusty embraces was a young Shropshire girl, only seventeen, very well-looked, her name was Elizabeth Parker. Poor being, she has had a sad time of it!' A few days later, he was at it again: 'At night I strolled into the park and took the first whore I met, whom I without many words copulated with free from danger, being safely sheathed. She was ugly and lean and her breath smelt of spirits. I never asked her name.'

ST MARGARET'S CHURCHYARD SW1

SLOW BURN

Visitors to Westminster Abbey might be surprised to learn that where they queue to enter its north door (in the churchyard of neighbouring St Margaret's) a man was most cruelly burned to death.

During Mass at St Margaret's on Easter Day 1555, former monk William Flower took exception to the ritual and as the priest was administering the Eucharist he 'did strike and wound him upon the head and also upon the arm and hand with his wood-knife'. Flower's actions were especially sacrilegious because the priest bled abundantly 'and the chalice with consecrated hosts being in his hand, were sprinkled with his blood'. Mass was well attended and 'people in great fear cried out lamentably, and thought they should presently have been killed', but the perpetrator was quickly overpowered, clapped in as many irons as he could bear, and incarcerated in the Abbey Gatehouse.

When summoned before prosecutor, judge and jury Bishop Bonner, Flower insisted that he despised his actions in savagely stabbing the priest, but could not condemn the devout faith that had driven him to do it. One man's piety was another's heresy and Bonner was responsible for

eradicating dangerous opinions such as this and strongly recommended that Flower recant, 'promising many fair things if he would do so', but his entreaties fell on deaf ears.

And so on 24 April 1555, Flower was delivered to the churchyard, where a stake had been erected. Merely putting him to the fire was not commensurate with his crime, so to first avenge the priest's injuries, Flower's right hand was held against the stake and hacked off with an axe. 'And thus fire was set unto him, who burning therein, cried with a loud voice, O the Son of God, have mercy upon me, O the Son of God, receive my soul three times; and so his speech being taken from him, he spake no more, lifting up, notwithstanding his stump, with his other arm as long as he could.'

Through either ineptitude or intent, there was insufficient firewood to complete the day's combustion, so Flower had to be cut down and laid in the embers 'which was doleful to behold … his lower part was consumed in the fire, whilst his upper part was without the fire, his tongue in all men's sight, still moving in his mouth'.

In contrast, no expense was spared for a banquet arranged by Bonner to celebrate the reconciliation of St Margaret's following its cleansing. The meal must have been of an exhausting character because the bishop and his guests worked their way through three capons, half a veal, four green geese, a dozen rabbits, a dozen pigeons, a sirloin of beef and two gallons of wine.

TAPESTRY COURT, MORTLAKE SW14

SPELL DISASTER

During the sixteenth century, a house between St Mary's Church and the river (later the site of a tapestry works) was home to philosopher John Dee. Perhaps the foremost scholar of his day, Dee had an insatiable thirst for knowledge, as evidenced by his library at Mortlake that contained in excess of 4,000 books covering disciplines from practical science – astronomy, geometry and botany, through theology and philosophy to alchemy and astrology. Mastery of such subjects would, according to Dee, allow him to unravel the mystery of God's creation and in this quest, wisdom could be gleaned as profitably from magic as mathematics.

His activities appeared sufficiently akin to sorcery for Queen Mary to summon him for interrogation; however, Elizabeth I considered Dee a trusted adviser. In the 1570s when a wax image of the Queen with a pin driven through its breast was discovered in a Lincoln's Inn dungheap, he reassured Her Majesty that its spell could be overcome – and things did not turn out too bad because Elizabeth survived until 1603 (though Dee's annihilation of the Spanish Armada by conjuring a storm also went some way to assist this).

But relentless intellectual enquiry still left him frustrated, so in 1582 when a man calling himself Edward Talbot (pictured) turned up at his door, Dee interpreted the event as a literal godsend. The stranger was a 'scryer', someone with the ability to perceive (or 'descry') apparitions in reflective objects such as mirrors, bowls of water, crystals or even polished fingernails, and within fifteen minutes Talbot was seeing visions in his host's 'show-stone'. Regrettably for Dee, he was unable to fathom this craft for himself, and though he may have harboured doubts about the visitor (not least for his confession that his real name was Edward Kelly and he lacked ear lobes, the consequence of conviction for forgery), he was not discouraged from inviting Kelly to become his collaborator, along with board and lodging for him and his wife chez Dee.

The men duly set about scrying and Dee was delighted when angels began to appear before Kelly, even more so when they seemed perfectly happy to answer any question he might wish to pose, and the inquisitor was soon on first-name terms with them. Thus, Mortlake became the workplace of perhaps the most eminent charlatan and scoundrel on record.

The character of Kelly's labours may be admired by an episode that took place some years later in Bohemia. Following some scrying that Kelly performed alone, it was with much trepidation that he informed his master how an angel had appeared naked and spoken about their wives – in particular how they might 'use them in common'. Dee was bewildered by the suggestion and sought clarification, asking his angelic sources if this was simply 'spiritual love and charitable care and unity of minds for the advancing the service of God' or whether it encompassed 'carnal use'. At this, a scroll appeared before Kelly bearing the Latin: *De utroq loquor* – I speak of both.

Over dinner that evening, the men's wives expressed unease with the divine directive and when Kelly undertook further scrying for Dee to query the matter, an angel replied that he 'did evil to require proof' (and this was by no means the first occasion in which an angel rebuked Dee for his incessant questioning). It was two in the morning before Dee climbed into bed that night 'where I found my wife awake, attending to hear some new matter of me' so he patiently explained the necessity of fulfilling the commandment: 'Jane I see that there is no other remedy but as hath been said of our cross-matching, so it must needs be done. Thereupon she fell a weeping and trembling for a quarter of an hour and I pacified her as well as I could.'

As luck would have it, the reassurance Dee sought arrived the following day; Kelly's scrying produced a series of letters that formed a simple cipher of some Latin. Notwithstanding some errors in its grammar, it was a message from God: 'You are chosen from the number of men to walk with him and to understand his mysteries … consider that if he find you obstinate, the plagues of heinous sinners and contemners of the gifts of God shall fall upon you … this is the last time of your trial.' The words were music to Dee's ears; God was testing him and if he was prepared to go against his better judgment and swap wives with Kelly, He would reveal the secrets of the universe.

Ever earnest and diligent, Dee drew up a covenant between God and the two couples, affirming their blind obedience, as well as silence – if any of them disclosed the arrangement they would be 'presently and immediately struck dead by thy Divine power'. Each solemnly signed it and in due course took to bed.

Dee's diary for the day following his spiritual trial reveals how the angels were eager to check whether 'cross-matching' had taken place, and a note records that both wives had been 'obedient'. But there is no mention of any profound epiphany beyond Dee's observation that shortly afterwards his wife stopped menstruating, and nine months later Jane Dee gave birth to a boy.

IMPERIAL WAR MUSEUM SE1

SEEK ASYLUM

The Bethlem Hospital's imposing new building opened in 1815 and two vast, four-storey wings radiated from what is now the museum entrance to accommodate some 364 patients – women to the east, men to the west, with blocks for the criminally insane behind each. Following a series

of damning reports on the institution, it was hoped that its
move to Lambeth would make a break with its brutal past.

But although mechanical restraint of patients was gradually superseded by less inhumane methods, old habits die
hard and improvements were thanks in part to a redefinition
of terminology. Padded cells were categorised not as confinement but 'isolation' – something so complete one patient died

from an epileptic fit after languishing unattended. Similarly, 'wet-packing' in which a patient was tightly sewn in a cold wet sheet, wrapped in blankets then secured to a bed with bands of webbing, was classified as a medical procedure. (Cold baths were thought beneficial for those of enfeebled mind and the wet pack a convenient means to prolong its efficacy with unruly patients – all day if necessary, irrespective of the needs of their bladder or bowels.) Basements were still reserved for those unconscious to the calls of nature who lay in loose straw on a stone floor that sloped towards a drain, while criminals were confined behind iron gratings 'like those which enclose the fiercer carnivora at the Zoological Gardens'.

By the 1850s, iron bars were being removed from windows, and manacles and chains superseded by the strait-jacket, gloves and 'strong dress', but what most horrified a visitor of the time was the wholesale intermingling of social classes among the criminal class:

> The unfortunate clergyman, the Rev. Hugh Willoughby who fired a pistol two years since at the judge at the Central Criminal Court is herded with the plebeian perpetrator of some horrible murder. Here also poor Dadd, the artist who killed his father whilst labouring under a sudden paroxysm of insanity, is obliged to weave his fine fancies on the canvas amidst the most revolting conversations and the most brutal behaviour.

However, medical science had come a long way since beatings and exorcisms, and a diverse new pharmacopoeia could now be secreted in patients' food, including hyoscyamine, chloral, digitalis and conium (hemlock), complemented by amyl nitrate and the ubiquitous morphine. Another innovation was galvanism, whereby increasing levels of electric current were applied between the nape of the neck and forehead – though with mixed results. One woman labouring under profound melancholia for possessing a beard enjoyed a full recovery while another's 'great sexual irritability' remained unbridled – although the treatment did clear up her acne.

The Imperial War Museum took over the building in 1936 – just in time for an opportunity to vastly expand its collections, although numerous unsolicited objects were acquired directly from enemy bombers.

WESTMINSTER ABBEY SW1

SCOT FREE

In 1296, while a warmongering Edward I was an unwelcome visitor to Scotland, he seized the Stone of Scone, the coronation seat of Scottish kings, and built around it what is now called the Coronation Chair, kept at the Abbey. This did not please Scottish nationalists, and a number of years later a cohort of four amateur burglars set off from Edinburgh to recapture it.

It was 23 December 1950 when ringleader Ian Hamilton hid in the Abbey after closing time with an assortment of house-breaking tools concealed about his person; however when a nightwatchman caught sight of him, he was obliged to shuffle out the door with a 'Merry Christmas'.

In the wee hours of Christmas morning, a different approach was adopted; as Big Ben struck four, the gang parked near the Houses of Parliament and Hamilton, Alan Stuart and Gavin Vernon crowbarred their way through a door to Poets' Corner. The crowbar was then employed to prise all 3,400 stone of the stone (15,240kg) out of the Coronation Chair, but in so doing, it broke in two. Legend has it, the block of Scottish sandstone was Jacob's pillow as mentioned in the Old Testament, so breaking it was less than ideal, but did at least make it significantly easier to shift. Hamilton offered the others his coat to drag the large piece, while he staggered to the door with the lesser lump.

But no sooner had he manhandled it into the car, getaway driver Kay Mathieson spied a policeman approaching; Hamilton leaped in, covered the stone and flung his arms around her. A sorry tale of how they were on holiday and arrived in London too late for a hotel seemed to satisfy the constable because he offered them cigarettes and suggested they resume their intimacies in a nearby car park. Mathieson joked that he could offer them a cell for the night but the officer let slip that he would rather not make an arrest because Boxing Day would be spent in court, to which Hamilton quipped that it must be an auspicious night for crime, prompting hearty laughter.

Their merriment helped to mask the peculiar scraping noise emanating from the Abbey as the other two, oblivious to the policeman's presence, hauled out the weighty piece, anxious that their colleagues' mirth signalled a loss of sanity. They were lucky to glimpse the officer just in time to jump into the shadows and watch their accomplices drive off.

A change of strategy was hastily settled upon: Mathieson would head north while Hamilton fetched the gang's other car, which was parked only a stone's throw away. But a fresh problem then presented itself; the car keys were in his coat.

Hamilton strode back to the Abbey, where he stumbled upon the stone – but of his accomplices and coat, there was no sign. Assuming that they had found the keys and gone to the car, he walked back to it, only to discover that they were not there either. So once again, he returned to the Abbey and in complete darkness began groping around on the floor. Visions of needles and haystacks were dispelled when, as luck would have it he found the keys – somewhat bent from the weight of the stone, and raced back to the car. Dawn was beginning to break so, throwing caution to the wind, he drove to Poets' Corner and wrestled the stone into the vehicle, unaware that the nightwatchman was simultaneously reporting its disappearance to police.

Hamilton headed south out of London but was soon hopelessly lost in back streets, and it was there that he spotted Vernon and Stuart. Not believing their good fortune but unable to all get in the car for fear of breaking the suspension, they abandoned Vernon and drove off. But as

the pair recounted their escapades, it dawned on them that Hamilton's coat was still lying outside the Abbey – with his name in it. With great reluctance they paid the Abbey one final visit to retrieve it – though not before dumping their booty somewhere in Kent.

A few days later when they returned to collect the stone, they were surprised to discover a gypsy camp set up beside it, necessitating some unforeseen negotiations. However, despite a nationwide search and police roadblocks along the border, the gang smuggled both pieces of their precious haul into Scotland. Not knowing what to do next, they laid them in the ruins of Arbroath Abbey.

When police learned of the stone's whereabouts, the dredging of the Serpentine was called off and a contingent despatched north to recapture it – which turned out to be timely because not long afterwards, Queen Elizabeth II needed to sit on it for her coronation (though some Scots gleefully asserted that the recovered stone was fake). To avoid political embarrassment, not one of the plunderers was prosecuted for their near treasonous crimes, much to the chagrin of the Abbey's Dean and Chapter, who were equally horrified by another craven ploy in 1996 when the Government unexpectedly chose to hand the stone back to Scotland. It now resides at Edinburgh Castle, though its guardians have promised to return it for future coronations.

RIVER THAMES, CHELSEA BRIDGE SW1

SKULL AND JUDGEMENT

When the first bridge at Chelsea was built during the 1850s, workmen looked on in alarm as bucket-loads of human skulls emerged from the northern riverbed. A serial killer was quickly ruled out because the crania were accompanied not by other bones but ancient weapons made from bronze and iron, inspiring an archaeologist to dub the site: 'our Celtic Golgotha'. The metalwork attracted a great deal of interest and the most spectacular find, the Battersea Shield, found its way to the British Museum while the skulls fell into the hands of dealers in curios and promptly disappeared.

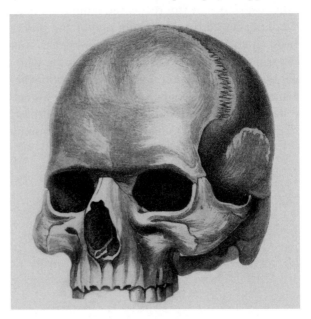

The subsequent discovery of other hoards of skulls at sites along the Thames (including more than 100 recovered near Kew Bridge) precludes the possibility that they originate from conventional burial sites exposed by erosion, or that Victorian navvies failed to recognise other bones or simply ignored them in favour of more saleable items. Radiocarbon dating confirmed that they date from the Late Bronze Age to the Iron Age, and though the presence of spears and swords might imply that a battle took place, a significant proportion of the crania were female and none showed evidence of trauma (although one found at Chelsea in 2001 had been trepanned, revealing that ancient people were not afraid to attempt major surgery). In fact, they were generally well preserved, something consistent with rapid submersion and suggesting that the river was considered an appropriate place to deposit the dead. But why only skulls have been found in such close proximity poses some unsettling questions.

Forensic research shows that when a complete corpse is placed in moving water, the head will readily separate from the body, so while the skull is unlikely to be found with other bones, it is also unlikely to be found with other skulls, let alone metal objects dropped at the same location. Further studies indicate that a skull dropped in moving water is likely to be carried away, while a fleshy head complete with its contents is apt to sink and become lodged in the riverbed. All of which points towards a deeply uncomfortable hypothesis; firstly that our ancestors decapitated the recently deceased, perhaps in funerary rites associated with their soul, which was thought to be seated in the skull. Then, because moving water might offer a boundary with the spirit world, they chose a specific region of the river, perhaps beside a jetty, and along with votive offerings of weapons they simply dropped the heads into it.

50 BERKELEY SQUARE W1

GHOST WRITERS

Correspondence in the scholarly journal *Notes and Queries* of 1880 told of an unpleasant incident at No. 50 Berkeley Square. One night, not long after a family had moved in, piercing shrieks were heard from an upper bedroom; the occupants rushed upstairs 'and found the unfortunate housemaid lying at the foot of the bed in strong convulsions. Her eyes were fixed, with a stare of expressive terror upon a remote corner of the chamber'. Unable to speak about her experience, she died the following morning.

The young woman's mysterious death led to understandable anxiety, and the account goes on to describe how a courageous young man volunteered to spend a night in the room to debunk talk of ghosts. As a precaution, he took a bell to summon help, and no sooner had midnight passed than 'a tremendous peal sounded through the house. Everyone hurried breathless to the haunted room. They found the guest exactly in the same place as where the dead housemaid had lain … his eyes fixed in horror upon the same spot'. He lived – but not to tell the tale: 'He never revealed his experiences. They were too awful, he said, even to mention.' What with further spine-chilling reports of an elderly couple locked in the basement and a tenant communicating with the dead, even *The Times* dryly noted: 'The house in question is known as the haunted house and it has occasioned a good deal of speculation among the neighbours.'

It may be understandable that ghosts felt more disposed to put in an appearance when locals had been made aware that the property was haunted, but even those oblivious to its notoriety fell victim. During the 1870s, two sailors on leave in London sought a place to sleep after squandering their resources on drink. Seeing a 'To Let' sign, the pair broke into the empty house and settled down for the night – but not for long. Woken by footsteps on the staircase, they recoiled in terror as the bedroom door opened slowly and a 'most horrible and wholly diabolical' figure entered the room. One able seaman was able to effect an escape out of the window, but the other was found in the square the following morning, deranged and incoherent.

Although these tales gave rise to No. 50's reputation as the most haunted house in London, it would be polite to issue forewarning of a spoiler because they are, of course, pure whimsy, spawned from a short story by Rhoda Broughton published in 1868. Although her eerie narrative centred on No. 32 of an unspecified Mayfair street, No. 50 was in a neglected and seemingly abandoned state and this, coupled with the notion that ghosts are apt to congregate around decrepit properties – especially ones in otherwise respectable neighbourhoods, led to its details becoming indelibly associated with the building. Subsequent embellishments of Broughton's story had manservants, soldiers, aristocrats, dogs and mothers-in-law all succumb to the invisible 'thing' in the cursed bedroom, and even long-deceased former Prime Minister George Canning, an earlier occupant, was belatedly endowed with a role. The scribbling frenzy was such that when the building was spruced up during the late 1880s, many writers lamented how it instigated the ghost's demise – although redecoration did not prevent the tale of the sailors first materialising in a book of ghost stories in 1924.

Happily, however, the facts are equally haunting. Those who saw faces at the windows or heard unexplained noises were blithely unaware that the house did have a tenant – Thomas Myers. He took the property sometime after 1859 and there is some suggestion that he did so on favourable terms because its dilapidated condition had already bestowed it with an inauspicious reputation. It had been home to a nonagenarian spinster, who thus unwittingly set the scene for more than a century of mass hallucination and fostered the notion of suspiciously inexpensive rent as a common motif among haunted houses. Myers began furnishing the property in expectation of moving in with his betrothed, but shortly before their marriage the lady in question ditched him for another man. Distraught, Myers left everything untouched and for the next twenty years lived as a recluse –

his association with the address only brought to public notice in 1873 for the prosaic reason that he failed to pay his rates.

The image of an eccentric, jilted fiancé living in a decaying time capsule might appear familiar. While some authors dreamed up ever more ghostly yarns, Charles Dickens was creating Miss Havisham of Satis House – forever in her bridal gown while cobwebs blanketed her wedding banquet. The novelist was known to use real people as inspiration for characters and a journalist friend, James Payn, who knew of Myers, claimed that he brought to Dickens' attention an individual who in *Great Expectations* 'appears for the second time to my eyes, as large as life indeed but not one whit exaggerated'. While other contenders have been suggested as the model for Miss Havisham, it is not a little tantalising to think that it might be the ghost of No. 50 Berkeley Square.

ST CHAD'S STREET WC1

TALKING RUBBISH

King's Cross was formerly the realm of rubbish tips and the most prodigious, which was thought to have first arisen following the fire of 1666, stood on land surrounding today's St Chad's Street. By the nineteenth century, the heap was strewn across 8 acres and formed the 'grand centre of dustmen, scavengers, horse and dog dealers, knackermen, brickmakers and other low but necessary professionalists' – as well as the birthplace of a significant proportion of London's flies.

Although this alpine range comprised mainly cinders and ash that were valuable for brick-making, a female army grubbed through the grime for sundry treasures to sell – rags for paper-makers, bones for soap-makers, pottery or shells for road builders and dead cats for furriers ('sixpence for a white cat, fourpence for a coloured cat, and for a black one, according to her quality'). And as well as dust there was dung: the locality's prevailing aroma derived from heaps of drying night-soil (chamber pot contents), which were combined with ash to produce fertiliser.

But the parable of riches among the refuse does not end there and a welter of respectable sources proclaim this bygone blot on the landscape an object of national pride. The story goes that following the burning of Moscow as Napoleon stood at its gates in 1812, homeless Muscovites somehow got wind of London's premier garbage heap, so purchased it and shipped the dust to Russia to make bricks for rebuilding.

Regrettably, the fable's foundations appear as crumbly as the purported cargo and first arose in 1825 when the dustheap was cleared and the land sold to developers for a reported £15,000. This figure quickly attached itself to the detritus and, likely encouraged by the fact that Alexander I visited London in 1814 (the first Tsar to do so since Peter the Great), it seemed clear that he had been eyeing it up for purchase. Flattering myths can be stubborn ones and by 1833 the sum coughed up by Russians had been elevated to a tidy £20,000, while in 1850, a short story in Charles Dickens' magazine *Household Words* upped the figure to a significantly more satisfying £40,000.

Aside from the fact that a version of events from the supposed purchasers is yet to materialise, it must be considered unreasonably ambitious to suspend disbelief that blighted Muscovites (who were not lacking cinders, as well as coal and timber, and a climate apt to encourage their combustion) might wish to part with even a nugatory sum of money for a mound of London debris that necessitated shipping to Russian waters, then conveying hundreds of miles by barge.

At best, it is possible that when the heap was purged, a portion was carried to the docks and used as ballast by Russian ships – likely inspiration for another tale that St Petersburg was built on waste from London's fire of 1666.

64–68 LADBROKE GROVE/ 35 LADBROKE GARDENS W11

CUT TO THE CHASTE

In 1858, surgeon Isaac Baker Brown established at No. 64 Ladbroke Grove 'The London Surgical Home for the Reception of Gentlewomen and Females of Respectability suffering from Curable Surgical Diseases'. The hospital numbered among its patrons Royalty, archbishops, peers and knights of the realm, members of Parliament and ambassadors – but treatment at Brown's hands was somewhat less distinguished.

Brown directed his attentions exclusively towards maladies that materialised between the feminine waistline and garter line, both front and back. Amongst this region were the ovaries, which he knew to cause countless ailments peculiar to women so advocated their extraction, and despite the disappointment of causing the death of his first three subjects, he performed the procedure on his sister. She survived, stimulating him to continue on hundreds more. But when it came to removing female parts, Brown had more than ovaries in his sights.

Intimate acquaintance with the female hinterland convinced Brown that hysteria and epilepsy were the result of masturbation: 'without doubt ... one of the most prominent causes is peripheral irritation of the pudic nerve'. He then became adept at identifying symptoms in gentle-women who engaged in such sordid practices: 'The patient becomes restless and excited, or melancholy and retiring; listless and indifferent to the social influences of domestic life. She will be fanciful in her food … often a great disposition for novelties is exhibited, the patient desiring to escape from home, fond of becoming a nurse …' Left unchecked, such wayward inclinations could rapidly escalate into mania, idiocy and death; yet the dangerous consequences of 'unnatural irritation of the clitoris' could be averted if he simply removed the irritated object.

'The clitoris is freely excised, either by scissors or knife,' Brown declared as he set to work, helpfully adding: 'I always prefer the scissors.' A grain of opium poked up the rectum allayed physical discomfort, while permanent relief required post-operative psychological therapy involving 'careful watching and moral training on the part of both patient and friends'. His notes reveal the simplicity and efficacy of the procedure: 'H.C.', a single woman of 20 who suffered epileptic fits, was admitted on 24 February 1864; 'March 3. Clitoris excised in the usual manner under chloroform. Was restless and hysterical for the first six days, when she improved daily, became cheerful and much more intelligent. She never had another fit and on April 13 being quite cured.' Seventeen-year-old 'M. N.' had enjoyed good health until she reached 15, when the onset of wandering womb coincided with her move to boarding school. Brown was wise to the tell-tale signs: 'Mr Brown ascertained from both her mother and herself that she had long indulged in self-excitation of the clitoris, having first been taught by a school-fellow. The next day after admission she was operated on and from that date she never had a fit.' Brown's records are silent regarding patient consent but few would have been inclined to publicly challenge him, least of all if they had to admit their shameful habit.

When Brown published the results of his snipping he found a champion among his ecclesiastical associates; the *Church Times* was fulsome: 'We desire to call the attention of the clergy especially to a little book which will enable them to suggest a remedy for some of the most distressing cases of illness which they frequently discover among their parishioners.' Brown's procedure was lauded as something available to all: 'The clergy will be doing a service, especially to their poorer parishioners by bringing [it] under the notice of medical men, any of whom can, if possessed of ordinary surgical skill, perform the operation with but slight assistance.' (Neither doctors nor clergymen ever reached the conclusion that surgery might offer relief to male sufferers.)

Imparting succour to impoverished masturbators caused no distress to Brown's cashflow because the hospital expanded into the three neighbouring properties to accommodate fifty in-patients and in 1866, emboldened by the approbation, he boasted how his scissor wielding could even cure lunacy. Many of his peers harboured doubts about his methods but this was the *coup de grâce*; as one psychiatrist put it: 'Mr Baker Brown begins his treatment of these cases at the wrong end.' Tales of horror began to emerge, including how he had performed his party piece on a woman suffering an anal fissure who, when she came round, was horrified to be suspected of 'a vice with the very name and nature of which she was alike unacquainted'. Turning his hand to the cure of nymphomania he had redirected his instruments from the clitoris to the labia, and even treated patients as young as 10. The medical establishment closed ranks and was unanimous in its condemnation, though as much in opposition to his handiwork as his inclination to discuss such sensitive realms so publicly. Brown was expelled from the Obstetrical Society, resigned from the hospital and even became an object of satire when one medic found comic mileage in his technique, suggesting kleptomania could be cured by cutting hand muscles and 'gyromania' (a morbid desire to waltz), by severing muscles in the lower body. The humiliation affected his health and he died penniless in 1873. Clitoridectomy was finally excised from the corpus of medical procedures in the twentieth century.

THE WARDROBE, RICHMOND TW9

ON THE THRONE

The bygone existence of a magnificent Tudor palace between Richmond Green and the River Thames is much overlooked, despite the fact that it played host to events of immense historical significance including performances by Shakespeare, the deaths of Henry VII and Elizabeth I, and the flushing of a toilet.

In 1596, courtier to Elizabeth I, Sir John Harington, penned a work entitled *A New Discourse of a Stale Subject, Called the Metamorphosis of Ajax* (and Tudor readers would chuckle over 'jax' or 'jakes' because it was slang for a privy). But Harington did indeed transfigure the toilet because, while the book was primarily a political allegory concerned with redeeming mankind from the mire, during a brief digression he discharged motion number two: a real-world exemplar of this filth-flushing objective and the precise manner in which to construct one. This entirely unfamiliar contrivance was designed by Harington himself and already in operation at his country residence near Bath.

To build your own sweet-smelling flushing privy, the author/amateur plumber recommended a 'stool pot' made from either brick, stone or lead with a brass plug sealing a 3in hole at its base so that it held several inches of water. A pipe from a cistern or barrel of water ran into the pot via a stopcock so that when the incumbent's evacuations were complete, the turn of a screw (concealed beneath a scallop shell so 'children and busy folk disorder it not') opened the plug, and sufficient water was released to sweep whatever lay in the vessel into a cesspit beneath – 'once a day is enough … though twenty persons should use it'. Thus, a dwelling was safeguarded from all but momentary contamination from the cesspit's pernicious stench. Harington suggested dressing the pot with pitch or wax to 'keepe it from taynting with the urine' and priced up each component – even recommending a City merchant who stocked the fittings. With the exception of an S-bend, it had all the makings of a modern flush lavatory.

Harington milked every opportunity for scatological levity in his book and could not resist jibes at courtiers including the Queen's late favourite, Robert Dudley. For this he was promptly despatched to Ireland on urgent and dangerous business, and it was two years before the stink had dissipated sufficiently to permit his return: 'Your book is almost forgiven, and I may say forgotten,' whereupon he discovered that Elizabeth had constructed his contraption at Richmond. Two centuries passed before another flushing lavatory was installed in London.

All that remains of the palace is its gatehouse, which stands over a road named The Wardrobe – which is appropriate because it was the chamber that commonly housed the latrine.

BRITISH MUSEUM WC1

FACTS AND ARTEFACTS

Public understanding of Ancient Egyptian curses has benefited greatly from the movie industry, which has raised
awareness of perils such as booby-trapped tombs bearing
injunctions of the kind: 'Death To All Who Enter', and
zombie mummies who crave human blood, etc. It is also
common knowledge that in 1923, Tutankhamen wreaked
vengeance on the Earl of Carnarvon for opening his tomb,
and the superannuated pharaoh even cruelly targeted the
Earl's faithful three-legged terrier, Susie. However, the
bloodcurdling story surrounding object EA22542, which
the British Museum acquired in 1889, predates these picturesque fables. The museum describes the artefact as the
inner coffin lid (or 'mummy board') of a high-ranking female
who lived around 950 BCE; others identify it as cursed.

In 1904, *Daily Express* editor Bertram Fletcher Robinson was
surprised to hear rumours about the object's sinister reputation from the Keeper of Egyptian Antiquities at the museum,
Ernest Wallis Budge. Robinson saw fit to investigate and
uncovered a horrifying saga for his readers; prudently keeping the identity of those involved anonymous, he related how
five friends had travelled to Egypt during the 1860s and while
exploring the necropolis at Thebes, one of the party, 'Mr D.'
was offered the coffin lid. Although he thought its face possessed 'a cold malignancy of expression unpleasant to witness',
he purchased it, but when the group departed for home with
their booty, misfortune began to strike: one of the friends was
shot, another died in poverty within a year, 'Mr W.' learned
that he had lost a large part of his fortune and promptly

expired, and Mr D. was shot in the arm, which then required amputation. The coffin lid was hastily passed to Mr W.'s sister, who, somewhat dismayed to receive confirmation of its malevolence from spirit medium Madame Blavatsky, sent it to a Baker Street photographer. Unfortunately, he also died suddenly in mysterious circumstances – though not before his photograph revealed not the face on the lid, but a real woman bearing a menacing expression. The lady was now glad to bequeath the item to the British Museum, which she

presumed to be far too scholarly an institution to trouble itself with the appeasement of indignant gods. Robinson's article had the eye-catching headline 'A Priestess of Death', though it closed by reassuring readers that she was quite content in her new accommodation and no longer sought vengeance.

But Robinson spoke too soon, because he died suddenly a couple of years later aged just 36, having told friends that he was still investigating the story. The priestess had signi-fied her displeasure in a most convincing manner and the die was cast. The curse now took on a life of its own and filled endless newspaper columns, including an article by notorious journalist W.T. Stead that was syndicated across the globe. Such exposure invited dramatic improvements to the narrative including new scenes featuring involving fur-ther victims who wound up dead at some point subsequent to a museum visit, and a fleshing out of the frustratingly vague details courtesy of sundry occultists and psychics.

But this paled into insignificance in 1912 when over supper one evening, Stead expressed doubts about the curse to his mealtime companions. Explaining how a ghastly death supposedly befell anyone who recounted the tale, he then proceeded to do precisely that, pointing out with satisfaction that he was very much alive when he finished. But not for long – the diners were aboard RMS *Titanic*.

A survivor's account of the conversation was all it took to trigger the coffin lid's impact on the world stage; to some, it was evident that the British Museum had attempted to rid itself of the artefact by selling it to an American collector and because a cursed sarcophagus would not be welcome on the *Titanic* shipping manifest (the lid had now matured into a fully-fledged mummy) it had been secreted onboard. Reason was now thoroughly untethered from its moorings and another elaborate tale explained how the disgruntled Egyptian initiated the First World War.

But events were not quite as Robinson described and his
source, Wallis Budge, spent much of the rest of his career
at the museum trying in vain to stamp out the doom-laden
gossip. The awkward truth was that Budge (and sometime
later, Stead) had heard the tale when invited to a soirée
hosted by a secretive association of spiritualists called The
Ghost Club, who gathered to share supernatural stories.
The fantastical yarn about the coffin lid and its reputation
for bringing calamity on all who crossed its path was spun
by amateur Egyptologist Thomas Douglas Murray (Mr D.)
who had indeed bought the relic when in Egypt with friends
including Arthur Wheeler (Mr W.), whose sister donated
it to the museum. Murray held his audience all the more
spellbound for the conspicuous proof of the curse – he was
missing his right arm. But in deftly blending fact with fancy,
he omitted to mention that he accidentally shot it off while
hunting quail at the Pyramids; he also lived until the decidedly less than blighted age of 70.

The British Museum wearily resigns itself, not without
irony, to calling object EA22542 the Unlucky Mummy and
those who dare may behold her self-satisfied expression in
Room 62.

INDEX